From White Australia to Woomera
The Story of Australian Immigration

There has never been a greater need for a sober, historically informed yet critical account of immigration policy in Australia. In this book, James Jupp, Australia's leading specialist on migration, surveys the changes in policy over the last thirty years since the seismic shift away from the White Australia Policy. Along the way he outlines the history of Australian immigration, compares the achievements of the Fraser, Hawke and Keating governments, and considers the establishment of the 'institutions' of multiculturalism and ethnicity. Jupp looks critically at the ways economic rationalism, the rise of Pauline Hanson and One Nation, and the environmental debate have impacted upon migration choices. The vexed issue of refugees and asylum seekers is also covered in great depth.

James Jupp is Director of the Centre for Immigration and Multicultural Studies at the Australian National University. His many publications include, as general editor, *The Australian People: An Encyclopedia of the Nation, its Peoples and Their Origins* (second edition, Cambridge University Press, 2001).

From White Australia to Woomera

The Story of Australian Immigration

JAMES JUPP

CAMBRIDGE
UNIVERSITY PRESS

PUBLISHED BY THE PRESS SYNDICATE OF THE UNIVERSITY OF CAMBRIDGE
The Pitt Building, Trumpington Street, Cambridge, United Kingdom

CAMBRIDGE UNIVERSITY PRESS
The Edinburgh Building, Cambridge CB2 2RU, UK
40 West 20th Street, New York, NY 10011–4211, USA
477 Williamstown Road, Port Melbourne, VIC 3207, Australia
Ruiz de Alarcón 13, 28014 Madrid, Spain
Dock House, The Waterfront, Cape Town 8001, South Africa

http://www.cambridge.org

First published 2002
Reprinted with corrections 2003
Reprinted 2004

Printed in Australia by BPA Print Group

Typeface Minion 10/12 pt, Monotype Strayhorn.   *System* QuarkXPress®   [PK]

A catalogue record for this book is available from the British Library

National Library of Australia Cataloguing in Publication data
Jupp, James, 1932– .
From white Australia to Woomera: the story of Australian immigration.
Bibliography.
Includes index.
ISBN 0 521 82424 9 (hbk).
ISBN 0 521 53140 3 (pbk).
1. Australia – Emigration and immigration – Government policy
2. Australia – Population policy. 3. White Australia policy.
4. Multiculturalism – Australia. 5. Asylum, Right of – Australia.
6. Refugees – Government policy – Australia.
7. Alien detention centers – Australia.
8. Illegal aliens – Government policy – Australia.
I. Title.
325.994

ISBN 0 521 82424 9 hardback
ISBN 0 521 53140 3 paperback

Contents

List of acronyms and abbreviations   ix

Introduction   1

Chapter 1 Creating an immigrant society, 1788–1972   5
A new Britannia   5
White Australia   6
Populate or perish   10
Planning and control   13

**Chapter 2 From assimilation to a multicultural society,
1972–2002**   21
Assimilation   21
The ethnic situation in 1972   23
Language and culture   24
Ethnic community organisation   27
The new proletariat   29
Ghettoes and ethnic suburbs   30
A political base   32
Social mobility   34
Asian settlement   35
A new middle class   36
An ethnic underclass?   37

**Chapter 3 The Fraser, Hawke and Keating governments,
1975–1996**   41
The Fraser government, 1975–1983   42
The Hawke government, 1983–1991   46

The Keating government, 1991–1996 — 49
The ministerial record — 52
Prime ministerial intervention — 53
Continuity and difference — 56

Chapter 4   Policy instruments and institutions — 61
The Immigration Department — 61
State government agencies — 67
The advisory structures — 69
Inquiries and reports — 72
Consultation and representation — 73
Research and advocacy — 75
The ethnic communities — 79

Chapter 5   Multicultural policy — 83
Australian multiculturalism — 84
The foundations — 85
The Galbally report — 86
Multicultural institutions — 89
The agenda of 1989 — 91
The reassessment of 1995 — 92
Settlement policy — 93
Language policy and multicultural education — 94
Access and equity — 97
The agenda of 1999 — 98
Indigenous peoples and multiculturalism — 99
Theorising multiculturalism — 101
Shifting emphases — 102

Chapter 6   The attack on multiculturalism — 105
Conservative criticism of multiculturalism — 106
Other criticism — 109
The bipartisan consensus ends, 1988 — 110
Australians Speak — 112
A developing critique — 113
Popular critiques — 115
Summarising the conservative critique — 116
Less conservative critics — 119
The survival of multiculturalism — 120

Chapter 7   The impact of One Nation   **123**
   The racist inheritance   124
   The arrival of One Nation   127
   Hanson's policies   129
   One Nation's immigration program of 1998   131
   One Nation support   134
   Graeme Campbell and One Nation   136
   The influence of One Nation   137
   Tragedy or farce?   138

Chapter 8   Economic rationalism   **141**
   Economic rationalism in immigration policy   141
   The overall economic impact   144
   The human capital approach   146
   Selection criteria   147
   User pays and cost-free immigration   151
   Settlement outcomes   153
   The 'uneconomic' immigrant   155
   The limits of rationality   157

Chapter 9   Sustainability and population policy   **162**
   Populate or perish   163
   Growing doubts   164
   Zero population growth   167
   A population policy   170
   Growth, limitation and devolution   173
   Ageing and decline   175
   Future stabilisation   176

Chapter 10   Refugees and asylum seekers   **180**
   The UN Convention and Protocol   182
   Refugee intakes since 1975   184
   The humanitarian programs   186
   Boat people, asylum seekers and mandatory
      detention   187
   The shift to temporary protection   190
   Tampa and the Pacific solution   193
   A tough solution for a small problem   196

Chapter 11 A past, present and future success?   **200**
    Immigration policy in a globalised economy   201
    Multicultural reality   208
    A glance at the future   213
    Changing attitudes and values   217

    Appendix I Chronology: 1972–2002   220
    Appendix II Ministers of immigration,
      departmental secretaries and gross annual
      settler intake, 1973–2002   224
    References   225
    Index   233

Acronyms and abbreviations

AAFI	Australians Against Further Immigration
ABC	Australian Broadcasting Commission (later Corporation)
ABS	Australian Bureau of Statistics
ACF	Australian Conservation Foundation
ACPEA	Australian Council on Population and Ethnic Affairs
ACTU	Australian Council of Trade Unions
AEAC	Australian Ethnic Affairs Council
AESP	Australians for an Ecologically Sustainable Population
AGPS	Australian Government Publishing Service
AIMA	Australian Institute of Multicultural Affairs (1979–86)
ALP	Australian Labor Party
AMEP	Adult Migrant Education (later English) Program
ANESBWA	Association of Non-English-Speaking Background Women of Australia
APIC	Australian Population and Immigration Council
ASIO	Australian Security Intelligence Organisation
ATSIC	Aboriginal and Torres Strait Islander Commission
BI(MP)R	Bureau of Immigration (later Multicultural and Population) Research (1989–96)
CAAIP	Committee to Advise on Australia's Immigration Policies (1988)
CALD	Culturally and Linguistically Diverse

CEDA	Committee for the Economic Development of Australia
CMEP	Child Migrant Education Program
COPQ	Council on Overseas Professional Qualifications
CRSS	Community Refugee Settlement Scheme
CSIRO	Commonwealth Scientific and Industrial Research Organisation
DEETYA	Department of Employment, Education, Training and Youth Affairs
DFAT	Department of Foreign Affairs and Trade
DIEA	Department of Immigration and Ethnic Affairs (1976–87, 1993–96)
DILGEA	Department of Immigration, Local Government and Ethnic Affairs (1987–93)
DIMA	Department of Immigration and Multicultural Affairs (1996–2001)
DIMIA	Department of Immigration and Multicultural and Indigenous Affairs (since 2001)
DSS	Department of Social Security
EAC	Ethnic Affairs Commission (State level)
ECC	Ethnic Communities' Council (State level)
ESL	English as a Second Language
FECCA	Federation of Ethnic Communities' Councils of Australia
GIA	Grant-In-Aid
HREOC	Human Rights and Equal Opportunity Commission
IOM	International Organization for Migration
IRT	Immigration Review Tribunal
LOTE	Languages Other Than English
LSIA	Longitudinal Survey of Immigrants to Australia
MAIS	Multicultural Australia and Immigration Studies
MFP	Multifunctional Polis
MRC	Migrant Resource Centre
NAATI	National Accreditation Authority for Translators and Interpreters
NESB 1	Non-English-Speaking Background (born overseas)

NESB 2	Non-English-Speaking Background (born in Australia)
NMAC	National Multicultural Advisory Council
NOOSR	National Office of Overseas Skills Recognition
NPC	National Population Council
NUMAS	Numerical Multifactor Assessment System
OECD	Organisation for Economic Co-operation and Development
OMA	Office of Multicultural Affairs (1987–96)
PM&C	Department of the Prime Minister and Cabinet
ROMAMPAS	Review of Migrant and Multicultural Programs and Services (1986)
RRT	Refugee Review Tribunal
RSL	Returned and Services League
SBS	Special Broadcasting Service
TAFE	Technical and Further Education
TIS	Telephone Interpreter Service (later Translating and Interpreting Service)
UNHCR	United Nations High Commissioner for Refugees
ZPG	Zero Population Growth

Introduction

Thirty years ago Australia finally abandoned its 'settled policy' of excluding all immigrants who were not 'white'. Instead of being the 'most British' country in the world it began to proclaim itself as the 'most multicultural'. One-fifth of its people were no longer of predominantly British or Irish descent. This radical change appeared to have been accepted with very little opposition. Mass immigration continued. Between one-third and one-half came from backgrounds which would have excluded them during the previous seventy years. In March 2002 Australia officially welcomed the six millionth postwar immigrant – a Filipina information technologist.

At the same time Australia was responsible for detaining Afghan, Iraqi and Iranian asylum seekers at remote desert and Pacific Island camps: Woomera, Curtin, Port Hedland, Nauru and Manus Island. Their fates were uncertain. There were repeated riots and disturbances at Woomera and elsewhere. Policy made on the run in the election atmosphere of late 2001 had left many loose ends. Many hundreds of desperate individuals, including women and children, who sought to escape from states denounced by the United States as 'the axis of evil' had become pawns in a bureaucratic and political game. There was a basic contradiction between the continuing desire to people Australia and the fear that matters might get out of control.

I have assumed that immigration policy has three facets: selection and control of the intake; services and support for those who have settled; and policies designed to manage the consequences of creating a multicultural society through immigration. All of these at various times have been the responsibility of the Commonwealth

Department of Immigration, which still proclaims them as its three functions.

It is argued here that, while Australian immigration and multi-cultural policy has been a success, it is also much more of a contested area than was previously supposed. The consensus between and within the political parties has broken down. A new party, One Nation led by Pauline Hanson, became very popular for a while. It built on accumulating grievances, among which was the retreat from ethnic homogeneity. A policy shift from 'populate or perish' to 'economic rationalism' moved the emphasis from numbers to quality. In the process some of the humanitarian aspects of previous policies were lost sight of. This trend reached its height with the furore over asylum seekers in 2001. The internment in remote desert camps and tropical islands, and the resulting protests from the inmates, sharpened the division between those wanting a liberal policy and those wanting to discourage and punish those who arrived without official selection.

Throughout this study of the years 1972 to 2002 I have used terms which are not universally accepted and which need definition. By 'racist', I mean a fairly complex position which argues that clearly identifiable races not only exist but are hierarchically graded. Thus, all members of a race are either superior or inferior to all members of another race. As an ideology, racism often argues for a worldwide struggle between races. This view was based on a misreading of Darwin's theory of evolution and was widely held in the nineteenth century. Its horrendous consequences under the Nazis discredited the theory and the term 'race'.

By 'xenophobic', I mean a simpler psychological reaction to people who originate in a different homeland and who are believed to be physically or culturally different. This is an almost universal condition but, like the urge to murder or steal, is necessarily controlled in a civilised society. On this definition far more people are 'xenophobic' than are 'racist'. It is a difficult word, unknown to many, but useful in describing attitudes which are not fully racist or based on physical appearance. Fear of another religion or language is xenophobia, not racism.

I use the term 'ethnic' as it is colloquially used in Australia, to mean someone not derived from the British Isles. This is not very scientific but is commonly understood and is used by 'ethnic' organisations and individuals. While attempts have been made in New South Wales to ban both 'ethnic' and 'Anglo-Celtic', they have not had much impact anywhere else. 'Ethnic' is a useful shorthand when discussing multiculturalism and the extent to which immigrants may, or should, assimilate to what is claimed to be the majority culture.

As it was used for most of the past thirty years, I have preferred the term 'non-English-speaking background' (NESB) to the new coinage 'culturally and linguistically diverse' (CALD). The latter is rarely used, even in official publications, although it was urged on ethnic organisations for a time by compliant public servants. Why such a change was needed was never explained by the Howard government which tried to introduce it.

As for the majority, or 'mainstream', I prefer the term 'Anglo-Australian' in a cultural rather than a racial or ethnic sense. The bare majority who are of third or earlier generations is overwhelmingly derived from the British Isles and speaks only English. 'Anglo-Celtic' will do, but 'Anglo-Saxon' is only a language. All permanent residents are, of course, equally Australians, especially if they have become citizens. I have distinguished between 'British/Irish' and 'Europeans', as did official policy until 1958 and to some extent until 1983. This is how all involved saw things and most still do. Australia was not settled by 'Europeans' but by the 'British', partly to keep 'Europeans' out! Its subsequent history was determined by that fact.

As a rule I use official terms where possible, although these often change. I refer throughout to the Immigration Department, as this has had five different names since it was founded in 1945 and this can get confusing (see Acronyms and Abbreviations). Unless otherwise indicated, the term 'minister' refers to the head of this department. I use figures derived from official sources, including the Census and the returns of the Immigration Department. Some of these are challenged by others and some are presented so as to make a particular case. But, generally speaking, Australia has some of the best official migration statistics in the world. I prefer to stick with them.

I have been personally involved in immigration and multicultural policy in Australia for much of the period discussed in this book. The opinions I express are my own and are based on discussions with a wide range of people in the course of conferences, committees, seminars and interviews. As the whole area is contentious and politicised, it will be clear that I prefer some viewpoints to others. As official departmental documents will not be available for up to thirty years, I have drawn on my own experiences and on a wide range of publicly available sources.

While there are several ways of discussing immigration, I have adopted the approach of a political scientist and a participant. I do not believe that immigration can be discussed without understanding the political context. Policy may be made by rational bureaucrats. But it is invariably developed within the political process and against a background of public opinion. While it is an aspiration of Australian policy makers to be rational and detached, the reality is rather different.

My own views should be quite apparent. I believe that Australia needs a continuing and planned immigration program into the future, that the sources from which immigrants are drawn make a multicultural approach to policy essential, and that policy should be shaped in the knowledge that human beings are involved and not just factors of production. I accept that politicians must work within limits set by public opinion. But I do not accept that majority opinion is always right. Changing public opinion is a necessary feature of democracy and, in this area, often essential.

1

Creating an immigrant society, 1788–1972

Australia is an immigrant society. Without continual immigration the modern, urbanised and affluent society of today could not have been created. Australia is also the product of conscious social engineering to create a particular kind of society. This distinguishes it from other immigrant societies such as the United States, Argentina or even Canada, where the role of the state was less apparent and where private initiative was more important. Almost alone, with New Zealand, Australian governments set out to create a specific model using immigration and the introduction of overseas capital and technology. They are still doing so today, although naturally the goals and methods have changed over the past two centuries.[1]

A new Britannia

Australia and New Zealand are the two 'most British' societies in the world outside the United Kingdom. Australia is the 'most Irish' society outside Ireland, although the United States attracted vastly more Irish immigrants to a much larger society. New Zealand might contest with Canada for the title of the 'most Scottish' society outside Scotland. The often repeated and incorrect claim that Australia is the 'most multicultural society in the world' does not bear close inspection. It is certainly much more multicultural than it was fifty years ago when the post-war immigration program began. It is even more multicultural than it was at Federation in 1901, when 20 per cent of its people were overseas-born and it had large German and Chinese minorities. But it is still much more a 'British' society than either Canada or the United States in terms of origins. Nor can it compare with such truly multicultural societies as India, Russia, Indonesia, Papua New Guinea or most of the states of Africa. Its social, intellectual, business and political élites are still overwhelmingly of British origin; three-quarters of its people speak only English; and a similar proportion subscribe, however nominally, to Christian denominations.

How, then, did Australia become so similar in its culture and ethnic makeup to a society at the other end of the world? Certainly not by accident. The whole thing was carefully and deliberately planned within the context of the worldwide British empire. It is still being planned now that the empire has gone, using immigration as a method of controlling population change. This has been just as true for governments claiming to believe in the free market as for those subscribing to planning and social engineering. The successes of Australian immigration are largely due to deliberate planning. The assumption that bureaucrats and politicians have superior wisdom lies behind public policy. This may be misguided but it has produced a better social outcome than a free market in labour or a succession of ad hoc reactions to international movement and local public opinion. It is not, however, a value-free process. Australia has long and strong xenophobic, racist and insular traditions and they have always influenced immigration policy. Policy has always been influenced by ideologies: imperialism, racism, utilitarianism, economic rationalism and humanitarianism.

Australian immigration policy over the past 150 years has rested on three pillars; the maintenance of British hegemony and 'white' domination; the strengthening of Australia economically and militarily by selective mass migration; and the state control of these processes. The first has become less important in recent years but still exercises some minds; the second has been challenged by those who believe the population is large enough already; but the third remains, even while governments move away from the concept of a planned and engineered society towards notions of free markets and personal initiative. Immigration remains one of the few policy areas where to be an 'economic rationalist' means to be a planner and organiser.

White Australia

Australia's nearest neighbours were non-Europeans, although many were under European, including British, colonial control. Emigration from Indonesia was rare and, like emigration from India, mainly organised for imperialist purposes to plantation economies. Emigration from China was growing from the 1840s when Britain established its colony in Hong Kong and forcibly 'opened up' China to world trade. Emigration from Japan was prohibited until 1866. The islands of the Pacific were sparsely populated and did not begin to come under direct colonial control until the 1870s and even later. The small Australian population saw its main threat as coming from China, which had a population of 300 million even in the mid-nineteenth century. The arrival of many thousands of Chinese on the Victorian goldfields in the 1850s ignited a fear which remained central to immigration policy for the next century and has not yet finally disappeared.

Attitudes towards race a century ago were based on several propositions, some of which are still influential. One was the idea of a 'tree of man' in which the various races – Caucasian, Negroid, Mongoloid and Australoid – occupied different levels. The white Caucasians were placed at the top because of their superior strength, technology, wisdom and, in many eyes, Christianity. At the bottom were the Australian Aborigines. This hierarchy of races was justified by a perversion of Darwin's theory of evolution, in which the fittest survived and the weakest were subjugated or eliminated. Darwin did not apply this theory to humans, but as 'Social Darwinism' it enjoyed much support and has not yet completely died out. It was further believed that interbreeding between races would drag the higher down to the lower, although this does not correspond to Darwin's observations of the animal world either. On this view, contact between races other than by conquest and subjection was undesirable. This was clearly a rationalisation of imperialism, where small numbers of British soldiers had conquered vast numbers of Indians.

The implications for immigration were that non-Caucasians should only be introduced for menial tasks, should be segregated from Caucasians and should not be allowed to remain permanently, to intermarry or to enjoy the same rights as others. The fullest version of this in practice in the nineteenth century was in the segregated states of the United States. The fullest version in the twentieth was in apartheid South Africa.

Few Australians rationalised their fear of non-Europeans in such theoretical terms. But many politicians and journalists did, including those supporting the new labour movement which gave rise to the Australian Labor Party in 1891. As in the United States, South Africa and elsewhere, the labour movement feared for working conditions and wages if inferior races used to inferior conditions were able to dominate the labour market. But it is a simple generalisation to believe that the White Australia policy was only a reflection of economic interest. Labor pioneers, including the most radical, were usually rabid racists by modern standards. They did not extend their condemnation to Aborigines, who they regarded as a dying race and no threat to working conditions. But their fear and loathing of the Chinese were often pathological.

In contrast to the United States, however, Australian racism was not particularly violent except towards Aborigines. In all the anti-Chinese disturbances from Buckland River (1857) onwards, there are few examples of violent deaths. Rather than relying on riots, murders and lynching, Australians looked to the state to exclude the inferior races by law. Immigration control, consequently, was at the heart of what became known from the 1880s as the White Australia policy. When the Commonwealth was founded in 1901 this control went to the new government, which immediately passed the Immigration Restriction Act through parliament. This remained in force until replaced by the Migration Act in 1958.[2]

The Act of 1901 nowhere mentions race or the White Australia policy. Equally, the Act of 1958 allowed the policy to be maintained for more than ten years, while also not mentioning either of these. It is still in force, with amendments, now that the policy has been dead for thirty years. This illuminates one of the stranger features of Australian immigration policy: the consistent denial by officials of something which everyone knows to be true – from 'There is no racial discrimination' to 'Detention centres are not prisons'. The reason for this original obfuscation was to satisfy the objections of the British government, which had to pass the Australian Constitution through the British parliament. As the majority of British subjects by 1900 were Indians or Africans, and as Britain had important trade and strategic interests with China and Japan, they objected to any overt hint of racial discrimination. Hence the insertion in the 1901 Act of the device of the dictation test.

The dictation test was probably the most hypocritical invention in the long history of Australian immigration, and there have been

several. It authorised an officer at the point of arrival to administer a dictation test of 500 words. It was understood, though
nowhere stated, that this should be in a language not known to the
immigrant. The test was removed from the 1958 Act and was only
used in fewer than 2000 cases, mostly in the first few years after
1901. By then shipping companies knew not to issue tickets to those
likely to be excluded and were penalised if they did. The threat of
the test was, however, extremely effective. A message was sent out
to the world that 'coloured' people could not settle in Australia.
They did not. By 1947 the non-European population, other than
Aborigines, was measured by the Census as 0.25 per cent of the
total. Australia had become one of the 'whitest' countries in the
world outside northwestern Europe.

After the passage of the Migration Act, which required landing
permits usually issued overseas, the officers of the Immigration
Department had the unenviable task of judging the degree of
'blood' in the veins of applicants for settlement. This was purely
racist and similar to Nazi and South African thinking. The pretence
of labour protection or cultural inferiority was replaced by an argument from social harmony. It was claimed by ministers and their
apologists that to bring into Australia anyone who looked different
would provoke social unrest in a totally homogeneous white British
society. The example of the United States was regularly quoted.
With the arrival of West Indians in England and rioting in London
and Nottingham in 1958, the British example (which was arguably
more relevant) became more popular. Official policy endorsed
popular prejudice rather than discredited Social Darwinist theories. Australia was to be protected from civil disorder by keeping
out those likely to provoke it, however innocent themselves. Exceptions were made for temporary residents and tourists, but they
were not allowed to remain permanently and were few in numbers.

White Australia had aspects other than immigration policy. The
expectation that Aborigines would either die out or that colour
would be 'bred out' was widespread. It was also contradictory.
Those most in favour of 'breeding out colour' were usually appalled
at the idea of 'half-castes'. It was the product of mixed marriages
who were usually taken from their parents to assimilate them to
white society. Non-Europeans were also denied naturalisation or,

towards the end of the policy, could only secure it after three times as long in the country as anyone else. As unnaturalised 'aliens' they were frequently denied welfare services or licences. Some of these restrictions were imposed by States and not by the Commonwealth. Non-Europeans were also barred from serving in the armed forces, although many did during the world wars.

Increasingly the policy was becoming untenable and even ridiculous. It was modified through the 1960s, especially by Harold Holt's administration on succeeding Sir Robert Menzies.[3] Finally it was declared as one of the first acts of the Whitlam government in 1972 that race, colour or creed would no longer be a basis for immigration control. No change in legislation was needed. This ended a long and increasingly embarrassing period when immigration policy had to be rationalised by hypocrisy, lies and evasions.

Populate or perish

Concern with racial purity has attracted more attention than the parallel concern with building the population in order to preserve the continent for its colonisers. In the early days the main threat to the British Australian population had been the intrusion of other European powers into the South Pacific. The Dutch had claimed Van Diemen's Land (Tasmania) as early as 1642, but they were satisfied with their Indonesian empire and increasingly allied with the British. The French might have claimed New South Wales had they arrived slightly before Captain Phillip in 1788. The Russians were in the Pacific well before the British. The Germans were more of a threat by the end of the nineteenth century. British soldiers withdrew from Australia in 1870, but the British navy was assumed to be quite capable of protecting Australia from its bases in Singapore and Hong Kong. Fear of the Chinese and Japanese was alleviated by the strict imposition of the White Australia policy, at least until 1941. But many Australians were conscious that they were a small isolated people, very far from their original homeland. Blainey's 'tyranny of distance' was only too real when it took weeks to get to England, as it did well into the 1960s for most people.

Edmund Barton's concept of 'a nation for a continent and a continent for a nation' dominated thinking at Federation in 1901.

Alfred Deakin opened his 1901 election campaign by favouring 'a White Australia, in which the absolute mastering and dominating element shall be British'. If vast and empty Australia were to be held by the British settlers it must not only be defended but also have enough human resources to defend itself. If the land were to be exploited it must have enough farmers, labourers and miners to work it. The clarion call of the national anthem – 'For those who come across the seas we've boundless plains to share' – was no joke, although it was made into one when Australia was punishing several thousand Afghans and Iraqis for daring to take up the offer in 2001. Even more persistent than the myth of White Australia in popular thinking has been the myth of the 'threat from the North'. A few boats appear on the horizon and public opinion, followed by public policy, goes into a tail spin.

The slogan 'populate or perish' was first used by Billy Hughes in 1937 and was revived by Arthur Calwell after the Second World War. In the First, Australia had sacrificed an exceptionally high number of its 4 million people. In the Second, it had faced air attack and potential invasion by the Japanese. Britain could not save Australia in 1942 and the United States had to be relied on to do so. Both wars were followed by planned immigration programs. That of the 1920s was aborted by the world depression and was still obsessed with the outdated aim of rural settlement. That of the 1940s still continues and has never been abandoned in fifty-five years.[4]

However, there have been two changes of approach to populating Australia. Before the 1980s immigrants were deliberately attracted by assisted passages, propaganda and recruiting drives by government, employers and some voluntary organisations. Since then no incentives have been held out and entry has become more difficult. The other shift, of course, took place between 1966 and 1972. Before then only 'white' and preferably British immigrants were sought. Since then policy has officially ignored race, colour and creed.

With the exception of the gold-rush years of the 1850s, Australian population has sharply increased in response to official programs. As with immigration everywhere, entrants decline in times of depression and increase in times of expansion. A growing number have responded to conditions at home – the aftermath of world wars, collapse of civil order, and dictatorship. This is the classic 'push–pull' model of migrant motivation developed from the experience of the United States. Even today some American social scientists argue that immigration is simply the sum of a host of individual decisions. However, in the case of Australia this overlooks the role of the state in turning the tap on or off and in favouring and encouraging some classes of immigrant over others. There are very powerful 'pushes' out of Afghanistan, Africa or Iraq, but they do not produce major inflows into Australia. In the post-war period there were fairly weak 'pushes' out of Scandinavia but much effort and money were spent in trying, with limited success, to attract 'Nordic' immigrants from countries which were often more prosperous than Australia.[5]

Britain had always been the source from which Australia sought to build its population. It contributed the largest single national group of immigrants each year from 1788 to 1996, when it was replaced by New Zealand, still remaining second. Until the 1960s it normally supplied at least half of the intake. Between 1949 and 2001 it provided 32 per cent of all immigrants, although this moves from a majority to a small minority over that period. But there were problems in attracting the British after the Second World War. There was full employment in both countries and a severe shortage of suitable shipping. Housing was probably the major motive for emigrating but there was also a housing shortage in Australia. Many British immigrants were housed in hostels into the late 1960s, which they resented.

The other major sources were the large number of Displaced Persons in European camps and the southern Europeans who were largely barred from the United States until 1965. In competition with Canada and the United States, post-war Minister for Immigration Arthur Calwell organised the selection of 170 000 Displaced Persons, the largest number of non-British yet to be accepted in a short period in Australian history. They were transported in former American troop ships, housed in former army camps in provincial areas and bonded to work at any task set by the Commonwealth. As Labor was in office they were to be employed at trade union rates and conditions.[6]

The Displaced Persons intake not merely added 170 000 to a population of 7.5 million, it also greatly enhanced the workforce, especially in construction and some agricultural areas. Work had to be accepted on pain of deportation, a threat very rarely used. Eventually many were able to secure their own employment. But initially most were classified as labourers or female domestics, the former going to construction sites in Tasmania or the Snowy Mountains, the latter often working in the camps. Consequently they did not appear in the major cities in most cases until well into the 1950s. In the meantime the Commonwealth had launched propaganda campaigns to gain public acceptance and also to persuade immigrants to become citizens and to assimilate. Much of this work was done through the Good Neighbour movement, which was organised between 1950 and 1978, when the Commonwealth withdrew financial support. Good Neighbour brought together existing charitable and community organisations but was reluctant to encourage ethnic organisations.

The Displaced Persons intake laid the foundations for a multicultural Australia, even while official policy favoured rapid assimilation. In 1947 the ethnic and immigrant proportions were at their lowest level before or since as there had been very little immigration since 1930. But the reservoir of 'New Australians' was finite. While the British intake remained high, the strong pressures from southern Europe could not be ignored. Agreements were signed with Italy in 1951 and with Greece in 1952. The basis for settlement was laid down in intergovernment agreements, which continued to be signed until 1970. Under them the Netherlands-born increased from 2000 in 1947 to 102 000 in 1961, the Greece-born from 12 000 in 1947 to 140 000 in 1966, the Italy-born from 34 000 in 1947 to 267 000 in 1966, and the Germany-born from 14 000 in 1947 to 109 000 in 1961. Although many were housed in camps they also had a presence in the cities. Opinion polling showed southern Europeans to be unpopular at this time and there was considerable controversy about 'ghetto formation' and crime. The southern Europeans were not effectively incorporated into the Good Neighbour movement , which was a factor in its eventual demise. Between 1947 and 1971 the Australian population rose from 7.5 million to 12.7 million, the larger part due to immigration.

Planning and control

To achieve the objectives of Australian immigration policy has required a greater degree of planning and control than was normal in other developed nations. Much migration control in other societies

was directed at preventing people from leaving rather than determining the conditions for attracting them. China and Japan both forbade emigration well into the nineteenth century. Some European
states, such as Russia and Germany, forbade emigration to those liable
for military service. Even Britain, until 1825, prohibited the emigration of skilled artisans, although this was not effectively policed. The
practice of forbidding emigration was most recently developed by
communist states following the Soviet model. A number of states still
require exit visas for those leaving.

This was not the approach of immigrant societies such as Australia, the United States and Canada, nor was it usual for Britain and
the British empire. Britain did not control the entry of foreign subjects until the Aliens Act of 1905, nor of British Commonwealth citizens until 1962. Neither of these controls was racially based in legal
terms. In practice they were designed to discourage Jewish immigration in the first case and non-European in the second. The United
Kingdom has never had a detailed migration program and much discretion is left to migration officers at the point of arrival. Family
reunion with resident British subjects, and work permits have been
the main instruments used. Until recently more have left Britain than
have entered. The United Kingdom has never controlled Irish entry
except in wartime. Citizens of the Irish Republic still constitute the
largest immigrant group, as they have done for 200 years.

The United States left much immigration control to the states.
While it legislated against Chinese entry as early as 1882, it was not
until 1921 and 1924 that strict controls were imposed. Even then
major exceptions were made for those from the Americas, and
Mexican immigration was actively encouraged during the Second
World War. Massive intakes before 1921 were simply processed as
they arrived and only rejected if diseased or criminal. After that,
national quotas were introduced, designed to maintain the ethnic
balance of a century before. These restrictions were lifted in 1965.[7]
Both Canada and New Zealand introduced 'white' migration policies which were directed mainly against Chinese and Indians,
although New Zealand has been much more liberal than Australia
towards Pacific Islanders.

Migration restriction in English-speaking countries has mainly
been directed against groups believed to be unassimilable or to

threaten social harmony or employment conditions. This was obviously the case with the White Australia policy enshrined in the Immigration Restriction Act (1901–58). Migration officers were given discretion, both overseas and in Australia, to determine whether an immigrant was 'coloured' or not. In some respects Australian control policy had contradictions. British subjects had virtually free access to Australia until 1983 – but only if they were 'white'. New Zealanders have always had free access and Maoris were acceptable but not other non-Europeans. While New Zealanders are nominally visaed on arrival and need a passport, they still constitute by far the largest gap in an otherwise universal system of entry control. Since 1996 they have replaced the British as the largest immigrating group. White non-British subjects were usually free to enter Australia until restrictions in the 1930s, reflecting the depressed economy and labour market. But they could be restricted from time to time. 'Enemy aliens' (Germans, Austrians and Turks) were denied entry between 1914 and 1925. Others had to provide landing money, to discourage poor southern Europeans who had been excluded from the United States in the mid-1920s. Official policy distinguished between 'British' and 'aliens' until both were redesignated in 1983 as 'non-citizens' until naturalised. By then the restrictions on land ownership or access to welfare services for non-British 'aliens', some of them imposed by States, had also ended.[8]

While immigration remained a colonial function there were some differences in practice. The Commonwealth took over constitutional control in 1901 under s. 51(xxvii) of the Constitution, but administrative control remained with the States until 1920. Even after that date some States, notably South Australia, pursued their own policies of attracting migrants within the overall Commonwealth legislation by offering land, housing or access to employment. Immigration control from 1901 until the 1970s had several basic features. 'Aboriginal natives of Asia, Africa and the Pacific' were kept out, regardless of the fact that they were not mentioned in immigration legislation. Those who came to Australia were returned home at the expense of the shipper, thus making carriers responsible for denying tickets. Some students or businessmen were exempted at the discretion of the Commonwealth but were not eligible for naturalisation or to bring in their relatives. All 'white' British subjects (including the Irish) entered freely and were only controlled if there were some security or criminal reason for doing so, which was very rare and sometimes controversial. This right was steadily removed but continues to be enjoyed by New Zealand citizens (now regardless of race). Non-British 'aliens' were admitted but could be subject to ad hoc restrictions mainly aimed at controlling their numbers. Refugees were admitted from specific situations and in numbers controlled by the Commonwealth, the largest intake being between 1947 and 1952.

Throughout this period Australia had a more effective system of control than Britain or the United States. The first let in anyone who was a British subject, which included nearly one-quarter of the population of the world. The Americans were very liberal towards immigrants from the American continent and especially Canadians. But the major factor in controlling entry was the distance of Australia from all other 'white' sources other than New Zealand. It was always cheaper to emigrate to North America or within Europe than to come to Australia. Even when the United States closed entry to many southern Europeans, they could still get to Argentina, Uruguay or Chile more cheaply than to Australia. Many moved with relative freedom within Europe, especially to France. There was no incentive for Americans or Canadians to come to Australia, as economic conditions in their homelands were comparable or better.

It was, then, unusual for immigrants to come to Australia from anywhere outside the 'white' British empire. Many within that category could not afford to come, a problem solved from 1831 by systems of assisted passages. Unlike control mechanisms, which are negative, assisted passages were positive. They were also unusual. New Zealand provided passages but not as regularly as Australia. Canada normally extended loans which had to be repaid. The United States needed no such incentives, as it was the goal of the great majority of European, Irish and even British emigrants until 1921. Assisted immigration built the Australian population in almost all years (other than wars and depressions) from 1831 to 1982. Far more Australians are descended from assisted immigrants than from convicts – probably a majority of those of British and Irish descent. Passages were subsidised by the United Kingdom but paid for from Australian resources, especially land sales. They were also organised from London, but with diminishing effect, by the Colonial Land and Emigration Commission. Consequently they were not available for non-British migrants until the colonies assumed complete control by 1870. No passages were normally available except for British subjects, with the exception of Queensland, which assisted Scandinavians and Germans. This remained the case until 1947.[9]

Assisted passages were a means of populating Australia while retaining its British character. The availability of passages was determined by colonial budgets, by economic conditions and by ethnic preferences. Some colonies, like South Australia, favoured British Protestants, while others, like Queensland and New South Wales, were more generous to Irish Catholics. All favoured agricultural workers and female domestic servants, the latter being expected to reduce the wide discrepancy between male and female numbers. Passages were not generally available for industrial workers or clerks, although exceptions were sometimes made for miners and building craftsmen. Families were favoured, but not those with too many dependent children. The disabled were excluded, as were 'habitual paupers'. The object was to build a healthy, economically viable, young and British people. Apart from Victoria, where the gold rush of the 1850s swamped the colony with unassisted immigrants, and Tasmania which was too poor to offer many passages, Australia was peopled to a large extent by those who had been paid to come. The greatest influx was to Queensland, when 100 000 were assisted between 1879 and 1888. Policy was largely determined by employers and land owners, who were well represented in the colonial legislatures.

The Australian population was thus planned and engineered to a greater extent than is true for almost anywhere else. Assisted passages continued to be used but were opened by international agreement to other nationalities after 1947. The largest number brought out in any decade was not until the 1960s, when 875 000 were assisted. By then both the occupational and the ethnic composition had changed, although the family basis remained important. Skilled workers were sought rather than labourers. The last major classification of immigrants as 'labourers' or 'domestics' was between 1947 and 1952 when these labels were applied to Displaced Persons regardless of their qualifications or experience. But by the 1960s manufacturing had become a much greater employer than agriculture. Europe had also become a much greater source of immigrants, and Britain correspondingly less important.

Nevertheless, the use of assistance to retain a British presence was still very important. Between 1958 and 1972 assistance was given to 77.6 per cent of United Kingdom arrivals and 75.7 per cent from Ireland. Preference was also shown to north Europeans, with 75 per cent of Austrians, 77.5 per cent of Danes, 61.6 per cent of Dutch, 60.7 per cent of Finns, 71.9 per cent of Germans, 66 per cent of Swedes and 60.9 per cent of Swiss coming out with assistance between 1945 and 1972. The figures for Displaced Persons were, of course, much higher: 80.6 per cent for Czechoslovakians, 85 per cent for Estonians, 80.6 per cent for Hungarians, 96.7 per cent for Latvians, 97.3 per cent for Lithuanians, 76.5 per cent for Poles and 97 per cent for Ukrainians over the same period. Most of these would not have come to Australia without public assistance. Others were less favoured. Only 33.8 per cent of Greeks, 19 per cent of Italians and 42 per cent of Portuguese were assisted, although the picture is different for Yugoslavs (58.1 per cent), many of whom were Displaced Persons, and for Turks (80.1 per cent) and Spanish (70 per cent). These two latter groups were recruited on the urging of the car and sugar industries, respectively. No Turks got assistance before 1964.

Despite the relaxation of the White Australia policy in the 1960s and the arrival of many thousands of Anglo-Indians and Ceylon Burghers, there was little or no assistance for non-Europeans. There were no assisted Chinese or Japanese nationals between 1945 and 1972, only two Burmese, three Indonesians and nine Ceylonese. There were tiny numbers from India, Lebanon, Singapore and Egypt, all of which were already sending large unassisted contingents. Essentially, assisted passages were a form of social engineering designed to keep Australia British, to increase the manual labour force, to redress the gender imbalance and to keep Australia white. While about half of those coming to Australia in the century and a half paid their own fares or had them paid by employers or relatives, the other half would probably not have come without assistance. No other society, at least before the creation of Israel in 1948, has been so consciously shaped by public authorities and resources.

Assisted passages (except for refugees) were abolished in 1982 by the Fraser government. They had become very expensive, especially in the peak years of the late 1960s. There was less need to encourage immigrants into a society which no longer had full employment. Nor was the basis of schemes in agreements with particular states compatible with the abolition of White Australia. The tradition of building a new society through state action remains. In some senses it has become even more central as entry to Australia becomes more restrictive.

White Australia and preference for the British have both gone. Some remnants of British preference remain: the open door for New Zealanders, only modified in 2001; the working holiday visas, which go mainly to young Britishers; the selection points allocation for English competence; and the maintenance in London of the largest overseas migration post. But these are only remnants, and the flow from Britain has levelled out at about 10 per cent of settlers. The 'British descended' component in immigration is still higher than for the United States and Canada, if only because of the escalating emigration from New Zealand and South Africa. English proficiency is an important qualification to gain points for admission. It was extended in scope when the 'concessional family reunion' category was merged into the 'skilled Australian-linked' one by the Howard government in 1997. Age, disability, unemployability are all barriers to admission, as they were for assisted immigrants from the 1830s.

Rather than engineering society by subsidising arrivals, as was the case until the 1970s, it is now engineered by selection and exclusion. This is rational and utilitarian. But it often weighs most heavily on those who have most reason to come to Australia – refugees, the poor, and their relatives.

Notes

1 Jupp, *The Australian People*; Jupp, *Immigration*; Sherington, *Australia's Immigrants*.
2 Lack and Templeton, *Sources of Australian Immigration History*; London, *Non-White Immigration and the 'White Australia' Policy*.
3 London, *Non-White Immigration*.
4 Lack and Templeton, *Bold Experiment*; Wilton and Bosworth, *Old Worlds and New Australia*.

5 Jupp, *Arrivals and Departures.*
6 Kunz, *Displaced Persons.*
7 Freeman and Jupp, *Nations of Immigrants.*
8 Jordens, *Alien to Citizen.*
9 Jupp, 'Seeking Whiteness'.
10 Jupp, *Immigration.*

2

From assimilation to a multicultural society, 1972–2002

The Australian experience of immigration was historically with those from the United Kingdom.[1] Before 1921 this included a large component of Catholic Irish, but these had almost ceased to arrive after the depression of the 1890s. England has always provided the largest number of the United Kingdom-born, followed by Ireland in the nineteenth century and Scotland in the twentieth. The English have remained the largest overseas-born group to the present. The Scots replaced the Irish by 1921 and were only replaced by Italians in 1961. Only in 1996 did New Zealand replace the United Kingdom as the single largest national source of newcomers.

As Sir Henry Parkes put it before Federation, 'the crimson thread of kinship runs through us all'. Himself an English migrant, Parkes ignored the Indigenous and Chinese populations who made up less than 5 per cent of the population. As premier of New South Wales in 1881 he warned Italians not to congregate together because it would delay their assimilation. He dispersed them throughout the colony as a condition of settlement aid. He was also hostile to Irish Catholic immigration and advocated its limitation. Most of his attitudes were widespread in late colonial Australia and represent majority opinion at the time of Federation in 1901.

Assimilation

As in many other countries, assimilation was seen as necessary to full acceptance into society. This society was, itself, always changing its character in response to new arrivals and it was not always clear what 'assimilation' might mean. To Parkes it meant acceptance of British Protestant dominance, which was scarcely acceptable to the large Irish Catholic minority. But even this minority favoured White Australia, seeing assimilation in racial rather than cultural terms. Policy towards the Indigenous minorities was very ambivalent. But by 1937 it was officially agreed at the national level that they, too, should assimilate. As they were also subject to discriminatory laws and to forced segregation, there was a basic contradiction. Non-Europeans, who were a small and declining minority, were also discriminated against and were popularly regarded as incapable of assimilation, even when they became Christians or spoke only English. They were unable to become naturalised and could not bring their relatives, including their wives, into Australia.[2]

'Assimilation' is a disputed term. To many it meant the disappearance of any characteristics which marked off individuals from each other. On this definition colour or facial features, which were inherited, made non-Europeans and their children unassimilable. This view was officially maintained well into the late 1960s as the basis for admission to Australia. The term also implied the adoption of majority culture, which was assumed to be uniform and self-evident. This attitude still surfaces in debate today. Most important was the adoption of the English language. Religious divisions are less important than a century ago, but non-Christian religions are looked on with suspicion by many. Clothing has become very varied, but some manifestly 'ethnic' dress may be criticised, from the long 'reffo' trench coats of the 1940s to the Muslim headscarves of today.

An example of assimilationism from the early post-war years was the official advice not to behave in any way which would attract attention. Assimilation would be complete when nobody noticed the newcomer. Similar advice had been given by Jewish organisations to those arriving as refugees from the Nazis in the late 1930s. Yet another example was the 'competition' at Good Neighbour conferences, when photos of selected children were displayed and delegates had to choose the 'Australian'. These measures of assimilation were very popular in the 1950s and muddled together physical appearance and cultural behaviour.

The term 'assimilation' is still used in the sense of becoming culturally Australian, although its use for physical appearance has waned as memories of White Australia fade away. What is really meant now is 'acculturation' – the most significant example being a shift to the use of English. Groups and individuals may retain such varied behaviour as religious adherence or food preferences, so long as they do so within the privacy of their own homes or communities. This was the often stated expectation of One Nation and other critics of multiculturalism in the 1990s.

The ethnic situation in 1972

British and European immigration had peaked in the 1960s with the largest number of assisted passages provided in any decade, at 875 000. Immigration agreements were in place with nearly all west European states and were extended to Turkey in 1968 and Yugoslavia in 1970. These agreements laid down the conditions under which assistance would be given but also obliged the Australian government to provide acceptable levels of settlement services and employment. While increasing numbers of 'mixed race' were coming from Asia in the 1960s, they did not normally receive assisted passages nor were they subject to official agreements between governments. They were almost invariably English-speaking Christians and were often easily assimilated into existing cultural and behavioural practices and institutions and especially the churches and suburban society.[3]

The original use of assisted passages to attract only British immigrants had become secondary, but the aim of encouraging white Europeans remained. The greatest threat to these aims was the reform of the US immigration system in 1965. Assisted passages had always been used to counter the attractions of North America. Canada competed with Australia and the US quota for British and Irish immigrants was rarely filled. Other Europeans were seriously limited by the 'national quota' system adopted by the United States in 1924. This had been aimed specifically against the 'new immigration' which had brought millions from eastern and southern Europe before the First World War. It set quotas for each nationality which were very small for such Europeans and negligible for the rest of the world other than Latin America. In 1965 the Immigration and Nationality Act of 1952 was amended, the national quota system was abolished and family reunion was given priority. This not only led to a rise in emigration to the United States but also redirected many who had previously looked towards Australia.

Thus, at the very moment when immigration to Australia from Europe was at its height, its future also became very uncertain. At the same time, the consolidation of the European Community in July 1968 redirected Italian migration towards other member states. This process continued with increasing economic success and the adherence of more EC members. Finally, in 1975, economic problems in Australia caused the Whitlam government to reduce intake to its lowest level from 1948 to the present. From then onwards European migration came predominantly from Britain, though declining, and from Yugoslavia.

These rapid changes between 1965 and 1975 froze the European immigrant communities. They were not added to, they consolidated their organisations and locations, and they steadily aged as the east Europeans had done before them. The Italian-born and the Greek-born peaked in 1971, the Maltese-born in 1981, the Spanish in 1976 and the Austrians in 1971. One effect of this was what is called 'cultural fossilisation' – the preservation of nostalgia for the homeland at a particular and increasingly distant time. This had previously been the experience of many east Europeans. It consolidated the ethnic communities while at the same time making it harder for them to retain the loyalty and interest of many of their children. These did not necessarily become 'Anglo-Australians' but developed subcultures of Italo-Australians, Greek Australians and so on. They changed from 'immigrants' to 'ethnics'. There is a contrast between those European ethnic communities which have been able to retain the support of the Australian-born and those which survive on nostalgia and a rapidly declining immigrant generation.

Language and culture

English is not legally the official language of Australia. It is so universally used that the issue of bilingualism or multilingualism scarcely arose before 1945. Unlike Spanish in the United States or French in Canada, there are no languages which present a threat. There are no Indigenous languages with more than 5000 speakers and half of those spoken in 1788 have disappeared. Thus, the pressures to abandon minority languages are strong and the resistance to this expectation is weak. Most of those normally using a language other than English are first-generation immigrants.

Once race had been abandoned as an official distinguishing factor, language became a central concern for policy makers. Apart from the Census of 1933, which tested the ability to speak English, there are no official figures on language use before 1976. By then twenty-five years of post-war immigration had created large communities speaking a language other than English (officially, LOTEs). These languages were seen by public agencies as the basis for 'ethnic groups', along with the traditional birthplace figures which had been recorded from as early as 1846. Policies were developed for those of non-English-speaking background (NESB 1) and their locally born children (NESB 2). These were often based on the so-called 'deficit' approach, namely that those not fluent in English needed compensating for the 'barriers' which prevented their full social participation.

Some immigrant languages had persisted over several generations, notably German and Cantonese. Italian had a continuing presence in north Queensland at least since the 1920s, and Greek was in use in Melbourne and Sydney from the same period. But most other languages withered as there was no community to support them. This was no longer the case by 1976. By then there were about 1 500 000 'regular users' of languages other than English. Details needed some adjustments, especially as most Yugoslav languages were classified as 'Slovenian', which was not the case and indicates the lack of expert advice used by the Australian Bureau of Statistics at the time. The major languages in 1976 have been estimated by Professor Michael Clyne as: Italian (444 672 speakers); Greek (262 177); German (170 644); the highly disputed Serbo-Croatian (142 407); French (64 851, probably an overestimate); Dutch (64 768); Polish (62 945); Arabic (51 284); Spanish (48 343); and Maltese (45 933).[4]

Even before multiculturalism had been effectively entrenched as official policy, there were already very large language communities in Australia. There were also very many new arrivals who could not speak English at all, including many who were still not fluent twenty years later. Census language figures obscure even greater complexity. The various languages of Yugoslavia were not fully detailed until 1986, nor were those of China until 1991. The many dialects of Italian have never been detailed, and distinct Indigenous languages were not listed until 1996.

By 1976 Australia had become multilingual. It needed enhanced translating and interpreting services and not simply the already well-established adult migrant and child migrant education programs, which were designed to teach English, and the more recent and limited telephone interpreter service created in 1973. At this stage there were only a few local commercial radio stations which broadcast in other languages, and Radio 2EA and 3EA which had begun 'experimentally' in 1975 and were the origin of the Special Broadcasting Service (SBS). Such broadcasting had been inhibited previously by an Australian Broadcasting Control Board regulation that only 2.5 per cent of time could be in a language other than English, including advertisements, and must have an English translation.

Official policy recognised that language variety presented problems which might be solved within a framework of English teaching, translation and interpreting. The variety of cultures was a different issue. Religious variety had existed since 1788 and was protected by section 116 of the Commonwealth Constitution. Complete freedom was limited by State laws on Sunday observance which were strictest in Victoria and South Australia. The main victims of these restrictions were the Jews and the Seventh Day Adventists, as there were very few Muslims in Australia. Assistance to religious schools from public funds had been implemented by the Commonwealth and the States since 1967 after three generations of acute and sometimes very bitter controversy. Free gifts of land were made by State governments to religious institutions. With the decline of tensions between Protestants and Catholics, and in the absence of many non-Christians other than the long-established Jews, religion was not seen as a 'cultural' issue. It was, however, the basis on which many ethnic groups were formed and languages maintained.

Many cultural manifestations were accepted within the limits of 'pasta and polka' activities. From the Displaced Persons choirs and folk dancers of the 1950s onwards, public displays of exotic culture were welcomed and officially encouraged. Folk costume performances were common at the annual Good Neighbour conferences, which were otherwise dedicated to assimilation. Most popular of all was 'gastronomic multiculturalism' – the growth of a restaurant culture in the major cities and of grocers and delicatessens. All of this made life more interesting without challenging Anglo-

Australian hegemony. Until 1976 almost all such cultural manifestations were by Europeans.

Other cultural activities were less welcome. There was a continuing fear of ethnic crime and violence, manifest particularly in anxieties about the Mafia which were most marked in the 1960s and 1970s. There were certainly traditions in southern Italy which lent credence to these fears and a significant southern Italian interest in marijuana, though not in other drugs. But it was quite unreasonable to extend these fears to the entire Italian population, many of whom were equally hostile to the antisocial minority which got them a bad name. All studies done then and since have shown most immigrant groups, including those from southern Europe, to have lower crime rates than the national average.

Political violence was also feared and denounced. Indeed, any political manifestation was viewed with suspicion. The regulations imposed on ethnic newspapers and commercial broadcasts until 1956 were mainly designed to prevent their use by extremist groups. This fear extended to public broadcasting once 2EA and 3EA became established and led to the abolition of the Melbourne community radio station 3ZZ by the Commonwealth in 1977.

The main problems involved the relationship between various national and political groups from Yugoslavia. Physical attacks and occasional bombings reached their height in 1970. The alleged role of Croatian groups in this led to the 'raid' on ASIO headquarters in Melbourne by Attorney-General Lionel Murphy in March 1973 in search of details withheld from him. Prior to the 1970s such limited political violence as erupted was mainly confined to east Europeans. However, the riots at Bonegilla hostel by Italians in 1961 saw an extraordinary reaction, including the mobilisation of army units at a nearby camp who did not, contrary to urban myth, actually march against Bonegilla.

Ethnic community organisation

Nearly all ethnic minority groups formed some sort of organisation soon after their numbers built up. They also published media in languages other than English. This is the experience of migration elsewhere, unless it is prohibited by the host governments. In

Australia restrictions on foreign language publications under the War Precautions Act of 1920 were imposed in 1934 and not fully lifted until 1956, but they have since been free to publish. Ethnic organisation was not caused by the adoption of multicultural public policy. It long predated that. The first non-English newspaper, *Die Deutsche Post für die Australischen Kolonien*, was established in South Australia in 1848. Welsh and Gaelic journals were first published in 1868 and 1857 and there were Chinese newspapers from the same time. Most of these eventually went out of existence as their public moved over to English or died out. The oldest surviving newspaper, *Le Courrier Australien*, has kept going since 1892 partly through sales to schools teaching French. But the *Hellenic Herald* has flourished since 1926. The same longevity is true for ethnic organisations. The Greek Orthodox communities of Sydney and Melbourne are over 100 years old. The Cornish Association of South Australia dates back to 1890, while the See Yap Society of Melbourne has survived since 1854, based on Australia's oldest Chinatown in Little Bourke Street.

No ethnic media or organisations received public funding until the 1970s and few have ever enjoyed much support. Between 1950 and 1970 the foundation for a variety of European ethnic organisations was created. In most cases this remains in existence. Newspapers created during this period and still being published include the *Dutch Australian Weekly* (1951), *Neos Kosmos* (1957), *Die Woche* (1957), *Magyar Elet* (1958), *La Fiamma* (1947), *Il Globo* (1959), *Australijas Latvietis* (1949), *Maltese Herald* (1958), *Tygodnik Polski* (1949) and *Edinenie* (1950), among others.

By the 1970s there was already a widespread network of ethnic organisations and media. The Department of Social Security, in its National Groups Section directory of 1977, listed almost 2000 organisations in all States and Territories. Many of these were very small or from small groups. But they included 38 Chinese, 35 Croatian, 133 Dutch, 23 Finnish, 60 German, 340 Greek, 55 Hungarian, 166 Italian, 96 Jewish, 56 Latvian, 62 Lebanese, 46 Maltese, 109 Polish, 31 Serbian and 106 Ukrainian associations. This suggests a very high degree of organisation among some of the Displaced Person communities, especially the Ukrainians and Latvians, and among the Greeks. When broad ethnic pressure groups began to form in the early 1970s, Greeks, Jews and east Europeans took an active role in their leadership. The Jewish community was already highly organised by the 1960s, and most Jews were able to live their lives within it in terms of schooling, socialising, marriage and recreation.[5]

The structure of ethnic organisations was already well established before official multiculturalism was launched in the early 1970s. To suggest that the policy was handed to immigrants who did not really want it is historically very dubious.[6] It may be true that many were not enrolled or reached by the ethnic networks. But in so far as 'communities' existed at all, they expressed themselves through these networks and media. Governments and other public agencies found it convenient to use the ethnic structures to consult on problems and as avenues of communication. It was mutually convenient for the communities and the public sector to deal with each other. This mutual convenience was the basis on which the ethnic communities' movements were launched in Sydney and Melbourne in 1975. From then on there was an organised 'ethnic lobby'.

The multicultural society was there, however, before either the policy or the lobby. By 1970, 20 per cent of Australians had been born overseas and that proportion increased slowly over the next thirty years to reach almost 25 per cent by 2000. Within that total, however, the British-born numbers rose only by 25 000 between 1971 and 1996, while New Zealand-born numbers rose by over 210 000.

The new proletariat

The ethnic groups formed by European migration between 1947 and 1972 were essentially working class, whatever their origins, although they often had middle-class leaders. They also wished to retain cultures which were changing in their original homelands, including dialects which were being modified into national languages and entertainment which was moving away from folk and rural forms towards expression through the mass media. There was a political divide between those who had come as refugees from communism and the larger number who had emigrated for economic reasons. Opinion polling still shows the former to favour the Liberal Party, while the latter are more strongly Labor than the Australian norm. There were also some political strains within ethnic groups, most notably with Greeks during the military dictatorship of 1967 to 1974.

European recruitment policy between 1947 and 1972 had favoured manual workers. By 1976, 61 per cent of male employed Greeks were tradesmen and labourers, 63 per cent of Italians, 77 per cent of Yugoslavs, 69 per cent of Maltese and 61 per cent of Poles. This compared with 37 per cent of the Australian-born and 45 per cent of the British. The opposite picture held for the professions, which included 10 per cent of the Australian-born but less than 2 per cent of the Greeks.

Immigration was creating a multicultural factory proletariat and pushing up many of the native-born into the middle classes.[7] The impact was most noticeable in Melbourne, Adelaide, Sydney and Wollongong and in the motor manufacture, clothing, textiles, footwear, construction, steel, food processing and catering industries. Migrant participation in mining was not so marked, especially in coal mining, and Newcastle and the Hunter was the least affected industrial region. There was very limited migrant settlement in rural areas, or in Tasmania or Queensland at this stage.[8]

Ghettoes and ethnic suburbs

Because most European immigrants up to the 1970s were, or became, working class, they settled in working-class neighbourhoods, close to expanding manufacturing industry. In the early stages these neighbourhoods were in the inner cities in housing built before 1914 or in the new far outer suburbs still being built, often by the immigrants themselves. The impact was greatest on Melbourne and Adelaide. This concentration reactivated fears of ghetto formation which had surfaced from time to time over the past seventy years. These fears were enhanced by violence and rioting in American ghettoes and by civil disorder in some areas of London settled by West Indians, such as Notting Hill and Brixton.

In general Australia does not have ghettoes in the American sense.[9] The inner city areas were soon deserted for more distant suburbs and many were gentrified by young Australian professionals. Most southern Europeans were anxious to own their own homes and did so at a higher level than native-born Australians or the British. The outer industrial suburbs could scarcely be called ghettoes at all. They were brand new, if often lacking such facilities as made roads, sewerage systems and public transport. No particular ethnic group predominated. In the years of full employment before 1975, families were able to earn high incomes, to buy their homes and to run cars – thus meeting their economic aspirations.

In so far as there were consistent settlement patterns, Italians and Greeks tended to arrive first in the inner suburbs and then to move outwards into adjacent and newer neighbourhoods. East Europeans favoured the outer 'green field' suburbs rather more, as did the Maltese. Jewish immigrants normally went to suburbs already settled by Jews, such as St Kilda and Caulfield in Melbourne or Bondi in Sydney. This was the most important example of settlement in middle-class areas by non-British immigrants. The British, Germans and Dutch all favoured the outer suburbs and tended to segregate themselves from other Europeans. There were, however, some British industrial districts, such as Elizabeth and Salisbury in Adelaide, Sunshine in Melbourne, Whyalla in South Australia and Kwinana in Western Australia. These usually resulted from recruitment by particular industries or by the allocation of State public housing specially reserved for the British. Until the 1970s much of this type of housing was not available for non-British immigrants.

By 1961 these patterns were already becoming apparent in Melbourne and Adelaide. Substantial proportions of southern Europeans were recorded in the inner Melbourne suburbs of Fitzroy, Brunswick, Richmond, Collingwood, the City of Melbourne (especially Carlton) and Prahran, and the inner Adelaide suburbs of Thebarton, St Peters, Kensington, Hindmarsh and the City. This was less marked in Sydney, except in the City itself, Leichhardt and Marrickville, and only visible in Perth at Fremantle. Mixed settlement by eastern and southern Europeans and the British was apparent in the Melbourne suburbs of Keilor, Altona and Sunshine, the Adelaide suburb of Campbelltown and the Sydney suburb of Fairfield. Apart from some rural districts in Victoria, Western Australia and Queensland, provincial settlement was mainly in the Canberra sister city of Queanbeyan and the steel city of Wollongong.

Distinct Italian, Greek and Maltese districts were emerging by 1971, following the mass migration of the 1960s. In Melbourne the adjacent cities of Brunswick, Coburg, Melbourne, Broadmeadows, Essendon, Fitzroy, Northcote, Preston and Whittlesea, to the north and west of the city centre, already contained 57 000 Italian-born by 1971; the neighbouring cities of Northcote, Brunswick, Collingwood, Richmond, Fitzroy, Broadmeadows, Prahran and Oakleigh contained 27 000 Greek-born; and the neighbouring Sunshine, Keilor and Altona, 12 000 Maltese-born. Other concentrations included 6000 Yugoslavs in Footscray. A new ethnic district was being formed in southwestern Springvale, where 32 per cent of the population was overseas-born in 1971. Apart from Springvale, Prahran and Oakleigh, these were all areas normally held by the ALP in State and federal elections. Immigration consolidated this loyalty and eventually spread this support to the newer southwestern industrial area around Springvale and Dandenong. These later attracted large numbers of Indochinese refugees passing through the Enterprise hostel at Springvale.

A political base

The concentration of southern Europeans in manual employment and working-class suburbs created a new political base for the labour movement. As in other immigrant situations such as the United States or Britain, immigrants and ethnic minorities tend to support the more reformist of the major parties. They rarely create their own parties and these do not prosper if they do so. Ethnic parties flourish where there is an historic concentration based on descent, such as the Parti Québécois in Canada or the Scottish National Party. Initial fears that ethnic groups would form distinct parties or unions were unfounded because immigrant and long-established communities do not behave politically in the same way. Ethnic politics by the 1970s was still concerned with homeland issues and often remained so for the immigrant generation. Not until the 1970s were enough former aliens naturalised to make much electoral difference.

British immigrants had always had a role in Australian politics and in 1901 they formed almost half the membership of the first Senate and House of Representatives. Numbers had dwindled by 1947, but the strong support of Irish-descended Catholics for the ALP was still easily measurable in opinion polls. The 'ethnic' element in Australian politics was essentially based on historic tensions between Catholics and Protestants. Usually half the Labor parliamentary representation was Catholic, while virtually all Liberal and Country Party members were Protestants. This division did not long survive the splits in the ALP between 1955 and 1957 but lasted essentially from 1916 to 1960.

Within twenty years of the start of mass European migration, many electorates were heavily influenced by ethnic voters. The great majority of these have consistently voted for the ALP ever since. In the national election of 2001 there were twenty federal electorates in which more than 30 per cent used a language other than English at home. These were all in Sydney (nine) or Melbourne (eleven). In five Sydney electorates an absolute majority did not speak English at home. Of these twenty, all but one (Menzies in eastern Melbourne) were held by Labor. A solid and unchanging base for the ALP was created by post-war immigration.

As immigrants became naturalised they were obliged to vote and a handful became active in the parties. Their experience was not usually very satisfying. Parliamentary selections were rare for immigrants, although more common for the second generation. The first Asian-born Commonwealth MP (Tsebin Tchen, Liberal Senator, Victoria) was not elected until 1998. An unusual feature of immigrant politicians has been their disagreements with their party, leading to expulsion or resignation. These include Andrew Theophanous, Franca Arena, Helen Sham-ho, Peter Wong and Paul Zammit. Although Labor holds nearly all of the ethnic electorates, it has been very reluctant to nominate immigrants to these safe seats. Discontent with the major parties and opposition to One Nation created Unity in 2000, with mainly Chinese and Vietnamese support. It had some success in Sydney municipal elections and elected Peter Wong to the New South Wales Legislative Council, but got very little support otherwise.

The major areas of non-British settlement, other than for the Chinese, are also a large part of the Labor 'heartland'. This is often overlooked in debates about the party's future, when the 'heartland' is conceptualised through outdated visions of the 'little Aussie battler', who is, of course, also believed to be of British or Irish descent. The consistent loyalty of these ethnic concentrations has been only grudgingly rewarded by Labor, and then mainly in Victoria. Only in Victoria has the party created an effective network of 'ethnic branches' since 1975. At the national parliamentary level, the two Coalition parties have normally returned more non-British immigrant members than Labor, although Labor is stronger among the second generation. At the municipal level, Labor has elected a range of immigrant councillors in Sydney and Melbourne. But unhappiness with some Labor councils in Sydney, such as Auburn, has recently strengthened the appeal of the minority Unity Party. In spite of all this, there is no doubt that Labor politicians, Commonwealth and State, have been much more likely to be answerable to immigrant voters than has been true for the Liberal and National parties.

Social mobility

Immigrants arriving between 1947 and 1972 were less rigorously selected than those coming afterwards, except on the basis of race. Australia has always favoured youth and discriminated against disability, right back to the bounty system of the 1840s. But most white British arrivals were either not subject to selection at all or were favoured in selection and assistance over the non-British. By the 1960s about one-quarter were returning to the United Kingdom. The British had few problems of acceptance, employment or language skills. But they were not marked by rapid social mobility and their children tended to remain in the same skilled manual occupations as their parents. The same was largely true for the Dutch and Germans, many of whom were also returning home in the 1960s as wartime hardships disappeared. British middle-class immigrants, many of whom came without assisted passages, formed a significant part of the professional and administrative classes. But this was not due to social improvement, as they had come from such classes in Britain.

There was a dichotomy among immigrants between those destined for manual employment, who were mainly Europeans, and those joining the middle classes, who were mainly British, North Americans or New Zealanders. But there was also a cultural divide which ran across class and occupation and was enshrined in the official designation 'non-English-speaking background'. Many Europeans who had been well educated in their homeland eventually moved out of the menial occupations which they first took up in Australia. The success of Jewish immigrants has been most fully documented in this respect. While there is little persuasive evidence, it seems equally likely that many Europeans with inadequate English suffered downward mobility. Their qualifications were often not recognised, a problem engaging official concern from the late 1940s until the present.[10] The occupations they sought increasingly demanded a level of English well beyond the 'survival' level to which the adult migrant education program originally aspired.

Asian settlement

In 1972 about 10 per cent of the settler intake was from Asia, excluding the Middle East. This temporarily passed 40 per cent in 1984 and touched 51 per cent in 1991 for one year only. For the thirteen years of the Labor government it averaged about 40 000 a year, or 39 per cent of settler intake, and this level has been sustained since the Coalition was returned in 1996. The 'colour blind' policy adopted from 1972 and the 'human capital' approach from 1988, were both at variance with popular perceptions of major differences between 'Asians' and 'Europeans', engrained in Australian history and culture. Over time the other perceived gap, between 'British' and 'aliens', became less important, especially as British immigration dropped towards only 10 per cent of the total. While official policy categorised immigrants in terms of visa classes, popular perceptions still saw them in terms of 'them' and 'us'.

Just as 'Europeans' might be divided between the mainly southern factory proletariat and the mainly northern skilled and middle-class workers, so 'Asians' were also very differentiated by skills and life chances. The picture is complicated by the large number of Asian students counted in the Census but not becoming permanent residents. Nevertheless, it remains true that Indian, Sri Lankan, Singaporean, Malaysian, Hong Kong Chinese and, to a lesser extent, Filipinos, Koreans, Taiwanese and mainland Chinese are much less likely to be working class than most southern and eastern Europeans. In many cases they have higher educational qualifications than the Australian average and higher incomes.

If fear of ghettoes had been rife for southern Europeans it was even more acute for non-Europeans. Immigration before 1972 had certainly produced large areas of concentration and very visible commercial centres for Italians and Greeks. Yet the tightest concentration for any ethnic group was for Jews in both Melbourne and Sydney, and the highest concentrations numerically were for the British in Perth and Adelaide. Neither of these attracted much critical comment. Dispersal over the years had spread Greeks and Italians into such new middle-class areas as Doncaster and Templestowe in Melbourne, Stirling in Perth, and Strathfield and Randwick in Sydney. Dispersal was less apparent in Brisbane but almost complete in Canberra. The 'Little Italys', such as Lygon Street in Melbourne or Norton Street in Sydney, were shopping centres, not crowded ghettoes, and very few Italians lived near them any more.

Australians had long been used to Chinatowns. By 1972 every major city except Adelaide had one. These had gradually lost their nineteenth-century reputation as sinks of vice, when the popularity of Chinese food increased. What Australians were not used to was large concentrations of Asians, especially in outer suburbs rather than city centres. Yet that is precisely where the expanding Asian population settled. The term 'Asian' covers even more variety than the term 'European'. This is reflected in quite different occupational and residential patterns. Many Chinese speakers are students and concentrations can be found around most universities, which was never true for European migrants. These students are likely to disperse as they return home or qualify as skilled immigrants and move out of student accommodation. Otherwise, Chinese speakers can be found throughout the major Australian cities: from relatively disadvantaged districts such as Cabramatta to affluent North Shore suburbs like Chatswood in Sydney, from working-class Richmond to bourgeois Doncaster in Melbourne, and spread quite evenly through metropolitan Perth.

A new middle class

In contrast to the mass immigration of the 1950s and 1960s, the slower and more controlled intake of the 1980s and 1990s did not create a new multicultural proletariat to the same extent. This was very different from the experience of the United States or the European Union. From the 1988 FitzGerald report onwards,[11] policy was directed towards enhancing 'human capital' rather than the manufacturing workforce. This conformed to analyses developed by the OECD, which argued that the future workforce would need a variety of skills appropriate to a 'postindustrial' society and that education was an asset in improving productivity.[12]

It is not generally realised that Asian immigrants, other than refugees, tend to be better educated, to secure better jobs and to live in more expensive suburbs than the Australian average. This is very different from the experience of Indochinese refugees in the present or the Chinese in the past. There are, then, two quite contrasting 'Asian' experiences and those who try to generalise about 'Asian' immigration are misleading themselves and others.

In 1996, 16.3 per cent of the Australian-born over 15 years old had higher qualifications, mainly degrees and diplomas. Of those employed, 27.2 per cent held administrative, managerial or professional jobs. Comparable figures for some Asian origins show that in most cases the level of qualification and of occupational status is higher. The China-born had 31 per cent with higher qualifications, Hong Kong-born 32 per cent, India-born 42.9 per cent, Fiji-born (more than half ethnic Indians) 20.5 per cent, Malaysia-born 40.5 per cent, Philippines-born 38.3 per cent, Singapore-born 35.3 per cent, Sri Lanka-born 33.8 per cent and Taiwan-born 24.3 per cent. Proportions in the workforce in administrative, management and professional jobs were: China (22.5 per cent); Hong Kong (39.3 per cent); India (36 per cent); Fiji (22 per cent); Malaysia (47.7 per cent); Philippines (17.4 per cent); Singapore (39.7 per cent); Sri Lanka (32.6 per cent); and Taiwan (41.5 per cent). The Filipino occupational figure reflects the fact that the majority are women, often married to Australians, and are probably employed below their level of qualification. Altogether this group of 560 000 immigrants, who would have been excluded under White Australia, have greatly improved the skills of the workforce in the very jobs likely to expand in the future.

An ethnic underclass?

Despite the tendency away from recruiting manual workers, some immigrant groups continued to concentrate in working-class suburbs and occupations. It remained true that most areas of non-British settlement returned Labor politicians. There were many less skilled jobs into which immigrants moved, as in other countries. These included catering, public transport, retail trade, construction, cleaning, food processing and a variety of service occupations.

Those recruited to these occupations were usually not native speakers of English and many had arrived under various humanitarian provisions. An unspoken aim of changes under the Coalition government after 1996 was to reduce this type of intake. Yet many such occupations were expanding, especially in catering and the retail trade. These could absorb many with less 'human capital' than high tech industries, but they were not organised as effective lobbies nor did they excite the imagination of politicians and bureaucrats.

Those making up this relatively small 'new proletariat' were faced with a higher level of unemployment than those recruited to manufacturing before 1970. They often competed with the less skilled Australian-born, with New Zealanders, with illegal overstayers and, of course, with each other. The problems of many immigrants were extended into the second generation, as unemployment, poor education and low skills often characterised the suburbs settled by immigrants from the Middle East and Southeast Asia in the 1970s. The children of the two major humanitarian intakes of that period were teenagers by the end of the century, living in areas with high unemployment and limited social mobility. This became an especially acute problem in the adjoining Sydney cities of Canterbury, Bankstown and Fairfield. Had more attention been paid to the large Vietnamese and Lebanese settlement in these areas from the 1970s, these problems might today be less serious.

Whether an 'ethnic underclass' is being formed, comparable to those in parts of Britain or the United States, has been inadequately studied. Most disadvantaged areas are rural and provincial and have low immigrant populations. Most disadvantaged social groups, such as single parents, are not predominantly drawn from immigrants. The most disadvantaged, by any measure, is the Indigenous population. Previous analysis, including that of Birrell, assumed that manual workers were disadvantaged.[13] But this overlooked the industrial arbitration system in Australia, which has been called the 'wage earner's welfare state' by Frank Castles.[14] A family with two or three members regularly employed was certainly not poor in the days before 1975 and would have accumulated enough home ownership and other savings to avoid poverty in later life. Some communities, such as the Ukrainians, developed effective co-operative savings systems, a practice also used later by many Koreans.

Migrant poverty was, however, present even in the days of full employment. Jean Martin's research for the Commission of Inquiry into Poverty reported in 1975 that 'the postwar migrant population as a whole is at present somewhere around an optimum situation so far as vulnerability to poverty is concerned'. However, she warned that, 'even if the proportion of the poor among migrants is less than in the rest of the population, it is still possible for certain sections of the migrant population to become fixed at the low socio-economic level at which the first arrivals entered the country. This will happen if the children of poor migrants suffer educational handicap, as many from non-English speaking families already appear to be doing.'[15]

In more recent years, with a higher level of unemployment and a reduction in the protection of the industrial wage-fixing system, the probability of poverty remains. A longitudinal study of disadvantaged children in 1992 pointed to 'the continuing and in some cases increasing economic disadvantage of children in NESB families in Australia in the early 1990s. It is evident that poverty among NESB families is not simply a short-term problem for newly arrived families, but is related to economic recession and restructuring as well as to long-term aspects of the migration process such as the impact of the refugee experience and of English-language proficiency.'[16]

In 1998 a Parliamentary Library listing of electorates by 'relative socio-economic disadvantage' showed Fowler (Cabramatta) as the worst and Gellibrand (Footscray) third. Both were areas of Vietnamese and Balkan settlement. Reid (Auburn and Granville) was an area of Muslim settlement and was ninth. But many other electorates with high ethnic populations were not particularly disadvantaged and there was no evidence of difference between 'European' and 'Asian' areas. Migrants in general are now spread across the social spectrum and many can be found in high-status areas of Melbourne and Sydney, such as Doncaster or Chatswood.

Notes

1 Roe, *Australia, Britain and Migration 1915–1940.*

2 London, *Non-White Immigration and the 'White Australia' Policy.*
3 Lack and Templeton, *Bold Experiment.*
4 Clyne, *Community Languages,* Table 1.
5 Rubinstein, *The Jews in Australia.*
6 Lopez, *The Origins of Multiculturalism in Australian Politics.*
7 Collins, *Migrant Hands in a Distant Land.*
8 Burnley, *The Impact of Immigration on Australia.*
9 Jupp et al., *Metropolitan Ghettoes and Ethnic Concentrations.*
10 Iredale and Nivison-Smith, *Immigrants' Experiences of Qualifications Recognition and Employment.*
11 FitzGerald, *Immigration – A Commitment to Australia.*
12 OECD, *Literacy, Economy and Society.*
13 Birrell and Birrell, *An Issue of People*; Birrell and Seol, 'Sydney's Ethnic Underclass'.
14 Castles, *The Working Class and Welfare.*
15 Martin, *The Migrant Presence,* 177, 182.
16 Taylor and Macdonald, *Children of Immigrants,* xiii.

3

The Fraser, Hawke and Keating governments, 1975–1996

The Whitlam government officially ended White Australia and gave its support to the concept of multiculturalism. But this had only a limited immediate effect. The most public enthusiast for multiculturalism, Minister for Immigration Al Grassby, was defeated in Riverina in the 1974 election in a campaign which included racist attacks on him and his policies.[1] His successors, Clyde Cameron and James McClelland, were in an older Labor tradition and promptly reduced the migrant intake at a time of rising unemployment.

Whitlam abolished the Immigration Department altogether in 1974. He recalls that Grassby found it 'incurably racist'. Functions were redistributed mainly to the Social Security, Education and Labour departments, with Senator McClelland as minister for labour and immigration from June to November 1975. Whitlam explained this as recognising a wider responsibility than organising intake: 'We had abolished the Department because in our view the Federal Government's responsibility for migrants did not end with recruiting them … but extended into all the areas where my government had taken initiatives, such as education and health and urban services'.[2] This continued to be the view of succeeding governments at least into the 1990s. But they operated with a revived and extended Immigration Department as well as through other relevant departments.

This abolition temporarily removed the core from migrant settlement services which had begun to be built and left multiculturalism with no clear administrative location. Grassby was, however, appointed as commissioner for community relations and his office became a focal point for developing multicultural and race relations policies until his contract ended in 1982. The abolition of the department was premature. Other departments had neither the expertise nor the willingness to take on a new constituency, the central problem of 'mainstreaming' which was to haunt all subsequent discussion of devolving services from Immigration. The adoption of 'access and equity' approaches ten years later was designed, more cautiously, to deal with these problems. In the meantime, the Fraser government also recognised a broader responsibility and extended the welfare and educational functions of the re-created Department of Immigration and Ethnic Affairs. This was validated and institutionalised by the Galbally report on migrant programs and services.[3]

The ending of White Australia had no immediate impact. Numbers admitted were so drastically reduced that the non-European component was almost negligible. In the financial year 1975–76 there were only 52 748 settler arrivals, of whom only 8200 were from Asia (excluding the Middle East). Whitlam had expressed his hostility to the admission of Vietnamese refugees after the fall of Saigon on 30 April 1975. While 130 000 fled from Vietnam during that period, the great majority went to the United States. It was not until the end of 1975 that refugees escaping by boat appeared in northern Australia. These were from East Timor, which Indonesia had invaded on 7 December, just one week before the Whitlam government was defeated at the general election. The first boatload of Vietnamese refugees did not arrive near Darwin until April 1976. Vietnamese already in Australia, who were mainly students, were granted refugee status, as were those arriving by sea.[4]

The Fraser government, 1975–1983

One of the first acts of the Fraser Coalition government was to re-create the Immigration Department under the new title of Department of Immigration and Ethnic Affairs. The second half of the title showed already that Fraser would encourage an emphasis on policy relating to settlement within Australia as well as to the conventional intake concerns of the previous department. There was no suggestion of returning to the White Australia policy. The two ministers with most influence, Michael MacKellar (1976–79) and Ian Macphee (1980–82), were known for their liberal views in this area. A further indication of the reforming approach to policy was the appointment as departmental secretary in 1981 of John Menadue, a former staffer for Gough Whitlam. While he was not exactly popular with most Coalition members, Al Grassby was allowed to work out his contract as community relations commissioner.

The net gain from migration under Fraser rose from the exceptionally low level in the last year of the Whitlam government, reaching a peak under Macphee of over 100 000 in 1981. In the first year of the Fraser government the ten major sources of immigrants were, in order: United Kingdom (27.1 per cent), Lebanon (17.2 per cent), New Zealand, Malaysia, Philippines, Yugoslavia, Greece, Italy, United States and Turkey. By the last year they were: United Kingdom (28.2 per cent), Vietnam (9.3 per cent), New Zealand, Germany, Poland, Cambodia, Philippines, South Africa, Malaysia and United States. These were not dramatically different, except for the temporary impact of Lebanese refugees in 1976 and of Vietnamese in 1982. Some 'traditional' European sources were still important in 1976, such as Yugoslavia, Greece and Italy. But the balance shifted towards Asia and the Middle East under Fraser, especially because of policy changes favourable to refugees. The British, New Zealand and North American component remained stable at just over one-third.

The Fraser government is best remembered for its humane approach to refugees and its creation of the institutions of multiculturalism. During MacKellar's ministry the Galbally report on migrant and multicultural programs and services was issued. Galbally reported directly to the prime minister and included some topics, such as ethnic broadcasting, which were not within the powers of the Immigration Department. The implementation of the report, however, rested largely with Immigration. An Ethnic Affairs Branch was set up in the department in 1977 and the Ethnic Affairs Council was appointed. Both had mainly settlement concerns. The first two migrant resource centres were established in Melbourne in 1977, ahead of the Galbally recommendation for a national network of MRCs.

In MacKellar's first year there were special visa arrangements for Lebanese and Vietnamese immigrants, responding to the political situation in those two countries. An amnesty for overstayers was implemented between January and April 1976. During that period 8614 applied for resident status, of whom the largest number were from Greece, Britain, Indonesia and China. Resident status was granted to Timorese refugees and to students from Indochina already in Australia. Reduction of refugee travel by boat was the stated aim of creating a refugee processing office in Bangkok in 1977. By then the department was already complaining of its growing workload caused by representations on behalf of migration applicants from sponsors, ethnic organisations and members of parliament.[5] The department adopted a new logo in 1977, showing welcoming hands gathering people into Australia. This logo was replaced under the Howard government by one of people rushing helter-skelter in all directions. During 1977 the last migrant ship arrived, ending nearly 150 years of seaborne travel for assisted migrants.

Pressures to emigrate to Australia alerted the department in 1978 to the need to formalise the migration program. Concern with the declining birthrate, expressed by the Australian Population and Immigration Council, also prompted relaxation of the family reunion program in June 1978. Nine principles of policy were stated by the minister, including that settlement should be permanent and that selection should be 'non-discriminatory' – this being a reassertion of the end of White Australia. At the same time policy began to move in another, 'discriminatory' direction by the development of a points system for 'general eligibility' based on social, educational and economic factors. The numerical multifactor assessment system (NUMAS) was accordingly introduced on 1 January 1979. It did not apply to family reunion or refugee admission but became increasingly developed until the present as a means of recruiting 'human capital'. The system was subsequently amended to reduce 'subjective' judgements (such as responsiveness and initiative) and to increase the importance of 'objective' factors such as employability, education and language capacity. Refugee settlement was addressed by the new Australian Refugee Advisory Council and with the creation of the Community Refugee Settlement scheme, which very modestly subsidised charitable and religious organisations to arrange for initial care through Australian families. The 'orderly departure' program was negotiated with Vietnam in 1979, thus removing the need to escape by boat at least until relations between China and Vietnam deteriorated in the mid-1980s. Migrant settlement councils were set up in each State to co-ordinate services and the Galbally Implementation Task Force researched and recommended policy arising from the 1978 report.

MacKellar left office in December 1979 to become health minister and was replaced by Ian Macphee until May 1982. MacKellar had seen the development of the department as a caring institution, implementing the settlement proposals of Galbally and tackling the growing problem of escape from Indochina. Macphee followed in the same tradition. By 1979 'Asia' had emerged as the largest regional source of immigrants (29 per cent), followed by Oceania (21 per cent) (mainly New Zealand) and Britain and Ireland (19 per cent). This was already arousing some criticism, but Macphee stood firm against any reduction of refugee intake or any suggestion of returning to 'traditional sources'. Many officers who had served under the White Australia regime retired in the early 1980s, making it easier to gain departmental acceptance of recent trends.

Macphee liberalised family reunion for 'concessional' relatives in addition to 'preferential' spouses, children and parents. Most of his tenure was taken up with implementing the Galbally report. Another amnesty was introduced in 1980 as the 'regularisation of status' program. Migrant intake began to increase, as did grants to ethnic welfare organisations and migrant resource centres. Consequently, the departmental budget rose from $72.6 million in 1979–80 to $104.5 million by 1981–82. Of this total, nearly one-third was spent on the adult migrant education program.

Macphee's tenure also saw the decision to abolish all assisted passages other than for refugees, ending 150 years of similar systems. This diminished the incentive to emigrate from Britain. New Zealanders were required to have passports for the first time. But, in general, entry conditions were liberalised, especially for relatives and for those coming from disturbed countries under the new 'special humanitarian' program from November 1981. The 'concessional' family reunion system was liberalised from April 1982 to encourage migration by non-dependent children, working age parents and brothers and sisters. Sponsoring relatives were expected to guarantee financial support, but this was inadequately enforced. Partly in consequence, the immigration intake rose to almost 120 000 in 1981–82, including New Zealanders. Macphee also undertook a series of national meetings to explain multiculturalism during 1982, often accompanied by his Labor 'shadow', Mick Young. It was at these meetings that the first ominous signs of organised racism began to appear.[6]

Ian Macphee is remembered as the most liberal and generous of immigration ministers. His policies, together with those of Michael MacKellar, were markedly more welcoming to refugees and family members than those of his Liberal successor, Philip Ruddock, after thirteen years of intervening Labor government. His reward was to lose his preselection for his Melbourne electorate and to be effectively driven out of politics by the new conservative forces in his own party.

The Hawke government, 1983–1991

Unlike the Liberal and National parties, the ALP rested heavily upon electorates in which NESB immigrants had been congregating since the 1950s. These were mostly historic Labor strongholds and remained in the hands of Anglo-Australian politicians, as most of them still do. While Fraser represented the monocultural rural electorate of Wannon, Hawke was returned for Wills in 1980, a north Melbourne area with the highest concentration of Italians in Australia, to whom were later added Greeks, Yugoslavs, Maltese and Lebanese. His Cabinets included several ministers representing similar electorates, including Keating (Blaxland), Young (Port Adelaide), Holding (Yarra), Duffy (Holt), Willis (Gellibrand), Dawkins (Fremantle), Howe (Batman), Hand (Melbourne) and West (Cunningham). Of his six immigration ministers, five represented strongly ethnic electorates and Senator Robert Ray was from Victoria, at the time the most ethnically diverse of all the States.

With such backgrounds the Hawke government might have been expected to be particularly sensitive to the needs and expectations of the immigrant voters, even if almost all ministers were Australian-born. Hawke's personal influence was strongly in favour of multiculturalism, which was not necessarily true for all his ministers. He was particularly close to the Jewish community and personally intervened to liberalise Soviet policy towards Jewish emigration. His political base in Melbourne sustained these attitudes and he was happy to work with, and listen to, those who had initiated multiculturalism under Whitlam and implemented it under Fraser. Influential individuals such as Walter Lippman, James Gobbo and Peter Abeles had direct access to the prime minister.

Immigration intake under Hawke built up steadily from a fairly low level of 93 000 in 1983 to a high point of 145 000 by 1989, the highest level for nearly twenty years. This rise was unusual in coinciding with a high level of unemployment. The Hawke government was sympathetic to refugees, continuing the example set by Ian Macphee under its predecessor. However, in 1990, the first boatloads of asylum seekers for ten years began to arrive off northwestern Australia. This prompted a panic scarcely justified by the small numbers involved, who mainly came from the rapidly deteriorating situation in Cambodia. This led to the adoption of mandatory detention for unauthorised arrivals and the opening of a detention centre at Port Hedland. This 'mandatory and irrevocable' detention policy haunted governments for the next decade.

Because ministers changed so rapidly under Hawke, it is harder to distinguish their policies than it was for MacKellar and Macphee. The greatest impact was from Senator Ray, who implemented the FitzGerald report of 1988 and introduced a 'rule based' system of selection. Stewart West's brief tenure from March 1983 to December 1984 involved the need to reply to the attacks on multiculturalism and immigration policy by Professor Geoffrey Blainey. He acquitted himself well, with the support of the prime minister. West was from the old socialist school of trade unionists and the industrial city of Wollongong. Intake dropped from the high levels of the Fraser government in response to an economic downturn. Refugee policy, although still dominated by Indochina, was adjusted to cater for Latin America, where oppressive governments were from the right rather than being communist as normally in the past. Reflecting the policies of the previous government, family reunion constituted 59 per cent of the 1983–84 intake (excluding New Zealanders) and humanitarian categories, 25 per cent.

West was succeeded by Chris Hurford, Mick Young and Clyde Holding, none of whom lasted for very long. This left the department relatively free to develop its own policies, mainly under the secretaryship of Bill McKinnon. McKinnon's experience had been with the Industries Assistance Commission and the Department of

Trade and Industry. Hurford, too, had a business background, then unusual in Labor politicians. For all of his tenure Hurford was also minister assisting the treasurer, a post in which he was probably more interested. He had to face severe criticism over the cuts in migrant settlement budgets in 1986. This period began the process whereby the Immigration Department became more centrally concerned with the economic viability of immigrants. The influence of professional economists on the bureaucracy was growing. As Michael Pusey has noted, that influence was mainly directed towards 'economic rationalism', including budgetary constraint, human capital and managerial autonomy.[7] Under Hurford the department developed its financial management improvement program, based on program identification and the determination of quantifiable key indicators. Accounting and management increasingly preoccupied the department from then on, together with the improvement of data collection which computers made possible.

Ray held office between September 1988 and April 1990, when he became defence minister. His tenure is noteworthy for his implementation of the FitzGerald report.[8] The Committee to Advise on Australia's Immigration Policies had been appointed by Clyde Holding in September 1987. While it ranged widely over settlement and multicultural issues, its main thrust was that the Department of Immigration needed to be professionalised and that the focus on intake policy should be on skills rather than on the humanitarian or family categories. The committee also spent some time in devising a model Migration Act, which was never implemented. 'The major thrust of the reforms was the restructuring of decision-making procedures, designed inter alia to limit ministerial and bureaucratic discretion … the central control function of the department was to be buffered from forces in an increasingly pluralist culture and volatile environment'.[9]

The rule-based system developed under Ray made rational selection easier than in the past. It discouraged regular lobbying by groups and individuals, although this has never disappeared altogether. Its basic assumption – that human beings could be fitted into limited categories – is typical of all highly developed modern bureaucracies. Yet this would only be possible with serious inflexibility. What has happened instead is the proliferation of so many different visas that only a professional lawyer or migration agent can understand the system. Kathryn Cronin, writing only three years after the new system was introduced, noted that there were 'eighty-five different visa classes and ninety-five entry permit types'.[10] The new system also militated against further amnesties and there have been none since, leaving many otherwise law-abiding 'unlawful' settlers in limbo. However, it also required an appeals procedure, institutionalised in the Immigration Review Tribunal (1989) and the Refugee Review Tribunal (1993).

Apart from changing to a rule-based system, the FitzGerald report also began the process of shifting emphasis from humanist concerns with family and asylum to an economically rational focus on the 'quality' of immigrants. This would be realised by submitting most of the intake to a points test rather than exempting the majority under family reunion. This recommendation was not implemented by Labor but is close to the abolition of the concessional family category by the Coalition in 1996. The report also aimed to upgrade the decision-making capacity of the department with a coherent research structure to replace that lost when Hurford had abolished the Australian Institute of Multicultural Affairs in 1986.

The FitzGerald report was the most important single influence on the Immigration Department for the next decade. It went against the Labor tide in criticising multiculturalism and family reunion and was questioned for doing so by the Office of Multicultural Affairs and by ethnic organisations. This aspect was not welcome to Prime Minister Hawke either. But it was what the department wanted, Ray was ready to implement it and the Liberal Opposition was happy to carry it through, should they be elected. They had to wait for another eight years, by which time 'economic rationalism' was almost consensual among economists and public servants.

The Keating government, 1991–1996

The Keating government was less influenced from Melbourne than were Hawke or Fraser. It was more interested in Indigenous issues and more inclined to stress that Australia was 'part of Asia' than was its immediate predecessor. While the Hawke government had its strongest constituency among southern Europeans, Keating was more closely involved with the Middle Eastern and Southeast Asian immigrants who had settled in Sydney. There was more controversy around these recent arrivals and less willingness to incorporate them within the ALP machine. The long-established Lebanese Catholics were an exception, but many of them were Liberals and they were much less prominent in the trade unions than were Greeks, Italians, Maltese or Yugoslavs. Keating's own electorate of Blaxland was a major centre of Lebanese settlement with a growing Vietnamese presence, as well as a native-born working class which resented these developments.

Immigrant intake under Keating dropped rapidly in the first few years, from 122 000 in 1991 to less than 70 000 in 1994 before rising again to 92 000 at the end of his government. This was a more cautious approach than under Hawke, but partly reflects the decline of refugee pressures from Indochina and China. Nevertheless, the humanitarian component of settler arrivals ranged between 13 and 17 per cent between 1991 and 1996 and was consistently higher than for the succeeding Coalition government. Unemployment reached its highest level, at 11 per cent, in 1991 and immigration was consequently reduced, which has always been normal for Australia as for many other societies.

The origins of immigrants during the Keating government continued to be largely from nationalities which would have been excluded under White Australia. The United Kingdom remained the largest single source but only provided between 12 and 17 per cent of the total. This was supplemented by New Zealanders, ranging from 8 to 12 per cent. Throughout the Keating period the other major contributors were almost all Asian, except for disintegrating former Yugoslavia and a small number from South Africa and the also disintegrating Soviet Union. Between 1990–91 and 1994–95, Vietnam added 39 000, Hong Kong 40 000, Philippines 24 000 and India 21 000.

Keating shifted the emphasis of government policy towards Indigenous issues, the republic and the notion of Australia as 'part of Asia'. This did not necessarily diminish activity in favour of multiculturalism. A massive Global Cultural Diversity conference was organised in Sydney in 1995 at a cost of $2 million. The impact of criticism of multiculturalism among conservatives was suggested by the refusal of corporate business to provide sponsorship, despite a serious attempt to attract it. The very large shortfall left by this was made up by the Commonwealth.

Keating had only two immigration ministers: Gerry Hand, whom he inherited from Hawke, and Senator Nick Bolkus, who took over from 1993 until the government was defeated in 1996. Both were from the socialist left of the ALP. More importantly, both had considerable influence with ethnic organisations in Melbourne and Adelaide, respectively, Bolkus being of Greek parentage. This continued the tradition of Labor ministers being 'minister for winning the ethnic vote'.

Hand was a trade unionist and party organiser, who had been largely responsible for organising the 'ethnic vote' around the victory of John Cain in the Victorian State election of 1982. For nearly three years he had been minister for Aboriginal affairs, where he developed the Aboriginal and Torres Strait Islander Commission after extensive consultations around Australia. Hand was seen on his appointment as more likely to be popular with the ethnic constituency than was Ray.

Hand had several strongly held prejudices – against lawyers, against the 'ethnic élite' and in favour of his departmental colleagues. Intake under Hand started high at over 100 000 a year but dropped to 80 000 by 1993 in response to the economic situation. Family categories made up more than half of this, but the humanitarian stream settled at about 12 000, where it has normally remained ever since. Hand also abolished the business migration program in July 1991, following a report critical of abuses, and substituted a points-tested business skills category.[11]

Refugee and illegal issues had become more prominent. For the first time, refugees and humanitarian cases were given four-year temporary protection visas rather than permanent residence, under the Migration Amendment Act of 1992. This was designed to deal with the large number of resident Chinese students remaining after the Tien-an-men Square repression of 1989 in Beijing. This new policy proved unviable and was ended in November 1993 under Bolkus, only to be revived again under the Howard government.

Hand's attitude towards refugees and asylum seekers seems ambivalent. In effect it was much more generous towards Europeans than Asians. The 'special assistance' program, which he introduced in 1992, was of great benefit to Yugoslavs fleeing from their collapsing country. But mandatory detention for boat people which he also introduced, in August 1991, bore very heavily upon asylum seekers from Indochina and, ten years later, from Afghanistan and Iraq.

Bolkus, like Ray and Hand, was something of a machine politician. This led him to intervene in the affairs of two agencies: the Federation of Ethnic Communities' Councils of Australia (FECCA) and the Bureau of Immigration Research. In neither case were the results very satisfactory. Bolkus, quite justifiably, felt that FECCA was not maintaining its previous level of research and submission to official inquiries. He also believed that the structure was out of date and that FECCA was in need of a drastic constitutional overhaul to make it more effective. His annoyance came to a head during a very public row at the official opening of the new FECCA headquarters in Canberra in 1994. Placing a departmental officer within the organisation with a brief to consult and to reform did not solve matters. This ended in a drawn-out and expensive wrongful dismissal case which left FECCA financially strapped for some time.

Bolkus also intervened in the Bureau of Immigration Research, attempting to dictate its list of conference speakers and attracting attention from its conservative critics by doing so. This was a factor in the resignation of the director, John Nieuwenhuysen, and was later used to argue for the bureau's abolition under Howard. Neither of these interventions was very productive.

The ministerial record

There were no fewer than seven immigration ministers during the thirteen years of Labor government, compared with seven in the twenty-three years of its Coalition predecessor and only one in the first six years of the Howard government from 1996. Change at the bureaucratic level was equally kaleidoscopic. Between 1948 and 1974 there were only three departmental secretaries. In the twenty-five years following the re-creation of the Immigration Department in 1975, there were nine secretaries and four changes of name.

In the formative years after 1945, the immigration ministry had been a stepping stone to higher office. Calwell and Snedden had become leaders of the Opposition, Holt prime minister, Lynch treasurer, Downer high commissioner in London and Opperman high commissioner to Malta. However, by the 1980s the position had less to offer. A succession of Liberal and Labor ministers ended their political careers rather than starting them. Grassby, Cameron, Macphee, Hodges, West, Holding and Hand made no further progress and Grassby, Hodges and Macphee lost their parliamentary seats altogether. MacKellar's career was cut short by the Labor victory in 1983 and he became director of a business lobby. Of Labor ministers, only Ray and Bolkus remained on the front bench after the defeat of 1996. They must necessarily await a Labor victory to continue their careers.

The ministerial record suggests that ministers with a long tenure or a strong personality can make a difference to policy. MacKellar, Macphee and Ray certainly did so, as has Ruddock in the Howard government. While normally represented in the Cabinet, the Immigration portfolio can, however, be a poisoned chalice. As with Aboriginal Affairs, also held by three ministers (Holding, Hand and Ruddock), it is subject to a high level of public criticism and controversy. Bringing in newcomers and changing the ethnic character of a society is rarely very popular. There is an immigrant constituency to please and a xenophobic public to placate. Neither major party has been completely consistent. As is often the case, the minister's most serious critics may be on the benches behind. It is very important to have the confidence and support of his or her leader.

Prime ministerial intervention

Within the normal practices of Cabinet government ministers are left to develop policy and practice with their departmental officials, and to seek approval from Cabinet for new departures or for anything likely to be politically controversial. Not all immigration ministers have been included in the Cabinet and their access has been consequently diminished. However, for most of the past thirty years they have been included. Under Whitlam all ministers sat in the Cabinet. Under Fraser, MacKellar and Hodges were not in the Cabinet. All immigration ministers sat in the Hawke and Keating Cabinets, but Ruddock was excluded from the first Howard Cabinet, to be brought in later.

Ministers have not always succeeded in gaining support for departmental policies and are always subject to the scrutiny of Treasury and the Department of Finance and their associated public expenditure review committees. When a finance minister is unfavourable towards departmental policy, as was Peter Walsh under Hawke, life becomes difficult.[12] When a prime minister is favourable, as was largely true under Fraser and Hawke, other ministers can be overruled. Examples of such obstruction and assistance were most apparent during the financial crisis of 1986.

Prime ministerial intervention was common when politically sensitive issues were involved. Whitlam had changed the relationship between the ALP Caucus and the ministry, giving more freedom to his government and himself than had previously been enjoyed by Labor governments. In the following years the Department of the Prime Minister and Cabinet became more powerful and developed offices within itself which supervised areas which were also the responsibility of other ministers. The most relevant example here is the location of the Office of Multicultural Affairs within PM&C in 1987, which was directly required by Hawke, and its removal and abolition in 1996, which was directly required by Howard.

Whitlam and Fraser gave strong leadership on issues which were not universally endorsed by their ministries or parliamentary parties. Whitlam broke publicly with the remnants of the White Australia policy which had been upheld by Labor for eighty years and most actively by his predecessor, Arthur Calwell. He gave full endorsement to the often controversial activity of Al Grassby, denounced the racism which cost Grassby his seat in 1974, and appointed him on a seven-year contract as commissioner for community relations. He had previously disciplined Fred Daly MP for his continuing support for White Australia, removing him as shadow minister for immigration in 1971.

Fraser enjoyed more nominal independence than Whitlam, although in practice there was little difference in the influence which they could wield. His active endorsement of multiculturalism was a departure from the assimilationist and Anglophile traditions of the Liberal and National (Country) parties. The appointment of two 'liberal' immigration ministers, MacKellar and Macphee, ensured that his policies were implemented. A new minister, John Hodges, who was openly unsympathetic to these policies, was publicly reprimanded by Fraser in 1982 for refusing to endorse a national languages policy at a large conference called for that purpose.

Hawke took a strong interest in immigration matters, replaced more ministers than anyone else, and was directly involved in the public controversies which broke out during his tenure. In 1986 he overruled his minister for communications, Michael Duffy, on the proposed amalgamation of the SBS and the ABC, and his minister for immigration, Chris Hurford, on cuts to the adult migrant education program. He also intervened actively in reforming the machinery for overseas skills recognition in 1988.

Hawke was personally involved in the removal of Ron Brown as departmental secretary in 1990 and his replacement by Chris Conybeare from PM&C. The transfer of deputy-secretary Tony Harris probably also involved prime ministerial intervention. Both changes were a response to concern that the department had become too restrictive under its previous minister, Robert Ray.[13] Hawke was readily accessible to several community leaders, had a very close relationship with the Jewish community, and in 1988 intervened in the conflict between Greeks and Macedonians as a conciliator. He was somewhat sceptical about the Immigration Department in general.

Keating's interventions were less apparent. The exhaustive study of his life by John Edwards does not have either 'immigration' or 'multiculturalism' in its index.[14] This suggests their relative unimportance to the prime minister. His concerns were rather broader, including Aboriginal reconciliation, the republic and placing Australia firmly within an Asian context. Hand's replacement by Bolkus in 1993 was caused by Hand's retirement from parliament and not by prime ministerial intervention.

Howard, however, was very active from the start of his accession in 1996.[15] Six departmental secretaries were replaced at once, including Chris Conybeare of Immigration. Howard immediately removed two institutions: the Office of Multicultural Affairs, and the Bureau of Immigration, Multicultural and Population Research. The latter abolition was not desired by his minister or the department. Howard refused to use the word 'multiculturalism' in public until the late 1990s. He publicly overruled Ruddock in accepting 'safe haven' temporary protection for 4000 Kosovars in 1999.

His most dramatic intervention was during the *Tampa* crisis of late August 2001, when a Norwegian container ship was forcibly boarded and its rescued asylum seekers removed to Nauru and Manus Island, New Guinea. Policy was taken completely out of the hands of the minister and the department and constructed by a small working party dominated by the secretary of PM&C, Max Moore-Wilton. Evidence presented at the Senate inquiry into the crisis early in 2002 suggested that Howard took a very active personal role in influencing policy. He staked his reputation on this in winning the November 2001 election.

Continuity and difference

With so many changes of minister under Labor it is hard to determine what Labor policy was over any length of time. This problem remained after 1996. Labor went into the 1998 and 2001 elections with almost no relevant policy at all and was badly caught out by the *Tampa* crisis. It had three shadow ministers between 1996 and 2001, none of whom had previously served in Immigration. The newly elected Howard Coalition government of 1996 seemed dedicated to undoing most of the 'Keating–Hawke agenda' in areas other than liberalising the economy. It turned its back on the earlier Liberal Party inheritance of Fraser, MacKellar and Macphee. Its term is not yet complete and final judgement must await its eventual demise. Its policies are interwoven into the discussion in the following chapters. Major shifts in emphasis happened quickly. The prime minister took an active interest in immigration and multiculturalism, as had his Labor predecessors. But his objectives were quite different and frequently opposite and were developed within a different ideological framework. In this he was supported by his minister, Philip Ruddock, who had previously been regarded as on the more 'liberal' wing of the Coalition.

Previous policies from which Howard and Ruddock moved away included support for multiculturalism, a program favouring family reunion, a vigorous monitoring of 'access and equity' for all Commonwealth services, a willingness to recognise humanitarian crises, and the frequent use of inquiries and consultation to ascertain the needs of the 'ethnic constituency'. Liberal and Coalition

politicians were subject to much less pressure from that constituency because of the nature of their electorates. While Ruddock
had built up a wide network of contacts, Howard and most of his
ministers had not. The strong influence of Sydney North Shore Liberalism, the partnership with the National Party, and the need to
win back votes that had gone to Pauline Hanson and One Nation
combined to limit still further the relationship between the new
government and the 'ethnic' voters.

Yet there were also elements of continuity, some of them arising
from within the bureaucracy and some of them willingly implemented by previous Labor ministers.[16] The practice of reducing government expenditure to keep taxes low was fully endorsed by the ALP
and the ACTU from the very start of Hawke's government in 1983.
While immigration costs had been greatly reduced by the termina-
tion of the assisted passage schemes, the costs of delivering services
such as English education, accommodation, translating and interpreting and localised welfare were growing. The first assault on these
came with the 1986 budget, denounced by FECCA as 'The Betrayal
of Multiculturalism'.[17] Severe cuts in the adult migrant education
program, which was administered through State agencies, were
denounced by New South Wales Labor Premier Barry Unsworth as
'plain stupid'. For the first and last time FECCA joined in anti-budget
demonstrations at Parliament House in Canberra, and was threatened with losing its funding for six months as a punishment.

With the active intervention of Bob Hawke, some of these cuts
were restored and regional offices in the Labor strongholds of Newcastle and Wollongong kept open. The Immigration Department
remained anxious to unload its grant-in-aid program on to other
'mainstream' departments. A policy position developed that the
department's responsibility for immigrants stopped after two years,
this being the minimum period for naturalisation. The 'access and
equity' approach was partly designed to ease such a transition by
ensuring that other departments were sensitive to cultural variety.[18]
However, the view of other service departments and of ethnic
organisations was that post-arrival services should remain with the
Immigration Department. The department was anxious to retain
the adult migrant English program, its largest single budgetary item.
Both the Review of Migrant and Multicultural Programs and

Services (1986) and the FitzGerald Inquiry (1988) recommended that this be transferred to the Education Department, but this has never been followed through.

Having failed to unload some of its welfare services, the Immigration Department began to press for cost recovery. This had always been an aim of the accommodation services, which were corporatised under Commonwealth Hostels Ltd. However, most such provision was confined to refugees by 1983 and they could not make much of a contribution to costs. The department finally sold off all of its hostels by 1994, retaining some flats and houses as an alternative. Other ways of raising revenue included charging public agencies, such as Commonwealth and State departments, hospitals and the police, for translating and interpreting services. This became effective by 1988. The department also introduced the airport departure tax to cover the costs of immigration control. It tried to introduce an arrival tax as well but failed to develop a system of collection and had to abandon it.

This still left many services unsupported. As the notion of 'user pays' captured the bureaucracy, legislation was passed by the Keating government introducing or increasing charges on previously free or cheaper services. This included the Migration (Health Services) Charge Act of 1991, the Migration Agents Registration (Levy) Act of 1992, and the Immigration (Education) Charge Act of 1992.

Apart from extending charges for services, the Labor governments began several processes which were to be built on further by the Howard government. Immigrants, other than in the humanitarian categories, were denied access to social welfare for the first six months after arrival. This policy came out of the Department of Social Security rather than Immigration. The Howard government immediately extended this to two years. All research had shown that the first two years were the most crucial in terms of securing housing and employment. This made life more difficult for many new arrivals, some of whom had to turn to private charities. While families undertook to support family reunion immigrants, this had proved difficult to police. Denial of welfare for a waiting period, guaranteed against a monetary deposit, was a more effective means of saving money which had previously been spent on unemployment benefits.

Labor governments were also concerned with illegal and undocumented immigration. The mandatory and irrevocable detention system for undocumented asylum seekers was introduced by Hand and supported actively by many ALP politicians. It left a very problematic legacy for the Howard government when numbers arriving began to increase from 1998. Hand's antipathy towards lawyers encouraged him to amend the legal and appeal rights of immigrants, a never-ending process followed actively by succeeding governments from Labor's Migration Legislation Amendment Act of 1995 through to the 'border protection' legislation of 2001 responding to the *Tampa* incident.[19] Unlike their Liberal predecessors, who had introduced amnesties for illegal overstayers in 1976 and 1980, Labor ministers refused to make such a concession and no government has done so for twenty years, except for a very limited 'regularisation of status' between 1990 and 1993.

The acceptance of 'human capital' and 'economic rationalist' approaches by the Canberra bureaucracy provided a line of policy continuity after the FitzGerald report of 1988. Much of the early research from the Bureau of Immigration Research after 1989 was concerned with the economic utility of immigration. While this was not influential enough to produce a major shift away from the family reunion and humanitarian programs, it laid the basis for such shifts upon the change of government. Budgetary stringency under Keating also laid the foundations for charging for English tuition, visa applications and appeal costs, all of which were made more expensive by the Howard government. As with all stable political systems, there was a degree of continuity which overcame changes of government or of minister. But the emphasis was markedly different under Howard – economically and financially stringent and with much less regard for humanitarian or settlement considerations. This did not reduce the departmental budget, as savings were eaten up by the escalating costs of mandatory detention and the 'Pacific solution' of 2001 and 2002, which was a response to the *Tampa* incident.

Notes

1 Grassby, *The Morning After.*

2 Whitlam, *The Whitlam Government*, 503.
3 Galbally, *Migrant Services and Programs.*
4 Viviani, *The Long Journey.*
5 DIEA, *Annual Report* (1977), 4.
6 DIEA, *Annual Report* (1982).
7 Pusey, *Economic Rationalism in Canberra.*
8 FitzGerald, *Immigration – A Commitment to Australia.*
9 Jupp and Kabala, *The Politics of Australian Immigration*, 118–19.
10 Jupp and Kabala, *The Politics of Australian Immigration*, 91.
11 Joint Parliamentary Committee of Public Accounts, *Business Migration Program.*
12 Walsh, *Confessions of a Failed Finance Minister.*
13 Jupp and Kabala, *The Politics of Australian Immigration*, 120.
14 Edwards, *Keating.*
15 Bean et al., *The Politics of Retribution.*
16 Birrell, *Immigration Reform in Australia.*
17 *Ethnic Spotlight*, no. 10, August 1986.
18 NPC, *Access and Equity.*
19 Crock and Saul, *Future Seekers.*

4

Policy instruments and institutions

The Immigration Department

Australia is unusual in having a distinct Immigration Department, which is normally represented in the Cabinet. In Britain, immigration is only one function of the Home Office, which is centrally concerned with policing and law and order. Similarly in the United States, the Immigration and Naturalization Service is part of the attorney-general's department. In Canada, immigration was previously the concern of the Department of Labour, while multiculturalism has been administered through a quite distinct agency. Italy, which has recently attracted mass immigration, has no specific agency responsible for immigration at all.

The existence of a specialist department for all but eighteen months (1975–76) since 1945 emphasises the bureaucratic planning role of the state in building and selecting population.[1] Distinct immigration statistics are developed by the department as an adjunct to its own planning. The Australian Bureau of Statistics duplicates this function to some extent. This has meant that Australia has some of the most detailed and meticulous migration statistics in the world. Its research capacity has also been considerable, especially between 1979 and 1986 through the Australian Institute of Multicultural Affairs and from 1989 to 1996 when the Bureau of Immigration, Multicultural and Population Research was producing a flow of information and analysis. This kept Australia in the forefront of immigration studies, given the lack of interest by most academic social scientists. While this research capacity has been substantially reduced, much analysis of immigration issues is still produced within the bureaucracy rather than by academics. This state domination of research currently directs studies towards economic criteria and the settlement outcomes of the various visa categories. There has been almost no 'social' or 'cultural' research funded directly by the Commonwealth in recent years.

Because it also manages a range of settlement services, the Immigration Department had encouraged studies of immigrant problems and adjustment, which elsewhere have mainly been the concern of academics or private research agencies. The responsibility for multiculturalism also gave the department an opportunity to widen its interest in the field of education, language policy and social engineering in general, although this interest has now contracted. While the Immigration Department has never been high in the bureaucratic pecking order, it is arguably more influential on policy than its counterparts in other countries and over a wider range of concerns than some other Commonwealth departments. However, in recent years it has limited its research and consultative functions and much less serious analysis is being done than was true in the 1980s.

All this may create the impression that immigration policy is rationally developed by a well-qualified department with access to the levers of power. That is certainly an aspiration within the bureaucracy and was strongly urged by the FitzGerald report of 1988, which the department welcomed. Policy was to be refined by creating a professional research bureau and freed from ministerial intervention by creating a rule-based system. Both were strongly favoured by the minister of the time, Senator Robert Ray. He was particularly anxious to clear his desk of the 10 000 or so cases sent up to him for final resolution by his department each year. It was expected that the creation of a strict rule-based system would reduce the constant lobbying which this involved and make decisions more rational. The creation of the Bureau of Immigration Research would give the department an effective instrument in refining policy where, according to FitzGerald, it had been amateurish.[2] This was particularly important in a rapidly changing policy environment influenced by globalisation and economic rationalism.

The Immigration Department underwent various structural changes to reflect different priorities. In particular, the budgetary domination of settlement services was reduced and reversed in the

1990s. Many of those services were privatised or limited and put on a full cost recovery basis. The compliance functions, which govern intake, were greatly increased, quite apart from the exceptional budgetary demands of the 'Pacific solution' in 2001 and 2002. From its origins in the post-war program, the department has always had two major functions: a 'policeman' who controls entry, and a 'parson' who looks after the welfare of those who have arrived, a growing concern between 1978 and 1988. The movement back from 'parson' to 'policeman' was already apparent by the early 1990s and escalated after 1996. After yet another restructuring in 1998, the department defined its functions as 'the managed entry of people to Australia, the successful settlement of migrants and refugees and the promotion of the benefits of citizenship and cultural diversity'.[3]

In the only exhaustive study of the Immigration Department by academics, Jeremy Bruer and John Power distinguished four phases: maximal bureaucratic controls, mid-1940s to mid-1970s; bureaucratic dislocation, early 1970s to mid-1970s; diversification of controls, mid-1970s to late 1980s; and towards rule-based administration since then. All these phases refer to what Kathryn Cronin has called 'the culture of control'.[4] On another dimension we might divide its functions as: nation building through assimilation, 1945–66; the transition to universalism, 1966–78; welfare, settlement and multiculturalism, 1978–88; and economic rationalisation and compliance since 1988. As with Bruer and Power's typology, there are transitional phases. Moreover, the functions of the departmental regional offices have remained more concerned with settlement than has the national headquarters in Canberra.

In 1976, its first year after being re-created, the Immigration Department was still primarily concerned with controlling and attracting immigrants. In a modest budget of $27 million it was still spending more than $7 million on assisted passages, by far its largest item other than general salaries. Many functions had yet to be transferred from other departments where they had been relocated after the abolition of Immigration in 1974.

Five years later (1980–81), the social and educational role had become more apparent. In a greatly expanded budget of nearly $97 million adult migrant education was now the largest item at $29 million, exceeding assisted passages at only $14 million. Grants to ethnic and welfare agencies were growing, following the Galbally report of 1978. Migrant resource centres were costing $1 million, the telephone interpreting service $1.5 million, grants for migrant welfare $1.7 million and the Australian Institute of Multicultural Affairs $1.4 million. Funding for the Good Neighbour Councils had almost disappeared. All of this marked a shift from the earlier concentration on selection and passage assistance to a greater concern with effective settlement. The department was also starting down the road of income generation, with receipts of over $18.7 million from the airport departure tax , covering nearly 20 per cent of its expenditure and falling on those leaving Australia rather than on immigrants.[5]

Five years further on and under a Labor government (1986–87), settlement services were now administered within an Ethnic Affairs division, headed by Peter Eyles. Outlays in this division totalled almost $90 million, from a departmental outlay in all programs of $180 million. The most important items were the adult migrant education program ($50 million), hostel and flats accommodation ($9 million), grants to welfare organisations ($6.5 million), translating and interpreting ($2.6 million) and migrant resource centres ($2 million). The full Galbally program was in operation and was taking up half of the department's income. The Federation of Ethnic Communities' Councils of Australia (FECCA) was receiving $120 000 and, to the annoyance of the Opposition, trade unions were being granted $455 000 'to assist migrants in industry'. There was almost no cost recovery in the Ethnic Affairs program, but charges were being made elsewhere for visa applications.[6]

This marked the high point of settlement service provision without cost recovery. It was the year in which cost cutting on migrant services was the budgetary response to a perceived financial crisis. Following the FitzGerald report of 1988 and under the influence of Immigration Minister Ray, there was an increasing emphasis on cost recovery and competitive tendering of services. By the last full year of the Labor government (1994–95), the department had radically changed its structure and accounting system, making comparisons with previous years difficult. The budget had reached $416 million. The settlement and ethnic affairs subprogram was still the largest at $109 million, and included the adult migrant

English program ($65 million), grants to organisations ($36 million), assistance to asylum seekers ($13.4 million) and refugee accommodation ($3.8 million). Over half of the costs of the telephone interpreter system were being recovered, but from Commonwealth and State governments rather than from individuals.

By 2001 the departmental budget and structure were reflecting the reduction of concern for settlement and multiculturalism and the increasing obsession with control and compliance. Detention, at $100 million, now cost more than the adult migrant English program, at $92 million. There was an executive co-ordinator of detention strategy and a detention taskforce headed by a first assistant secretary. Two separate divisions dealt with refugee and humanitarian policy, border control and compliance. Both were headed by first assistant secretaries. Only one division dealt with migration and temporary entry and one with multicultural affairs and citizenship. This latter had only small sections dealing specifically with settlement and multiculturalism. The eight State offices still retained a strong interest in settlement and were responsible for administering grants-in-aid and the migrant resource centres. They were, however, relatively remote from the policy makers in Canberra. Of first assistant secretaries in Canberra in 2001, two dealt with internal management, four with selection and control, and only one with the whole range of post-settlement services and issues.[7]

Despite having a higher proportion of its staff from ethnic backgrounds than any other Commonwealth department, Immigration remained predominantly Anglo-Australian at the top. The only departmental secretary of 'ethnic' origin was Peter Wilenski, who was born in Poland. His tenure as secretary of Labour and Immigration was brief in the last year of the Whitlam government. In 2001 three of the department's ten overseas regional directors, two of its seven first assistant secretaries, and the senior officers responsible for the humanitarian program, settlement and multiculturalism were from ethnic backgrounds. This was certainly more representative of Australian society than in other departments. But most important decisions, including those relating to the crises around asylum seekers, were made by the Australian-born of British origins and final decisions were often taken in other departments, especially PM&C. Blainey's 1984 thesis – that immigration policy was made in a 'secret room' at Belconnen (Canberra) – over-looked the probability that this hypothetical room was filled with people from the same background as himself.[8] Despite regular restructuring and the normal selection of the departmental secretary from outside, many decision makers have passed through the three locations of overseas posting, regional office and Belconnen over the years. They have lived out their professional lives within the department. They tend, therefore, to share a departmental culture, based on the interchange of views, attitudes and experiences within its confines.

The culture of organisations has become a major concern of administrative theory but is hard to measure without a series of interviews which public servants are now very reluctant to undertake.[9] In the eyes of Whitlam, Grassby and Wilenski, the original Immigration Department was so committed to White Australia as to be beyond redemption. After twenty years of political control favouring multiculturalism and a universalised intake, this cultural inheritance has probably disappeared. However, the increased emphasis on control and compliance may have reactivated any prejudices which officers might privately hold. As with the police, compliance, selection and control officers may develop a jaundiced view of their customers. Many senior departmental officers have risen through those ranks. Certainly the 'countries at risk' criteria for restricting visas works overwhelmingly against Asian and Pacific applicants. The capping of parental reunion also mainly affects Asians. Apart from a handful of east Europeans, all those interned under the mandatory detention system since 1991 have been from Asian or Middle Eastern countries. Conversely, the business migration program has usually worked to the benefit of ethnic Chinese.

There is little concrete evidence of 'racism' within the Immigration Department compared with its prevalence thirty years ago. But the social and economic situation in many countries outside Europe or North America makes more probable some form of discrimination against immigrants from them. A culture of control certainly exists and is usually shared by the minister, regardless of party. That nobody should enter without visa clearance, that there should never be an amnesty for overstayers, and that unvisaed asylum seekers should be interned awaiting final clearance or deportation marks out Australia as having one of the most restrictive control systems of any democracy. This is maintained by frequently changing the rules to close loopholes, in an elaborate bureaucratic game of snakes and ladders.[10]

A culture of control also implies a culture of suspicion. Because a small minority of applicants practise fraud, whole categories are subject to excessive scrutiny and restrictions. Prospective spouses are awarded a two-year temporary visa until their marriage has proved 'permanent', and they are subject to detailed and sometimes humiliating questioning. Parents are only admitted if they establish that the 'balance' of their family does not live outside Australia and only 500 are now admitted each year, pending acceptance by the Senate of regulations which would admit other parents on payment of very considerable prepaid bonds. Visas are very difficult to obtain from 'countries at risk', which are judged by the proportion of overstayers rather than the gross number. This suspicion contrasts with previous naivety about business and student migrants who bring money into the country, not to mention the admission of war criminals who have escaped such scrutiny.

Repeated changes of minister and secretary may have damaged departmental morale between 1983 and 1996. The minister most respected in this period was Robert Ray. There was considerable unhappiness with the removal of Ron Brown as departmental secretary in 1990, which was seen as responding to the 'ethnic lobby'. There was also some unhappiness about developments surrounding asylum seeker policy in 2001 and 2002. Minister Ruddock has, however, had a long association with departmental officers in Opposition and government, and his expertise in this area is respected as superior to that of many of his Labor predecessors.

State government agencies

Under the Australian Constitution the Commonwealth is empowered to legislate 'for the people of any race' (s. 51(xxvi)) and for immigration (s. 51(xxvii)). These powers have been extended to cover multiculturalism without any demur from the States. Broadcasting, including the ABC and SBS, is also a Commonwealth power through its control of the telegraph (s. 51(v)). The colonies had all organised immigration control, assisted passages and settlement services before 1901. They continued to do so in co-operation with the Commonwealth for the next twenty years.

Following the First World War the Commonwealth took over effective control of selection and assistance, and this was reasserted by the post–Second World War Labor government, which tended to be centralist in this as in other areas. State Agents-General offices in London continued to advertise and encourage emigration, most notably South and Western Australia. From 1946 State Migration Offices were set up to process immigration proposals from the United Kingdom. But non-British migration was regarded as a Commonwealth responsibility from the 1920s onwards under its power over aliens (s. 51(xix)). The States did, however, co-operate with the Commonwealth in delivering the adult migrant education program from the 1940s through their educational facilities.

As numbers of immigrants built up in Melbourne, Sydney and Adelaide from the 1950s, the State governments of Victoria, New South Wales and South Australia needed to consider their non-British populations as clients for education, hospitals, employment and other major policy areas which rested wholly or largely with them. This recognition took twenty years to institutionalise and was pioneered mainly by Labor State governments. This reflected the electoral base which Labor had established in ethnic areas as well as a commitment to social justice by such premiers as Neville Wran (New South Wales), Don Dunstan (South Australia) and John Cain (Victoria). Non-Labor premiers, especially Joh Bjelke-Petersen (Queensland), Sir Thomas Playford (South Australia) and Sir Charles Court (Western Australia), were much less responsive. Tasmania, which received few immigrants, has maintained a small office within the premier's department with limited functions and resources.

The first, and usually the strongest, State agency was the Ethnic Affairs Commission of New South Wales, now renamed the Community Relations Commission after a controversial intervention by Premier Bob Carr. This was created by the Ethnic Affairs Act of 1976 in fulfilment of an election promise in the successful Labor campaign of Neville Wran.[11] The commission's 1978 report, *Participation*, became the most influential State-level strategy in parallel with the national Galbally report of the same year.[12]

State agencies, usually answerable to the premier, were created over the following decade until every State and Territory had an equivalent. In Queensland even the Bjelke-Petersen National government established a Department of Ethnic Affairs in 1981. These agencies were normally recruited and staffed from immigrant and ethnic Australians and were also responsible for funding and working with the Ethnic Communities' Councils. The Cain Labor government in Victoria had presented a detailed ethnic affairs policy to the electorate in 1982, legislated for an Ethnic Affairs Commission at the end of that year and received the major report *Access and Equity* in July 1983.[13] Like the New South Wales report this ranged widely, emphasising particularly the need for translating and interpreting services, language teaching, grants to ethnic organisations and the monitoring of other government departments. The importance of the State agencies is that they gave a direct voice to immigrant communities in defining the services which their members needed. As the Commonwealth reduced its commitment from 1996, they became the main public sector defenders of multiculturalism.

The advisory structures

In the early post-war days the Commonwealth created advisory committees to discuss and refine immigration and settlement policy. These were chosen from individuals and interests believed to have a stake in the outcomes. Prior to the 1970s these were composed almost entirely of the Australian-born. The interests which had to be persuaded of the value of immigration included business, the unions and returned servicemen. Women, as elsewhere in the consultative structures of the time, were rarely represented. The thought of including Indigenous representatives probably never crossed the mind of the selectors. Partisan patronage was not usually important and unions and businessmen sat together without much tension, the former being less enthusiastic than the latter about increasing the labour force.

The earliest Immigration Advisory Council was set up in 1947 by Arthur Calwell and reconstituted by the new Liberal minister, Harold Holt, in 1950. It held its last meeting in August 1974 following the temporary abolition of the Immigration Department by

Whitlam. Its sixteen members in 1950 included several trade unionists, such as Rex Broadby, Percy Clarey, H. O. Davis and Albert Monk. Organisations represented were listed as: Air Force Association, Associated Chambers of Commerce, Associated Chambers of Manufactures, Australian Council of Employers Federations, Australian Council of Trade Unions, Australian Legion of Ex-Servicemen and Women, Australian Workers' Union, National Council of Women, National Farmers' Union, and Returned Sailors', Soldiers' and Airmen's Association. The chairman, Colonel R. S. Ryan, was the Liberal MP for Flinders. This council was to be concerned broadly with settlement issues (including 'non-European migration') and assimilation. Its counterpart, the Immigration Planning Council, had a more specific concern with economic, industrial and developmental aspects. This division between 'social' and 'economic' advice was to continue in the future.

Twenty-five years later, following the shift from assimilation to multiculturalism, the composition of advisory councils was quite different. Multiculturalism was a new concept in the 1970s and was often criticised as vague and undefined. The agencies developing policy included the Department of Immigration, the newly formed ethnic communities' movement, the political parties, influential individuals in the ethnic communities, educational and welfare institutions and a handful of academics. Policy was also developed on the national and State levels and by government and non-government agencies. Business corporations and most trade unions and ex-service organisations were not so directly involved as in the 1950s. There was a sufficient variety of interests to make for debate and confusion.

The division between 'social' and 'economic' advice was maintained with the creation of the Australian Population and Immigration Council (APIC) by the Whitlam government. For most of the Fraser government there were three advisory councils, but they were amalgamated into the National Population Council by Hawke in 1984. The APIC was joined by the Australian Ethnic Affairs Council (AEAC) in 1977. This began the process whereby immigration and settlement policy advice came mainly from the ethnic constituency rather than from established Anglo-Australian individuals and institutions. It also marked the increasing use of academics and the diminishing role of conservative partisans, despite appointment by a Liberal government.

The AEAC of 1977 was chaired by Polish-born Professor Jerzy Zubrzycki and included three other academics, Susan Kaldor of the University of Western Australia, Chilean-born Professor Claudio Veliz of La Trobe University and George Papadopoulos of Royal Melbourne Institute of Technology. Its members included many who remained favoured by governments of both persuasions and at both levels for the next two decades. These included Papadopoulos, Uri Themal, Bill Jegorow and Josephine Zammit. There were four women members out of twenty-four, not ungenerous for the late 1970s. But most important of all was that almost the entire council was of ethnic background. As continued to be the case, one union representative (Bill Colbourne) and an industry representative (Brian Noakes) were not. Council members were advised that they were not 'delegates' or 'representatives', which remained the normal practice. But the AEAC effectively institutionalised ethnic community organisations as a normal part of the Commonwealth advisory structures.

The parallel APIC similarly drew on the ethnic constituency. But it had a much larger academic component and was more directly concerned with immigration and population issues than with settlement or multiculturalism. It was chaired by the minister, Michael MacKellar. Academics included Professor Mick Borrie, who had chaired the national population inquiry of 1975, Professor W. P. Hogan, Professor J. D. B. Miller, Dr Max Neutze, Dr Alan Richardson and Professor R. J. Walsh. Business organisations sent three members while the unions also sent three, including then president of the ACTU, Bob Hawke. The legal profession was also represented, most notably by James Gobbo, who was later to chair the first National Multicultural Advisory Council under the Hawke government. Only four members were of ethnic background and none were women. This composition suggests, within the prejudices of the time, that the APIC was expected to deal with more serious matters than the AEAC.

The consultative structure was reformed again under the Hawke government, when the National Population Council was set up in 1984. This was dominated by members of ethnic organisations and

academics. It was consequently well equipped to develop policy and
to advise on settlement issues. But it no longer had the earlier function of co-opting economic and social interests. As with previous
arrangements it was divided between a Migration and an Ethnic
Affairs and Settlement committee. Its two co-chairmen after 1987,
Glenn Withers and David Cox, were both professors. It was undoubtedly the best qualified and most ethnically diverse of the consultative
committees answering to the Immigration Department. Its reports
on access and equity, population policy and refugees included
important pieces of original research. This did not save it from abolition by the minister, Gerry Hand, at the end of 1991.

It was replaced by a Settlement Advisory Council of predominantly 'ethnic' membership and narrower concerns. On the election of the Howard government there were only limited advisory
councils appointed on multiculturalism and refugee settlement.
Policy advice from outside the Immigration Department was much
less actively sought, being replaced by contract research or for-
malised consultations. Departmental officers and the minister's
personal staff became more important sources of guidance, which
was not always an improvement.

Inquiries and reports

The use of inquiries and reports was a major instrument for refining policy under the Fraser, Hawke and Keating governments but
has been much less commonly so under Howard. Such inquiries
were also a form of consultation. They normally called for expert
witnesses and professional consultants, together with submissions
by organisations and members of the public. With a secretariat
chosen from the relevant department they were also useful in vali-
dating policies which had already been planned or were in train.
Multicultural policy at the Commonwealth and State levels was usually determined by such exercises.

Among the most important such inquiries since 1975 have been:
under Whitlam – the National Population Inquiry of 1975 (chair
Mick Borrie); under Fraser – the review of Post-Arrival Programs
and Services for Migrants of 1978 (Galbally) and its evaluation by
the Australian Institute of Multicultural Affairs in 1982, and the

survey of Information Needs of Migrants of 1980 (WD Scott & Co.); under Hawke – the review of the Australian Institute of Multicultural Affairs of 1983 (Cass), the review of the Special Broadcasting Service of 1984 (Connor), the inquiry into the Adult Migrant Education Program of 1985 (Campbell), the review of Migrant and Multicultural Programs and Services of 1986 (Jupp), the National Policy on Languages of 1987 (Lo Bianco), the discussion paper on the National Multicultural Agenda (1988), the Committee to Advise on Australia's Immigration Policies of 1988 (FitzGerald), and the Inquiry into Racist Violence of 1991 (Moss and Castan); under Keating – the Access and Equity Evaluation of 1992 (OMA), the Population Issues Committee of the National Population Council of 1992 (Withers), the parliamentary inquiry into the Refugee and Humanitarian System of 1992 (Theophanous), the parliamentary inquiry into Asylum and Border Control of 1994 (McKiernan), the inquiry into Population Carrying Capacity of 1994 (Jones), and the parliamentary inquiry into Access and Equity of 1996 (Morris).

This was an extraordinary research and consultation effort which has had no parallel before or since. The only comparable major review under Howard was the consultation leading up to the multicultural agenda of 1999. All ministers also hold annual consultations over the planned intake. The regular complaint that there was no discussion about immigration and multiculturalism under Hawke and Keating is clearly ridiculous. Nor were those consulted drawn only from bureaucrats and professionals. Most inquiries sought public participation, often through press advertising. These major inquiries do not include many lesser surveys undertaken within the research programs of the Australian Institute of Multicultural Affairs and the Bureau of Immigration Research, which also frequently included public consultations.

Consultation and representation

Commonwealth and State advisory councils have largely been drawn from established interests, and from ethnic organisations, academics, lawyers and the professions in general. Since the 1980s they have broadened to include women and a handful of Indigenous members. As their ethnic component increased, the business and trade union representation declined and became marginal. The Immigration Department built up a reserve of 'ethnic leaders' for service on relevant councils and committees. These normally included the FECCA president after 1979. Party patronage was a factor in selection from the 1980s, but the financial benefits of membership were confined to a modest sitting fee, travel, and accommodation in equally modest hotels. The early councils certainly included many who later made successful careers, including one prime minister. But membership on Immigration Department councils was rarely a major factor in their advance.

Advisory council membership usually required proficiency in English and an occupation which allowed flexibility in attending meetings throughout Australia. The basic problem in this was that the needs of a predominantly working-class constituency were not necessarily understood by professional or business people of the same ethnic background. Nor were the trade unions effectively in touch with that part of their membership. Advice on policy might well come from such councils, although it was usually steered gently through by departmental officials, but the often urgent needs of many immigrants could only be ascertained at the local level and by direct communication. As needs were greatest where English proficiency was least, advisory council members were not necessarily the best conduit for consultation. This view was strongly held by at least two Labor ministers, Gerry Hand and Nick Bolkus. Hand launched out on an exhaustive and exhausting round of consultations designed specifically to by-pass the 'ethnic élites'. It was based on his previous experience with Aboriginal affairs, where such localised consultations are unavoidable. Bolkus preferred to attempt the reform of FECCA, which he felt was not fulfilling its role of transmitting the demands of its constituency.

Consultation with the ethnically diverse constituency reached its height under Hawke and Keating. All ministers in recent years have held consultations on the annual immigration program, although that, too, rests with a selected group rather than mass meetings. Under the Howard government, consultation has become much less important. Apart from the Council for Multicultural Australia, there is none of the regular advisory structure which existed in the past. That council has a small budget and a limited role. Large conferences, which provided a forum for public debate, ceased to be funded by the Commonwealth when the Bureau of Immigration, Multicultural and Population Research was abolished in 1996. Crises within FECCA for most of the late 1990s limited its role as a sounding board, although it continued to be funded by the Commonwealth for that purpose.[14]

The Howard government did not strengthen the advisory structures, which had tended to be run down under Keating. A new Refugee Settlement advisory committee was created which included a representative of the Refugee Council of Australia as well as others working in the field of refugee settlement. The National Multicultural Advisory Council worked on the Agenda of 1999 and was then reconstructed as the Council for Multicultural Australia on a similar basis. But there was no re-creation of the National Population Council or of the monitoring and research structures abolished in 1996. Consultations on the annual immigration programs continued through ministerial visits around Australia, utilising the department's network of migrant resource centres and the Ethnic Communities' Councils (ECCs). But the advisory role of FECCA was fairly marginal and it never fully recovered from the trauma surrounding the attempt to reform it under Senator Bolkus. Because the Liberal and National parties did not have the grassroots or trade union networks of the ALP they tended to draw on professional and business people for advice and to be less sensitive to social and economic issues. Very few of their politicians represented electorates with large immigrant populations, although one who did was John Howard. The plethora of consultations, inquiries and reports which characterised the Hawke and Keating governments was not repeated.

Research and advocacy

Before the development of official research agencies in the late 1970s, the main centre for immigration research was the Demography department of the Australian National University. The elaborate consultation and inquiry processes of the Hawke and Keating governments gave immigration and settlement policy a research base comparable to any in the world. This was complemented by two agencies: the Office of Multicultural Affairs (1987–96) and the

Bureau of Immigration Research (1989–96). These were preceded by the Australian Institute of Multicultural Affairs (AIMA), set up in 1979 in response to the Galbally finding that 'If we are to achieve the benefits of a multicultural society, its development must be guided, supported and given direction by independent experts of high calibre'.[15] These three agencies produced much excellent research before falling victim to partisan intervention. Throughout this period the Immigration Department also sustained its library and statistical services, produced a stream of publications and developed a very informative website.

The fates of AIMA, OMA and the BIR suggest that governments and bureaucracies are uncomfortable with independent but publicly funded research and advocacy. This tends to be dominated by academics, whereas submissions to inquiries can always be accepted or rejected by the public servants staffing the secretariat. Departmental publications are, of course, always subject to ministerial control and approval. Nevertheless the Galbally finding is as relevant now as it was in 1978. Publicly funded research on immigration and its consequences had been of world standard in Australia from the 1970s. Private research, through universities and think-tanks, has been very limited and has declined almost to marginality since 1996. Research through State government agencies has also tended towards the publication of newsletters, although some useful factual and directory material is often produced.

The AIMA, located in Melbourne, was governed by its own legislation (the Australian Institute of Multicultural Affairs Act of 1979) but answerable to the Department of Immigration for its budget and general guidance. For most if its seven years it was directed by Petro Georgiou, the main inspirer of the Galbally report, who was dismissed by Minister Hurford in 1986 and went on to direct the Victorian Liberal Party and to be elected for the safe Liberal seat of Kooyong. This partisan identification earned him the enmity of the Melbourne group which had largely been responsible for gaining acceptance of multiculturalism under Whitlam.[16] They centred around the journal *Migration Action* and the Ecumenical Migration Centre. However, AIMA employed George Papadopoulos, one of this group, and Georgiou was succeeded by Peter Sheldrake, a member of the ALP.

The Act gave AIMA wide scope to engage not only in research but also in promotion of multicultural objectives named in the Act. It provided advice to the Commonwealth on relevant matters. In practice it concentrated on settlement issues, including a major evaluation in 1982 of the Galbally report. It did not enjoy good relations with many academics, other than Professor Zubrzycki, and was subject to a hostile evaluation when Labor came to office in 1983. Despite a recommendation by the 1986 Review of Migrant and Multicultural Programs and Services that it continue, Minister Hurford abolished AIMA in the burst of budget cuts in that year. It was clearly a victim of partisanship but was also probably undermined from within the Immigration Department. Although its council and membership included many from ethnic organisations, it got little support in the end from FECCA or the ECCs.

The 1986 review and the 1988 FitzGerald report both advocated a higher degree of research, monitoring and advocacy than was left after AIMA was abolished.[17] The process was started all over again, although it could have been built upon a retained AIMA under new leadership. The Office of Multicultural Affairs was originally conceived of as within the Immigration Department. Wilenski advised that it was better for it to be where it was wanted than in Prime Minister and Cabinet where it was not. PM&C was very concerned not to get responsibility for grant-in-aid allocations to ethnic welfare groups. This was left with Immigration, making the distinction between 'multicultural' and 'ethnic affairs' which puzzled many. Under Peter Shergold, an academic and a former research officer of FECCA, the OMA got off to an excellent beginning. It developed a multilingual consultancy system, completed the only professional survey of opinion on a range of relevant issues, and laid the foundations for monitoring public service performance in taking account of a varied clientele – the 'access and equity' strategy which had been developed since 1985.

The OMA was not directly answerable to Immigration. Its response to the criticism of multiculturalism in the FitzGerald report of 1988 was not particularly welcome there. Shergold was transferred eventually and went on to a highly successful public service career. His successors saw the OMA gradually fade away, losing its research functions to the Bureau of Immigration Research and being mainly focused on public service management issues through the access and equity strategy. Its last two directors were both Labor patronage appointments, its orientation was unacceptable to the new Coalition government, and it was abolished as one of that government's first acts in 1996.

The third research and advocacy agency – the Bureau of Immigration Research – was also located in Melbourne but was part of the Immigration Department, with control over its library and statistical services in Canberra. It established a much better relationship with academics and ethnic communities than had AIMA. Its budget of about $500 000 for competitive contract research was very useful for academic institutions specialising in the area. It also undertook in-house research. The publications output of the BIR, both in quantity and quality, equalled anything comparable in the world. Its regular mass conferences helped to build a clientele from ethnic communities and the public sector. It was undoubtedly the most influential research agency on immigration, settlement and multiculturalism which Australia has ever had. Towards the end of its life, population policy was added to its responsibilities.

Yet the BIR, too, was abolished by Howard and nothing was put in its place. Howard took a personal role in the abolition, as he had done with the OMA. The BIR had researched various 'problem' areas not usually of direct interest to the department, such as the ethics and politics of immigration and social issues such as relative disadvantage or discrimination. Its eventual nemesis probably had most to do with the growing attack on the immigration intake using 'zero sum' arguments, and its commitment to multiculturalism. Its enemies were close to Howard and the conservative element in the Liberal Party, just as AIMA's enemies had been part of the 'social justice' element in the ALP. Indeed, some saw the abolition of the BIR as a payback for the previous abolition of AIMA.

While the period between 1976 and 1996 saw a massive output of research material, this is no longer the case. Control over research rests entirely within the Immigration Department and is mainly concerned with the settlement and employment prospects of different visa classes. Advocacy, access and equity monitoring and social and economic research are back under departmental control, but greatly diminished. Few research projects are now submitted to competitive tendering, although they may be responses to approaches from academics or research consultancies.

The ethnic communities

At least 3 million Australians are undeniably 'ethnic' in the sense of normally using a language other than English. A further 1 million at least are likely to identify with this large minority, if only through parents or other relatives. The loose use of terms such as 'the ethnic community' or 'NESB' obscures the fact that this large part of the electorate does not have very much influence unless governments want it to. There are far fewer 'ethnics' in parliament or in policy-making public service positions than these figures might suggest. Those who are in a position to influence policy are drawn from a wide variety of backgrounds. Many are fully acculturated or arrived in Australia as children. They have often made their careers in spite of their ethnicity rather than because of it. In contrast to the United States, there are few organised ethnic lobbies with direct access to government and fewer still seeking to advance their members within the policy-making frameworks.

Despite this, many opponents of developments under Fraser, Hawke and Keating argued that policy was being driven by a 'powerful ethnic lobby'. This was said to be the main beneficiary of the 'multicultural industry'. Whether a lobby is powerful or not often depends on the petitioned government allowing it to be influential (trade unions have little influence on the Coalition). The 'ethnic lobby' arose at a time when there was much discussion of 'social movements'. These were believed to be replacing the conventional business, commerce, labour and ex-service lobbies which had influenced policy in the past and had been incorporated in advisory structures for many years. From another perspective – public choice theory imported from the United States – lobbies were 'rent seekers'. They distorted policy by asking for favours which less well-organised citizens could not extract. The idea of ethnic groups as 'social movements' was more influential on the left of politics, while their description as 'rent seekers' entered into the vocabulary of the Coalition.

Ethnic groups, communities, media and churches existed well before the 1970s. Looking to the American example many assumed that ethnic lobbying would become increasingly important in Australia.[18] Many deplored this as bringing 'old world battles' into local affairs. This argument was strengthened by Balkan-oriented disputes in the 1970s and 1980s. It was given further credence by accusations of ethnic branch stacking in the ALP in the 1980s and 1990s and more recently in the Liberal Party.

However, the American model was not followed. Once again the state intervened, making ethnic peak bodies into semi-public agencies. Ethnic Communities' Councils had been created in Sydney and Melbourne at the end of the Whitlam period, drawing much of their support from within the Labor Party but being overtly nonpartisan. These were based on the affiliation of ethnic groups, with limitations to prevent the larger ethnic groups from dominating. FECCA, the national body, was set up in 1979. Each State and Territory was equally represented, which greatly distorted the reality that two-thirds of the ethnic population lived in New South Wales and Victoria. Immigration Department officers assisted in creating the structure and the department was willing to encourage applications for public funding. This was approved in the last days of the Fraser government in 1982 but was implemented under Labor, which naturally took the credit.

From 1983 until the present, FECCA has received a substantial annual grant of more than $350 000 to maintain its office. This was delivered by the Immigration Department from 1983 until 1988, when it was transferred to the OMA, returning to Immigration in 1996. State ECCs were usually funded by the State government, New South Wales providing $261 000 in 1998. The Commonwealth subsidised the Queensland ECC for several years, as the Bjelke-Petersen government refused to do so, continuing to support the elsewhere defunct Good Neighbour Council.

The ethnic lobby, then, was paid for by the governments which it was lobbying. This practice was increasingly widespread under the Hawke Labor government as a means of consultation. It might also be seen as a way of controlling and subduing any ethnic radicalism. However, FECCA, the ECCs and most ethnic organisations were not radical and some were quite conservative. Because Labor was nationally in office for thirteen years FECCA tended to be closer to that party. But State ECCs had good relations with Coalition governments, especially after the retirement of Bjelke-Petersen in 1987.

FECCA and the ECCs were 'pan-ethnic' organisations and had to avoid favouritism between different ethnic groups. They were dependent on public funds and had to avoid partisanship. They refused to play the 'numbers' game when opposition to high immigration levels was building up in the 1990s. The areas on which they lobbied were largely confined to family reunion, access and equity, ethnic-specific services, language policy, and education, welfare, health and other social provision. Their lobbying method was mainly through submissions to government inquiries rather than through the media or demonstrations. They were reasonably effective while Labor was in office, frustrating the amalgamation of SBS and the ABC in 1986 (along with the Democrats) and criticising some aspects of the FitzGerald report in 1988. But as economic rationalism took hold and services were either limited or charged to recipients, their influence waned. After a period of internal dissension and reconstruction in the mid-1990s, it would be hard to say what FECCA was achieving under the Howard government except its own preservation. It was a useful organisation in maintaining an ethnic presence in the public policy arena, especially for smaller groups which did not have access to politicians. However, the Howard government was fairly unsympathetic to 'rent seekers' and FECCA's influence on it was not very apparent.

Throughout the Fraser, Hawke and Keating governments there was a substantial input from ethnic organisations and individuals into multicultural and settlement policy. This became much less significant under Howard, especially as Commonwealth commitment in these areas was reduced. At no time was it true that immigration policy in general was driven by the 'powerful ethnic lobby'. Eventually even those areas of ethnic concern, such as family reunion, became quite uninfluenced. Ethnic influence continued at the State level. But at both levels the influence of public servants and politicians remained more important and, indeed, increased as major ethnic organisations lost their impetus or became frustrated at slow progress. The 'ethnic lobby' lacked a strong parliamentary base in the major parties and could not command a distinct electoral following. It was incorporated within the official structures which funded it and expected its collaboration.

Notes

1 DIEA, Annual Reports, 1976–95.
2 FitzGerald, *Immigration – A Commitment to Australia*.
3 DIMA, *Annual Report 1997–98*, Secretary's Report.
4 Jupp and Kabala, *The Politics of Australian Immigration*.
5 DIEA, *Annual Report* (1981).
6 DIEA, *Annual Report* (1987).
7 DIMA, *Annual Report* (2001).
8 Blainey, *All for Australia*.
9 Pusey, *Economic Rationalism in Canberra*; Weller, *The Mandarins*.
10 Crock and Saul, *Future Seekers*.
11 Murphy, *The Other Australia*.
12 Totaro, *Participation*.
13 Sheppard, *Access and Equity*.
14 FECCA, Annual Reports.
15 Galbally, *Migrant Services and Programs*, para 9.18.
16 Lopez, *The Origins of Multiculturalism in Australian Politics*.
17 Jupp, *Don't Settle for Less*; FitzGerald, *Immigration – A Commitment to Australia*.
18 Jupp, *Arrivals and Departures*.

5

Multicultural policy

Multiculturalism is a neologism, a term recently invented to describe something for which there was no previous satisfactory description. It was coined and developed in Canada in response to political pressure from minority cultures, especially the Ukrainians and other Slavs. The official formulation of 'two founding nations' (British and French) left other cultural groups feeling that they had been overlooked, despite their important presence especially in western Canada. The 'Bi-Bi' report (the Canadian Royal Commission on Bilingualism and Biculturalism of 1970) in volume four considered 'the contribution made by the other ethnic groups to the cultural enrichment of Canada and the measures that should be taken to safeguard that contribution'. While there would be only two official languages, multiculturalism was designed to cater for a multiplicity of other cultures, including those long-established as well as those of more recent immigrants.

From the beginning, Canadian multiculturalism accepted that cultures had relevance beyond the immigrant generation. This was not so obviously the case in Australia, where responsibility for multiculturalism has rested for all but nine of the past thirty years with the Immigration Department. The Canadian Commission researched two questions:

> To what degree have Canadians whose origin is neither French nor British integrated with anglophone or francophone society? To what degree have they remained attached to their original cultures and languages?

Australian multiculturalism

The Australian approach, which followed the Canadian in less than five years, was quite different. It has been argued by Mark Lopez, in his detailed study of the origins of multiculturalism, that little attention was paid to the Canadian model even while the terminology was accepted.[1] Policy development was seen as concerned with the immigrant generation. Indigenous Australians were not regarded as relevant until 1989. Religious minorities were not taken into consideration either. Language was seen as the core of ethnic diversity. The basic question asked in Australia was, therefore, how to ensure that non-British immigrants were integrated into Australian society. The term 'non-English-speaking background' (NESB) was coined to describe the target group. While policy development by 1982 argued that 'multiculturalism is for all Australians', this was never effectively implemented or understood.

The term 'multiculturalism' has been defined in different countries in accordance with the local situation. It was reluctantly adopted in the United States where it has also endured the most consistent attacks. In the United States, human rights and ethnic relations have been defined and determined to a large extent in the courts, acting on the wording of the American Constitution and in response to political agitation. This has led to such innovations as school bussing, ethnic quotas in public appointments, and the drawing of electoral boundaries to take account of ethnic distribution. None of these has been the case in Australia. Yet much of the conservative attack on multiculturalism from the early 1980s was simply transferred from the United States as though the two situations were the same. A central claim of American critics is that multiculturalism endorses cultural relativism and thus denies the basic liberal principles upon which society and its institutions depend. This has never been the case in Australia. All official formulations have stressed the supremacy of existing institutions and values as well as of the English language. Some have advocated cultural relativism in traditional Indigenous affairs, but this has never been true for the immigrant communities.[2]

Australian multiculturalism puts less emphasis on civil rights and constitutional protections than does the American variety. It puts far less emphasis on cultural maintenance than in the Canadian case. It does not endorse distinct cultural development, as in South Africa. Comparisons are often made with societies such as Yugoslavia to establish that 'multiculturalism does not work anywhere'. These are quite bogus and dishonest. Australian policy is not based on distinct enclaves but rather on what Al Grassby originally called 'the family of the nation'. In other words, everyone would work together towards common purposes in exchange for common treatment. This was, however, a vague idea in its early stages and there has been a consistent attempt to define the essence of multiculturalism, most recently in 1999. Rather than multiculturalism being undefined it has been repeatedly redefined, without avoiding repeated attacks from critics who are often quite ignorant of these official reformulations.

The foundations

Multiculturalism was first officially defined by the Australian Ethnic Affairs Council report of 1977, *Australia as a Multicultural Society*. This council was appointed by the Fraser government. But the origins of multicultural policy lie with the Whitlam government and with advisers who were predominantly Labor supporters. The enthusiastic adoption of multiculturalism by Fraser ensured bipartisan support but also led some of the Labor originators to criticise subsequent developments and especially the Galbally report of 1978. As Lopez has remarked, most 'multiculturalists' in Melbourne were Labor supporters 'in a state of disarray' at the Coalition victory of 1975.[3] Some of them continued to be critical throughout the Fraser years, while others made their peace. Grassby, Whitlam's minister responsible for the acceptance of multiculturalism, continued as community relations commissioner under the Fraser government until his contract expired in 1982. While his main responsibility was to monitor racial discrimination, it also allowed him to develop some aspects of multiculturalism such as advocacy and education. This work was continued and expanded by the race discrimination commissioner, Irene Moss, under the Labor government elected in 1983.

Lopez asserts that the origins of multiculturalism were largely in Melbourne among supporters of the ALP and the Australian Greek Welfare Society. While undoubtedly correct, this overlooks much that was happening in Canberra and Sydney and within organised ethnic communities. Melbourne certainly remained at the heart of multiculturalism for many years, and the Victorian Labor and Liberal parties were more responsive than their New South Wales counterparts. Yet Labor politicians such as Whitlam and Grassby in New South Wales or Don Dunstan in Adelaide were also driving a multicultural agenda by the late 1960s. The east European communities were resisting assimilation and influencing the Liberal and Democratic Labor parties accordingly. Most importantly, the massive southern European immigration of the 1960s had challenged the assimilation assumptions which guided the Good Neighbour movement and the Immigration Department. Ethnic discontent with existing policy created the ethnic communities movement in Sydney and Melbourne by 1975, which was to become the most enthusiastic supporter of multiculturalism over the next twenty years. The Ethnic Communities' Council of New South Wales held its first conference in June 1975, attended by Prime Minister Whitlam and Opposition leader Malcolm Fraser. Poles like Zubrzycki and Jerzy Smolicz, and Jews like Walter Lippman, were influential in their own communities and there was strong support among Melbourne Greeks. By the time that the Ethnic Affairs Council formulated its definitions there was already a much larger constituency for multiculturalism than when it was first advocated by Grassby in 1973. At the core of this constituency were a wide variety of Australians of 'ethnic' background.

The 1977 definition of multiculturalism was handed down through committees and reports for the next twenty years, amended but never repudiated. It was mainly drafted by Zubrzycki and Dr Jean Martin, both of the Australian National University. They concluded: 'What we believe Australia should be working towards is not a oneness, but a unity, not a similarity, but a composite, not a melting pot but a voluntary bond of dissimilar people sharing a common political and institutional structure'. This approach they called 'cultural pluralism'.[4]

The Galbally report

While the report of 1977 laid down broad principles it had few specific proposals and these were mainly concerned with schooling and languages. At the time these were mainly within the province of State governments. The real foundation document of multiculturalism was the report presented to the prime minister in April 1978 by Frank Galbally, a Melbourne barrister who had previously been active in the ALP. He had drifted away towards the Liberals, partly in response to the split in the Victorian ALP in 1955 and its subsequent shift to the left and towards anti-Catholicism. The report was uniquely published in Arabic, Dutch, German, Greek, Italian, Serbo-Croatian, Spanish, Turkish and Vietnamese. A major influence on the report was 30-year-old Greek-born Petro Georgiou, who went on to a career in the Liberal Party.

The Galbally report was intended, by its broad terms of reference, to concentrate on the provision of migrant settlement services by Commonwealth and non-government agencies. In practice it went well beyond this, especially in developing a 'multicultural' approach, a word which did not appear in the terms of reference at all. The guiding principles of the report were to reappear throughout the history of multiculturalism to the present. They were:

a) all members of our society must have equal opportunity to realize their full potential and must have equal access to programs and services;
b) every person should be able to maintain his or her culture without prejudice or disadvantage and should be encouraged to understand and embrace other cultures;
c) needs of migrants should, in general, be met by programs and services available to the whole community but special services and programs are necessary at present to ensure equality of access and provision;
d) services and programs should be designed and operated in full consultation with clients, and self-help should be encouraged as much as possible with a view to helping migrants to become self-reliant quickly.[5]

The report stated clearly that those most in need of help were 'those who arrive here with little or no understanding of the English language'. Previously, considerable assistance had been available to British migrants through the Good Neighbour Council, churches and charities. After Galbally, migrant assistance was discussed and delivered predominantly to non-British migrants. One consequence was the withdrawal of Commonwealth funding from the Good Neighbour movement (recommendations 31 and 32). In Galbally's view the movement had a cumbersome and increasingly irrelevant structure. But 'more serious ... has been its inability to take account of the growing capacity and desire of ethnic organisations to provide their own services'. This criticism reflects the influence of Australian Greek Welfare and Australian Jewish Welfare. But its genesis was also in increasing conflict between the Victorian Good Neighbour Council and some of the activists associated with the early development of multiculturalism under Whitlam and now involved in the new Ethnic Communities' Councils. Most of these were Labor supporters, whereas many Good Neighbours were Liberals.

The central importance of the report lay in its recognition that 'ultimately ethnic groups themselves must take on the task of advising government of the needs and priorities of migrants, and ensuring that ethnic cultures are fostered and preserved' (para 6.41). One agency for achieving this was the already existing grant-in-aid scheme of the Immigration Department, which was greatly expanded after Galbally. This provided funding for ethnic organisations to deliver advice and services. Another instrument created by Galbally was the migrant resource centres, with management committees 'drawn principally from local ethnic and community organisations', which would be 'multicultural and available to all groups' (paras 6.7 and 6.8).

It was this network of ethnic welfare delivery which was later to be attacked as costing 'billions' in 'divisive' support for ethnicity. Neither in theory nor in subsequent practice was this criticism even remotely near the truth. The additional cost of grants-in-aid was estimated at $1.7 million over three years and for migrant resource centres, at $1.34 million. Over the same three years the ending of Good Neighbour funding would save $2.81 million, an almost direct transfer from 'mainstream' to 'ethnic specific' funding (Appendix I).

The Galbally report goes well beyond a new structure for migrant welfare delivery in its discussion of multiculturalism and the media. The report 'rejects the argument that cultural diversity necessarily creates divisiveness. Rather we believe that hostility and bitterness between groups are often the result of cultural repression' (para 9.7). If multiculturalism was to succeed it needed an educational program, the fostering of cultures and languages, the development of relevant knowledge, greater effort by the Australia Council, and cultural agreements with other societies. These themes were to be repeated for the next twenty years with modest results. Of more lasting impact was the recognition of the importance of the media. The report laid down the principles on which the Special Broadcasting Service in radio and television was created at a modest cost of $10.77 million over three years. SBS was to expand and flourish to become one of the most successful and expensive of all multicultural agencies.

Multicultural institutions

The creation of the Australian Institute of Multicultural Affairs (AIMA) in 1979 established a well staffed and funded agency with responsibilities detailed in legislation. These were defined in the Australian Institute of Multicultural Affairs Act (154 of 1979) as: to develop an awareness of the diverse cultures within the community and an appreciation of the contributions of these cultures; to promote tolerance; to promote a cohesive Australian society; and to promote an environment that affords the members of the different cultural groups and ethnic communities the opportunity to participate fully in Australian society. This would be achieved by providing advice to the Commonwealth government; commissioning research; reporting to the minister; making information available to the community; conducting educational and promotional activity; and establishing a relevant library. AIMA had no responsibilities in the area of Indigenous studies or policy, which was the province of the Australian Institute of Aboriginal (and later Torres Strait Islander) Studies.

AIMA was a response to the Galbally recommendation (9.18) which claimed, correctly at the time, that 'there is very little information available on multicultural developments in Australia ... If we are to achieve the real benefits of a multicultural society, its development must be guided, supported and given direction by independent experts of high calibre.' Its first chairman was Frank Galbally, its first director Petro Georgiou and one of its seven council members was Jerzy Zubrzycki. The secretary of the Immigration Department was always a council member. Otherwise, AIMA enjoyed a degree of independence from Canberra. Its early leadership was closer to the Liberal Party than to the Melbourne group which pioneered multiculturalism under Labor. This was to create problems when Labor was elected nationally in 1983. AIMA was well staffed, with twenty-six employees in 1980, rising to forty-five by 1984. Its staff was largely of non-English-speaking background and its council of eighty overwhelmingly so. Whatever might have been true of the group which initiated multiculturalism under Whitlam, by 1980 policy was largely being made from within the ethnic constituency, if always with the participation of public servants and with an element of party patronage.

The development of multiculturalism rested with a number of other agencies appointed by the Immigration Department, starting with the Ethnic Affairs Council, chaired by Zubrzycki and reporting to Michael MacKellar in 1977. These agencies, unlike AIMA, were staffed by the Immigration Department and their members were part-time. As with all subsequent councils, the great majority of its members were of non-English-speaking background (twenty-three of twenty-six). Others, as with subsequent councils, represented industry and the unions, although it was officially held that all members were not 'representatives' but individuals.

A feature of policy development through such councils has been that there is almost no continuity of membership. Zubrzycki was not appointed to any councils under Labor but was a member of the National Multicultural Advisory Council (NMAC) later appointed under the Coalition. Party patronage was not a major factor, although some members were undoubtedly more acceptable than others to the ruling government. On the Coalition's 1977 Ethnic Affairs Council, Bill Colbourne, Bill Jegorow and George Papadopoulos were all Labor activists. On Labor's 1989 Advisory Council on Multicultural Affairs, Sir Nicholas Shehadie and Sir James Gobbo sat comfortably alongside Simon Crean and several other ALP members. On the 1994–97 NMAC, former Liberal minister Ian Macphee took part along with Martin Ferguson of the ACTU and under the chairmanship of Mick Young, a Labor politician with whom he had jointly campaigned for multiculturalism in the early 1990s. Nobody actively identified with the ALP or the unions was a member of the 1999 NMAC, which was probably the most politically conservative of any advisory body since the Galbally committee of 1978.

The ethnic composition of these advisory councils was carefully chosen to represent changes in the composition of the target population. It was also chosen on the basis of representing all States and Territories, which meant the under-representation of the two major immigrant concentrations of Sydney and Melbourne. There was Aboriginal membership of all three councils between 1989 and 1999. Union and business representatives, in common with most other 'non-ethnic' members, took a limited role, with the exception of Sir William Keyes of the Returned and Services League who was a valuable and active member of the first NMAC. Essentially the agendas and policy statements between 1977 and 1999 were worked over by appointees active in ethnic organisations, chosen by the Immigration Department. There were few academics. Female representation increased to one-third by 1995 but declined again by 1999. There was a marked shift towards Asian membership, with only one Chinese and one Arab on the 1977 council but seven Asians on the 1999 council. Greeks were represented throughout, although more strongly under Labor. All councils were serviced by public servants from the Immigration Department or the Office of Multicultural Affairs (OMA). Lack of continuity between councils gave these officers considerable influence over the agenda and recommendations. But each council contained enough experienced and determined members to ensure that they were not simply rubber stamps.

The agenda of 1989

One issue which was not favourably resolved was the proposal for a Multicultural Act, which had been referred to the NMAC as a requirement for developing the agenda. Canada had passed a Federal Multiculturalism Act in 1988 and copies were available to the council in 1990. Multiculturalism had also been enshrined in the Canadian Charter of Rights and Freedoms of 1981. However, in 1988 the Liberal leader, John Howard, had broken the consensus on multiculturalism with his speech to his party at Esperance in June.

This was the culmination of several years of conservative criticism. By 1990 this was so strong that many were prepared to abandon the word, an issue which also came before the NMAC ten years later.[6] The Canadian Act had been passed unanimously, but this seemed improbable in the newly hostile Australian atmosphere. Multiculturalism had previously had a legal basis in the 1979 AIMA Act. But this had been repealed by Labor on the abolition of the institute in 1986, revealing how fragile such legislation could be. Although strongly supported by the Federation of Ethnic Communities' Councils (FECCA), it was decided not to pursue new legislation. While this might have given a statutory basis to OMA and to the access and equity strategy, multiculturalism had become too controversial by 1990 to ensure unanimous parliamentary approval.

The reassessment of 1995

Senator Nick Bolkus was the only immigration minister of direct 'ethnic' origin, born in Adelaide of Greek parents and maintaining close links with the Greek community and with Greece. The reassessment of 1995 went beyond the agenda of 1989 in looking at issues of power and influence rather than simply tolerance and equity. Entitled *Multicultural Australia: The Next Steps*, the NMAC report of 1995 was designed to move beyond the original 1989 agenda without repudiating its major thrust. It was launched by Prime Minister Paul Keating and thus took on the status of an 'agenda', although it was not formally called that.[7]

The report was compiled by a small NMAC committee set up in 1994 under the chairmanship of Labor MP and former immigration minister, Mick Young. The subcommittee was overtly bipartisan, including Ian Macphee, Janet Powell, leader of the Australian Democrats, and two academics, Professor Stephen Castles and Dr My-Van Tran. Despite its bipartisan appearance, it was probably the most radical of the various committees recommending multicultural policy. It was serviced by OMA, rather than by Immigration as for the 1989 and 1999 agendas.

The NMAC report was supported by considerable research data comparing native-born, English-speaking (ES) and non-English-speaking (NES) immigrants. It also indicated the growing proportion of the Asian-born, without using them as a distinct category.

This research showed the impact of unemployment to be closely related to non-English-speaking background, especially for the young. Most controversially it examined the number of advisory and political appointees in terms of ethnic background. This finding led to recommendation 11 – favouring 'a more multicultural Australian Public Service', and to recommendation 12 – for both levels of government 'to take cultural diversity into account in appointments to advisory boards and government positions in all areas of public sector management'. This addressed the 'vision' that 'all Australians participate in the major public institutions and processes of society to the level of their capacity and interest and, where appropriate, these institutions and processes reflect the cultural diversity of the society'.[8] Minister Bolkus later took this to mean that 15 per cent of all advisory appointments should be from non-English-speaking backgrounds. This did not have time to be tested before the election defeat of Labor in 1996. A similar, but unquantified, recommendation was made in the 1999 agenda.[9]

Settlement policy

Australian multiculturalism is best understood as an aspect of immigrant settlement policy. It grew out of a concern with settlement rather than with cultural maintenance, which has largely been left to the ethnic communities. While it officially validated such maintenance against assimilationism, from the Galbally report in 1978, through the access and equity strategies of the 1980s and on to the agendas of 1989 and 1995, the central focus has been on alleviating problems faced by non-English-speaking immigrants.[10]

The basic difficulties faced by new arrivals with inadequate English have always been finding a job, finding a house and learning the language. Other problems of adjustment, including the frequent psychological problems of refugees, have been less adequately addressed by public policy. Australia has had migrant settlement programs from colonial times, originally pioneered by Caroline Chisholm in the 1850s. These expanded into the 1920s but were always focused on British immigrants. The work of the Good Neighbour Councils between 1950 and 1978 also included British immigrants but did not effectively reach most Europeans. All these services included co-operation between public and private agencies, as is still the case.

By the 1970s the Immigration Department was providing on-arrival accommodation, often in old army barracks but increasingly in custom-built hostels; teaching English to adults through the adult migrant education program; employing professional social workers; subsidising the Good Neighbour Councils; and working with organisations such as the Red Cross and St Vincent de Paul.[11] As there was full employment there was only a limited need to give assistance with finding work and this was often left to ethnic networks where necessary.

The Galbally report moved settlement services towards a greater participation of ethnic groups and a lesser concern with British migrants. This process continued to the point where considerable assistance was given to non-English-speaking migrants but very little to the British, who essentially did not need much help in a full employment economy. The Immigration Department subsidised these groups; added child migrant education to its functions in 1970; developed the telephone interpreter system after 1975; built more hostels (but sold them off by 1994); and began holding consultations with ethnic organisations and other client groups. By the 1980s settlement policy was well developed and compared favourably with that in most other immigrant societies. Services were, however, limited by the Immigration Department's small budget. Other major service providers were much less sensitive to ethnic diversity, most notably the Commonwealth departments of Education and Social Security. However, the growth of State government Ethnic Affairs Commissions after 1978 provided another increasingly important dimension to service delivery. All policy after Galbally intertwined settlement and multicultural issues. The client base was ethnic, consultation was through ethnic organisations, and subsidies went to ethnic-specific welfare deliverers and were fiercely defended as one of the few areas where the voice of immigrants was given high priority.

Language policy and multicultural education

The growth of ethnic-specific services in the 1980s allowed many ethnic groups to have a modest access to public funding and decision making. This was enhanced by the relationship between Labor Commonwealth and State governments and many ethnic communities. Despite this, cultural maintenance has been a priority of many ethnic organisations but not of the Commonwealth government or the Department of Immigration. It is more controversial than settlement services and goes against more than a century of assimilationism. Government policies have normally been directed at improving human capital or enhancing commercial contacts, rather than supporting immigrant cultures. Language policy moved rapidly away from developing community languages to favouring English literacy and the 'languages of commerce'.[12]

Education has been a major arena for developing multicultural policies. Initially it was believed that the school system would be a major assimilative force, as it had been in the United States. Not until 1971, under the Immigration (Education) Act, did the Commonwealth take a direct role, aimed at teaching English to migrant children under the child migrant education program. This important reform had little to do with multiculturalism, as it was assimilationist and utilitarian. However, it remained as a priority which eventually damaged attempts to develop policy relating to other languages. The multiplicity of languages used in Australia also militated against public funding, as this could not be universally available at a useful level.

Despite the adult and child education programs, many migrants have never learned English beyond the 'survival' level – and some (mainly southern European women) have never reached that level. The number of languages used increased along with the need for translating and interpreting. As multiculturalism was widely accepted by the 1980s and Australian links with other societies were growing, it was argued that a national language policy was needed to counter the dominant monoglot Anglophone tradition. This was a policy debate in which FECCA had a major role. However, this was a highly contested area. The most coherent attempt to bring some order into policy was the National Policy on Languages developed by Jo Lo Bianco in 1986 for Education Minister Susan Ryan. The guiding principles were: English competence; maintenance and development of other languages; services in other languages; and opportunities for language learning.

At the same time, a National Advisory and Co-ordinating Committee on Multicultural Education was devising a multicultural education policy. Both these exercises were largely aborted – the first by a change of minister from Ryan to John Dawkins, and the second by Ryan herself. There were too many conflicting claims and too much resistance to change for such innovative programs to be accepted. The Immigration Department was running its own research, 'The Language Question', conducted by Mary Kalantzis, Bill Cope and Diane Slade, and was using the research capacity of the adult migrant education program (AMEP) for the same purpose. This was probably a pre-emptive move to prevent the Education Department from taking over all of Immigration's language and teaching services, as Dawkins recommended in 1990.[13]

Language is an emotive issue in many societies and was the basis for defining 'ethnic groups' in Australia from the Galbally report onwards. Three major policy concerns and organised interests were involved: the teaching of English, where the Immigration Department had a major stake through the AMEP; the teaching of other languages, where teachers were well organised, especially in the main European languages; and the maintenance and use of 'community languages' – those actually used by immigrants and their immediate descendants – where FECCA and the ethnic organisations had a major interest. Governments tended to see these three areas in utilitarian terms and to play off the different interests to secure an optimum economic and budgetary return. Teaching English to migrants was obviously of economic value but expensive. Many remained illiterate in English, joining existing Anglo-Australian and Aboriginal illiterates.

Education Minister Dawkins, who was openly unsympathetic to immigration and multiculturalism, used his influence to redirect language policy away from 'community languages' and towards literacy, English and 'languages of commerce'. In this latter aim he was supported by organisations favouring emphasis on Asian languages rather than European. Eventually a limited number of languages were given priority in funding, with only modern Greek being essentially a community language, while Italian received support through 'insertion classes' and from the Italian government. Small subsidies to weekend schools managed by ethnic groups were all that the ethnic lobby could extract. The language maintenance function of SBS radio and television was limited to imported movies. Eventually the major language groups, such as Italian,

Greek, Arabic and Chinese, developed their own commercial media without public funding.

The late 1980s mark the high point of trying to develop language and multicultural education programs on a national scale. Competing interests and differing aims proved too resistant. Language teaching continued to decline in schools and universities. Official pressures were directed to commercially useful languages, improved literacy and computer training. The enthusiasm for Asian languages had waned by 2002, when the Howard government prematurely ended an annual subsidy of $30 million to support their teaching in schools.

Access and equity

Following the creation of the network of services recommended by Galbally, the next problem was to ensure that migrant clients were being well served over the whole range of service delivery outside the Immigration Department. These clients have normally been regarded as the responsibility of Immigration by others. The persistence of assimilationist attitudes and a lack of cultural sensitivity meant that many were unable to access services to which they were entitled, often because they did not know these existed. It became a major function of the Office of Multicultural Affairs from 1990 to monitor what was happening across the board. Despite the still controversial ethnic-specific services endorsed by Galbally and funded by the Immigration Department, most migrants dealt for most of their needs with mainstream departments. These frequently did not use interpreters, although they were increasingly available; had no understanding of religious or other cultural differences, which had become more marked as immigration moved into Asia, the Middle East and Africa; and frequently referred non-English-speaking clients back to ethnic or multicultural agencies, which were not specialists and were designed to refer migrants onwards to mainstream service deliverers.

The access and equity strategy was designed by the National Population Council in 1985 and ratified by the Review of Migrant and Multicultural Programs and Services in 1986.[14] OMA instituted a mandatory reporting system within the Commonwealth government and published these reports. There was considerable resistance from departments which did not see themselves as delivering services, especially Treasury.

With the abolition of OMA in 1996, access and equity has become less emphasised and its administration has been returned from PM&C to Immigration. It is now governed by the rhetoric of a Charter of Public Service in a Culturally Diverse Society. This charter, endorsed by Commonwealth and State governments, calls for access and equity reports to be made to the Immigration Department, using performance indicators.[15] It was claimed in 1996 that 'the message about access and equity appears not to have been well understood by relevant stakeholders'.[16] In so far as this was true, it reflects the resistance of many public agencies already surveyed in the extensive evaluation of 1992.[17] The general finding of this evaluation, based on fieldwork research, was that access and equity was well understood at the higher administrative levels but had not been transmitted to counter staff and others dealing directly with clients. It is an interesting comment on the resistance to multicultural reality that the situation continues to remain the same.

The agenda of 1999

As with the two previous agendas, although on a more modest scale, the 1999 agenda was launched by the prime minister. The difference was that the prime minister concerned, John Howard, had a long record of opposition to the concept of multiculturalism. The councils of 1989 and 1995 had also, of course, been much closer to the ALP. Despite this, the new agenda not only endorsed the same principles but also argued strongly for retention of the word 'multiculturalism'. It urged the restoration of a monitoring agency similar to the disbanded OMA. This was immediately rejected, along with any suggestion of independent funding for multicultural projects. The new agenda did not have even the rather blunted teeth of those which preceded it, nor any mechanism for implementing its recommendations.

Despite these limitations, the 1999 agenda reaffirmed multiculturalism as government policy after fifteen years of often acrimonious public debate. NMAC was 'optimistic about Australia's future as a culturally diverse society and is confident that Australian multiculturalism will continue to be a defining feature of our evolving national identity and contribute substantial benefits to all Australians'.[18] This was a fairly firm reaffirmation in the light of the prime minister's well-known attitudes. Adding the word 'Australian' was a concession which made little real difference. An emphasis on 'inclusiveness' did not depart from the original notion that multiculturalism was 'for all Australians'. Moreover, the 1999 agenda called for 'leadership' in defence of a multicultural society, which might well be taken as a pointed reference to those politicians who had been criticising the concept for the past fifteen years.

What distinguished the 1999 agenda from the 1978 Galbally report was that many of its concrete recommendations were not implemented, even if its general rhetoric was unquestioned by government. The most important unimplemented recommendations (21, 24 and 30) urged greater funding for multicultural advocacy, increased cultural diversity on public boards and agencies, and the creation of a central co-ordinating agency. This would have restored the situation as it was under Keating and Hawke, reversing the policy of the Howard government too drastically for this to be acceptable.

Indigenous peoples and multiculturalism

Multiculturalism was often criticised because it did not seem to be concerned with Aboriginal issues. This was not strictly true. The agenda of 1989 included Indigenous people within its compass, as did the access and equity strategy as amended in the same year. Control over this agenda and the strategy was in the hands of OMA, situated in PM&C, rather than in the Department of Immigration. In preceding years, Aboriginal and 'ethnic' affairs had been kept strictly apart as they were the responsibility of two distinct departments. Indigenous organisations were not affiliated to FECCA. There was limited communication between ethnic and Indigenous organisations until the 1990s. One issue on which there was some co-operation was the national language policy, as many Aboriginal languages were under threat of extinction. There was Aboriginal representation at the national conference called on this issue by the Fraser government in 1982. The evaluation of 1995 also devoted attention to

Indigenous issues. Finally, the 1999 agenda recommended that the work of Aboriginal reconciliation should be carried forward by 'government, individuals, [and] private and community organisations'.[19]

The evaluation of the access and equity strategy in 1992 concluded that 'the differences in backgrounds, circumstances and needs of people of non-English speaking background and Aboriginal and Torres Strait Islander peoples are considerable'. An evaluation study in Port Hedland found that while there was a reasonable knowledge of the strategy among immigrants, 'few of the Aboriginal participants … including ATSIC officials, had heard of the A&E Strategy'.[20] This underlines the extent to which many aspects of multiculturalism were the 'property' of either the Department of Immigration or OMA. This created indifference or even hostility in other departments and agencies whose policies were being monitored from outside.

A shift in priorities from the Hawke to the Keating government gave greater emphasis to Indigenous issues and to the work of the Aboriginal and Torres Strait Islander Commission and the Land Councils. OMA correspondingly lost influence in this area. Its research capacity was reabsorbed by the Immigration Department and it was abolished altogether as one of the first acts of the Howard government. Finally, at the end of 2001, the Immigration Department took over the existing Department of Aboriginal Affairs to become the Department of Immigration and Multicultural and Indigenous Affairs. It had created a 'ministry of other people', with the prospect of 'mainstreaming' urban Aboriginal welfare services. This ran contrary to most public declarations of Aboriginal organisations and spokespersons in the past. However, there was very little public comment.

The inclusion of Indigenous issues within multiculturalism was always incomplete. Because this policy area was associated with the Immigration Department or its minister, it was seen by others as only concerned with immigrants. In recent years, objectives have been extended to embrace 'diversity'. This includes not only the Indigenous people and immigrants but also women, the disabled, gays and lesbians, provincial dwellers and almost any group seen as disadvantaged or subject to discrimination. FECCA has also broadened its constituency in this way, seeking alliances outside the ethnic communities.

In several senses the access and equity strategy can be usefully applied to groups other than immigrants. But to leave the area within the ambit of the Immigration Department is to inhibit this extension. Moreover, it blurs the focus and blunts the impact of pressure upon government and public agencies. The same could be said for the emphasis on productive diversity, which stresses the economic benefits of immigration rather than problems needing solution. This is especially relevant to the years since 1996 when 'special interests' have been attacked as 'rent seekers' looking for special privileges not available to the 'mainstream'. That was not what multiculturalism was originally about. It aimed to extend rights and privileges to immigrants which were already enjoyed by the native-born, without requiring the abandonment of cultures, languages and religions not derived from Britain or developed in colonial Australia. There is still plenty of scope for public policy in this area, without confusing the issue with a broad tolerance towards a variety of groups with little in common.

Theorising multiculturalism

Australian multiculturalism was developed as a method for dealing with the consequences of ethnically diverse immigration. The main influences came from public servants, ethnic organisations and politicians. Consequently these influences were mainly pragmatic. Multiculturalism did not live up to its appearance as an ideology, except in the eyes of some of its opponents. Nevertheless, as elsewhere, there have been attempts to develop theories analysing change from a monocultural to a multicultural society, justifying that change as a necessary improvement or criticising it as divisive. The main influences on public policy and elaboration have stressed that multiculturalism is essentially a liberal democratic creed, based on tolerance of diversity within the principles and practices of Australian public life.[21] Differences of emphasis have centred around cultural maintenance and social justice, although these are not necessarily incompatible.[22]

Most of this work has been done by Australians of 'ethnic' background or by those professionally engaged in immigrant studies. These have included Zubrzycki, Smolicz, Martin, Jayasuriya, Jakubowicz, Bottomley, Castles and Kalantzis. A critical approach has been taken by Kukathas, Betts and Birrell. Among major issues canvassed have been: the extent to which 'tolerance' can be extended into 'active citizenship'; the nature and extent of the values, institutions and practices which will bind together a multicultural Australia; contradictions between equality and equity; the accommodation of different value systems and beliefs; the role and nature of ethnic groups; the intersection of class, gender and ethnic relations; and the social and economic value of cultural diversity.[23]

In recent years multiculturalism has been analysed from a postmodernist perspective, with special reference to literature.[24] While this has had an influence on cultural studies it has not been incorporated into policy. Indeed, the experience with trying to develop a multicultural education policy in the mid-1980s suggests that theoretical debate clouds the issue to the point where policy makers simply walk away from implementation altogether. Academics who have served on committees developing multiculturalism have included Stephen Castles, Laksiri Jayasuriya, David Cox, Chandran Kukathas, Ghassan Hage, George Smolicz, Jerzy Zubrzycki, Helen Hughes, Charles Price, Colin Rubenstein, Trang Thomas, Jo Lo Bianco, Mary Kalantzis and the author. Their views have been many and various.

Shifting emphases

A remarkable feature of multicultural policy development has been the constancy with which the basic principles of 1977 have been repeated, despite the intervening dissension and debate. The 1999 agenda includes an appendix listing major reports over that period which is a good guide to the basic principles of official Australian multiculturalism.[25] However, there have been some shifts in emphasis over the years, without departing from the basic approach. These include the development of the idea of 'productive diversity', associated particularly with Professor Mary Kalantzis and Bill Cope, last director of OMA. This moved the discussion away from settlement and welfare issues and towards the contribution which a multilingual and skilled immigrant workforce can make to the Australian economy in a globalising world. This approach also appeals to corporate business to a greater degree than the 'access and equity' service delivery issues.[26]

Organisationally many settlement and multicultural programs are now more important at the State than at the Commonwealth level. By 2002 all States and Territories were under Labor control and all had functioning agencies concerned with multicultural programs. New South Wales, Western Australia and Victoria had important translating and interpreting services, especially in the health and legal areas. Multicultural Affairs Queensland was active and innovative and had secured recognition and support for the long-neglected South Sea Islander community. South Australia and Victoria have, for many years, developed language and education programs recognising cultural diversity.

State governments are less remote and depersonalised than the Commonwealth and they do not have immigration control functions. All State multicultural agencies hold regular consultations with their ethnic constituency. Unlike the Commonwealth, which usually confines its concerns to the overseas-born, the States have no inhibitions about catering for cultures and communities which have been established for several generations. Because multiculturalism in the States has been consistently bipartisan, these policies have not been so subject to attack as at the national level.

Notes

1 Lopez, *The Origins of Multiculturalism in Australian Politics*, 223–4.
2 Jupp, *Understanding Australian Multiculturalism*.
3 Lopez, *The Origins of Multiculturalism in Australian Politics*, 443.
4 AEAC, *Australia as a Multicultural Society*, 18.
5 Galbally, *Migrant Services and Programs*, para 1.7.
6 OMA, *National Agenda for a Multicultural Australia*.
7 NMAC, *Multicultural Australia*.
8 NMAC, *Multicultural Australia*, 12.
9 NMAC, *Australian Multiculturalism for a New Century*, recommendation 24.
10 Jupp, 'Immigrant Settlement Policy in Australia'.
11 Jordens, *Alien to Citizen*.
12 Lo Bianco and Wickert, *Australian Policy Activism in Language and Literacy*.
13 Lo Bianco and Wickert, *Australian Policy Activism in Language and Literacy*.
14 NPC, *Access and Equity*; Jupp, *Don't Settle for Less*.

15 DIMA, *Charter of Public Service in a Culturally Diverse Society*; DIMA, *Access and Equity Annual Report*.

16 DIMA, *Annual Report* (1996), 7.

17 OMA, *Access and Equity Evaluation Report*; Jupp and McRobbie, *Access and Equity Evaluation Research*.

18 NMAC, *Australian Multiculturalism for a New Century*, para 3.4, 76.

19 NMAC, *Australian Multiculturalism for a New Century*, rec. 12.

20 Jupp and McRobbie, *Access and Equity Evaluation Research*, 49, 62.

21 Castles, *Multicultural Citizenship*.

22 Hage and Couch, *The Future of Australian Multiculturalism*.

23 Cope and Kalantzis, *A Place in the Sun*.

24 Clark et al., *Multiculturalism, Difference and Postmodernism*.

25 NMAC, *Australian Multiculturalism for a New Century*.

26 Cope and Kalantzis, *A Place in the Sun*; Hay, *Managing Cultural Diversity*.

6

The attack on multiculturalism

Multicultural policy in Australia was developed by the Immigration Department, by most State governments and by individuals and groups involved in immigrant affairs. It remained within the Immigration portfolio from 1975 until 1987 and was returned to it in 1996. At the State level, where immigration is not a government function, it usually rested with the premier's office. It has not been essentially concerned with 'culture' in the conventional sense, so much as with immigrant settlement services. Not until 1989 were Aboriginal issues brought under the multicultural umbrella. This remained controversial and was not welcomed by many Aboriginal activists or organisations. They saw the Indigenous peoples as distinct and not merely one among many ethnic groups of recent settlement. Not until 2001 was Indigenous policy brought within the scope of the Immigration Department, which was renamed the Department of Immigration and Multicultural and Indigenous Affairs (DIMIA). This acknowledged the responsibility for Aboriginal reconciliation transferred to the minister, Philip Ruddock, some months before. Responsibility for multiculturalism was then undertaken by a junior minister, Gary Hardgrave. The Labor shadow ministry also separated immigration from multiculturalism in 2001.

Multiculturalism replaced the long-standing support for assimilation. Yet it was not particularly controversial in the first decade when it was confirmed as Commonwealth public policy by the Galbally report of 1978 and reconfirmed by Malcolm Fraser in 1981. Early critics were mostly academics, including Lauchlan Chipman in 1980, Geoffrey Partington in 1981, and Frank Knöpfelmacher and Raymond Sestito in 1982. These were not directly associated with a major political party, although Knöpfelmacher had been close to the Democratic Labor Party in the 1960s. The conservative journal *Quadrant* became an avenue for criticising multiculturalism from the early 1980s onwards, particularly around the bicentenary of British settlement in 1988.

The basic arguments of these early critics were that multiculturalism was divisive; that it denied the distinctive Australian heritage based on British origins; that it was simply a response to the 'ethnic vote'; that it would encourage separatism with the resulting possibility of ethnic and racial strife; or, as Dame Leonie Kramer claimed while chair of the ABC, that it had never been defined and was an intellectual muddle. In fact, multiculturalism has been officially defined many times. It is true that very few academics, other than Stephen Castles or Chandran Kukathas, have analysed it in depths as a philosophy.

Most of this was based on an abstract understanding of multiculturalism often drawn from controversies in the United States. It rarely looked at actual policies operating in Australia. Both Lauchlan Chipman and Brian Bullivant argued that multiculturalism was inapplicable to education, which should concentrate on improving skills rather than emphasising cultural differences. Apart from this, the early critics were very general in their critiques. Knöpfelmacher was strongly influenced by his experience in Czechoslovakia and the collapse of that state in 1938 through German ethnic separatism in the Sudetenland. This inappropriate transfer from other situations became common with the breakdown of Yugoslavia in the 1990s. Otherwise, the early critics were mainly concerned with the preservation and advance of mainstream Anglo-Australian culture, which they assumed, though did not necessarily state, to be superior to introduced minority alternatives.

Conservative criticism of multiculturalism

Many conservatives were probably inhibited by the enthusiastic support for multiculturalism of Prime Minister Malcolm Fraser. With the defeat of the Coalition in 1983, criticism of multiculturalism became more popular with conservatives. Previous critics had included reformists and radicals associated with the ALP who regarded the Galbally provisions as a cheap way of delivering services which should have been undertaken by state agencies. Some also saw the approach of Galbally and Zubrzycki as unduly stressing cultural maintenance rather than economic and social disadvantage and life chances. They contrasted this 'culturist' approach to the 'social justice' aspirations of the original Melbourne ethnic rights movement of the early 1970s. The first multicultural agenda under Hawke in 1989 clearly identified with this position: 'multiculturalism expresses and complements the Government's broader social justice strategy which is designed to ensure that the benefits flowing from its economic policies are fairly distributed throughout the community'.[1]

With the transfer of Liberal leadership from Fraser to Peacock in 1983, a succession of leaders (Peacock, Howard, Hewson and Downer) all at various times criticised multiculturalism and the Labor immigration program. Peacock, who was regarded as the most 'liberal' of these, accused the Labor government in 1984 of undermining bipartisanship, but did not attack the changing ethnic composition of the intake. The conservative attack on multiculturalism became most bitter in the mid-1980s when it seemed that Labor under Hawke could remain in office for some years. Liberal leadership passed to John Howard between 1985 and 1989. Criticism of multiculturalism was encouraged by the growing tension between the Greek and Macedonian communities. This led Blainey in 1988 to accuse Hawke of 'turning Australia into a nation of tribes'.[2]

Two influential and widely quoted attacks on multiculturalism were launched by David Barnett in 1986 and Stephen Rimmer in 1988. Both concentrated on the cost of grants to ethnic organisations, a theme taken up later by Pauline Hanson and described at the time by Blainey as 'ethnic payola'. Barnett attacked 'the bloated ethnic industry' which was 'dividing Australia'. In his view, 'tens of millions of dollars' were being 'spent on ethnic groups by a vast army of bureaucrats ... Millions of dollars are sloshing around among federal and state bureaucrats, migrant organisations and the trade unions'.[3]

Two policy papers from conservative think-tanks – the Centre for Independent Studies and the Australian Institute for Public Policy – developed a more complex critique. Raymond Sestito, drawing on the American political theorists Mancur Olson and

Anthony Downs, argues that multiculturalism as public policy was catering for artificially created and self-interested groups. In his view, 'Australia's political parties have become the initiators of multiculturalism, rather than responding to group pressure ... parties compete to see who can promise the most to migrants'.[4] While this has helped to bring real issues onto the political agenda, it is also dangerous in his view. Demands escalate as the parties compete and public policy caters for groups rather than individuals. Much of this is not unreasonable. But his final conclusion is that legal limits should be placed on promises made by parties to interest groups. This formulation, made in 1982, became increasingly popular with conservatives, leading to Howard's promise in 1996 to govern 'for all of us' and to Pauline Hanson's attack on 'special interests'.

Rimmer's criticism, six years later, took up the claim that vast sums were being expended on divisive policies. Like Sestito he acknowledges the influence of Michael James, an economic rationalist at La Trobe University. Rimmer quotes Sestito's pamphlet with approval and also seeks support in the recently issued FitzGerald report on immigration policy. Noting several varieties of multiculturalism, including a conservative one, Rimmer argues like others that 'the denial of the legitimacy of Australian culture is supported by multiculturalism'.[5] He wrongly asserts that multiculturalism regards all cultures as equal, a critique of multiculturalism as cultural relativism which was becoming popular in the United States.

Rimmer at the time was an economist with the Australian Chamber of Commerce, whose president, Andrew Hay, claimed in the same year that 'multiculturalism was a dangerously misguided policy which had resulted in social divisions between new Australians and longer-term residents'.[6] Rimmer attempted to measure the costs of multiculturalism, a task which he found well beyond him. He admits that 'governments do not know how much they are spending on multicultural services'.[7] Unfortunately his own calculations border on the absurd. By including all costs which might even remotely be caused by immigration, and estimating those for which there were no figures, he was soon into the 'billions' which were later claimed by Pauline Hanson. This was very far from the modest few millions which were directly attributed to multiculturalism in Commonwealth and State budgets. It included the estimated costs of 'ethnic crime' but omitted the large and increasing cost of subsidising religious schools.[8]

The most persistent critic of multiculturalism during the crisis year of 1988 was Geoffrey Blainey, who had a weekly column in the *Australian*. To him, 'multiculturalism, as espoused by both parties, is utterly shoddy. Morally, intellectually and economically it is a sham.'[9] Blainey's concern was with the protection and advancement of a distinctively Australian culture. Any challenge to this, however modest, was divisive. Blainey remained the most influential of all the conservative critics and was highly regarded by John Howard.

Other criticism

Not all critics of multiculturalism have been associated with conservatism. Lopez distinguishes four different 'ongoing versions of multicultural thought'.[10] These were: cultural pluralism, associated with Zubrzycki and Jean Martin; welfare multiculturalism, associated mostly with David Cox; ethnic rights, associated with the Melbourne group of Alan Matheson, George Papadopoulos and George Zangalis; and 'ethnic structural pluralism', associated most with the ethnic communities' movement. In the early days the approach of Fraser, Galbally, Georgiou and the Australian Institute of Multicultural Affairs was consistently attacked by the Melbourne ethnic rights group. These were mostly members of the ALP and became influential after the election of John Cain's Victorian government in 1982 and the Hawke victory in 1983. In the end they achieved the abolition of the institute in 1986 after Georgiou had been removed as its director. Papadopoulos became director of the Victorian Ethnic Affairs Commission. Matheson, who was the ACTU ethnic liaison officer, served on the FitzGerald committee of 1988. However, they were not alone in influencing policy and the Immigration Department remained closer to the 'ethnic welfare' approach and to David Cox. 'Cultural pluralism' was often denounced as 'culturist' by left critics and Zubrzycki was not appointed to any positions of influence under Labor.

All of these critics agreed that a multicultural policy was desirable but disagreed on its precise nature. A more general attack came from the FitzGerald committee, appointed to review immigration policy by the Hawke government. FitzGerald was close to Labor, having been appointed by Whitlam as first ambassador to Communist China. The committee of six also included Professor Helen Hughes, an economic rationalist, who was later to emerge as a strong opponent of multiculturalism.

Its many recommendations, submitted to Clyde Holding in July 1988, were not primarily concerned with settlement and multiculturalism. The report concluded that support for immigration was faltering and that one factor in this was confusion and hostility about multiculturalism: 'Multiculturalism, which is associated in the public mind with immigration, is seen by many as social engineering which actually invites injustice, inequality and divisiveness'.[11] FitzGerald followed this up in newspaper interviews in which his criticism of multiculturalism was more wide ranging. This was not welcomed by Hawke, and the newly created Office of Multicultural Affairs within his department criticised this aspect of the report. It was the first instance in which a commissioned policy report of considerable influence had openly attacked multiculturalism, if only by inference.

The bipartisan consensus ends, 1988

Bipartisan agreement on multiculturalism and immigration ended in 1988.[12] The turning point was a speech by party leader John Howard to the Esperance conference of the Western Australia Liberals on 30 June that year. In it he attacked trade union power and the idea of an Aboriginal treaty, and he defended the notion of 'One Australia'. He made no reference to Asian migration but developed this issue during the next few months. He had previously declared that bipartisan consensus on immigration was over, in response to issues raised in the FitzGerald report. The year was also marked by a discussion of national identity stimulated by the celebration of the bicentenary of British settlement.

Howard had begun an onslaught on multiculturalism as soon as the FitzGerald report appeared. Addressing the Canberra Press Club he stated that 'there are profound weaknesses in the policy of multiculturalism. I think it is a rather aimless, divisive policy and I think it ought to be changed.'[13] Howard followed this up by refusing to sponsor the Bicentennial Multicultural Foundation, chaired by Sir James Gobbo. This essentially conservative body has flourished, nevertheless, doing unobtrusive work including advising police forces on relations with ethnic communities.

Howard's petty response was rejected by Liberal premiers Nick Greiner and Jeff Kennett but was consolidated into party policy by his Esperance address. He announced the ideal of One Australia, which 'respects our cultural diversity and acknowledges that we are drawn from many parts of the world but requires of all of us a loyalty to Australia at all times and to her institutions and her values and her traditions which transcends loyalty to any other set of values anywhere in the world'. In Howard's view, 'we are too apologetic'. These themes were to remain central to his rhetoric for the next fifteen years. He strengthened his remarks in the following week by saying of Asian immigration that 'it would be in our medium term interest and supportive of social cohesion if it were slowed down a little so the capacity of the community to absorb were greater'.[14]

By May 1989 the shadow minister for immigration, Alan Cadman, was stating that the Liberal Party was 'moving away from multiculturalism to something we think is more all-embracing'. He added that under the Coalition the term 'multiculturalism' would not be used.[15] This was in defence of Howard's concept of One Australia. However, Howard's support in the polls had dropped rapidly after his Esperance speech and subsequent remarks on Asian migration. Media treatment was unfavourable. By the end of the year he had been replaced by Andrew Peacock again. One of his last public appearances as leader was at the December FECCA conference in Canberra where he was heckled, while Ian Macphee enjoyed a standing ovation.

Peacock had replaced Howard in 1989 partly due to Howard's remarks on Asian migration and his attack on multiculturalism. Nevertheless, he was especially critical of the Multifunctional Polis scheme of 1990. His successor, John Hewson, was also critical of multiculturalism. Other conservatives outside the Liberal leadership joined in, including Brigadier Alf Garland, RSL president. His view, expressed in July 1989, was that 'Australia needs multiculturalism like it needs a hole in the head'. During the March 1990 election he called for a national referendum on the immigration mix and was also critical of the Multifunctional Polis scheme. Both he and Peacock argued that the MFP would be an Asian 'enclave', contrary to long-established settlement policy. The mass circulation *Daily Mirror* at the same election published pages of readers' letters attacking the MFP, foreign investment and Asian migration. In Queensland a precursor of One Nation, Bruce Whiteside's Heart of a Nation, was founded in 1988 on the Gold Coast, mainly in opposition to Japanese property ownership. Professor Blainey also criticised this at the same time. Whiteside's campaign collapsed when he was revealed as a New Zealand citizen. He reappeared ten years later as organiser of the Pauline Hanson support groups.

Australians Speak

By 1990, when Hewson became Liberal leader, conservative attitudes towards multiculturalism had shifted markedly and the influence of Fraser and Macphee had waned. Hewson, an economics professor, came from outside politics, unlike the other three Opposition leaders between 1982 and 1996. He instituted a major survey of opinion, *Australians Speak*, which claimed to represent the views of 4000 Australians. No indication of the methodology was given, but it seems from the responses on many issues to have been heavily dominated by Liberal activists, small business, farmers and the professions. One of its major purposes was to canvass support for a goods and services tax, the issue on which Hewson largely lost the 1993 election. However, it also included a segment on 'a united country', which is an interesting guide to conservative thinking outside the narrow range of professional politics. It concluded that 'the single most perplexing issue … is the issue of multiculturalism'.[16]

As with the rest of the report, this section stressed the need for shared values. More than 40 per cent of respondents had raised multiculturalism and immigration as an important issue, most wanting a 'rational debate' without accusations of racism. A concern was that multiculturalism would work against the development of an identifiable Australian nationalism. Some directly supported assimilation. Others held that there was too much emphasis in immigration on refugees and family reunion, and that multiculturalism was divisive and had got out of hand. 'Some racial or religious groups might continue to perceive that their first loyalty is to a culture, or a country, rather than to Australia.' The underlying theme was that multiculturalism was encouraging cultural 'ghettoism' and that Australia should decide its own cultural direction. Respondents were quoted as opposing a 'salad bowl' or 'jigsaw puzzle' concept of Australia. One issue which had already been raised in Queensland was the exhibition of signs in foreign languages outside shops and restaurants.

The attitudes displayed in 1991 echoed to some extent those expressed by Howard three years before or by Blainey in 1984. They reappear not only in speeches by Liberal leaders after 1996 but also in those of Pauline Hanson. They are not specifically 'racist' and some tried to distinguish between 'multiracialism' and 'multiculturalism', with the second being less acceptable than the former. By the early 1990s, conservatives had developed a critique of multiculturalism which was to shape policy when the Coalition regained power in 1996. They had moved away from any lingering sentiment for White Australia or even for the New Britannia. But they were adamant that Australian culture must be uniform and based on universally accepted values. While the first proposition ran contrary to Labor definitions of multiculturalism, the second was incorporated into all official formulations of Labor and Coalition governments from 1989 to 1999.

A developing critique

Between 1983 and 1995 the Liberal Party was rent with leadership contests and ideological debate. The most consistent critic of multiculturalism remained John Howard but others took up the issue, especially as elections drew close. At the same time there was a growing clamour outside the party system from journalists and commentators. This was not directly related to the feuds within the Liberal Party, although some like Barnett and Blainey were personally or intellectually close to Howard. It often reflected debates in the United States, where the so-called 'culture wars' were raging around concepts such as 'political correctness', Christian values, the right to bear arms and the increasing cultural variety of the United States caused by immigration, affirmation of minority rights and competing lifestyles.

Blainey, having raised the issue of Asian immigration in 1984, also became one of the most influential critics of multiculturalism as practised by the Hawke government. In his apologia, *All for Australia*, his emphasis remained on Asian migration. Labor had only been in office for eighteen months and had yet to develop a different approach from Fraser. He deplored the decline in British immigration and the new government's defunding of the Big Brother movement which had been sponsoring British youth migration since 1925. This was evidence that 'the word multicultural has increasingly come to mean anti-British'. Further, 'the multicultural policy, and its emphasis on what is different and on the rights of the new minority rather than the old majority, gnaws at that sense of solidarity that many people crave for ... The policy of governments since 1978 to turn Australia into a land of all nations runs across the present yearning for stability and social cohesion'.[17]

Blainey, as a historian, was very concerned with what he saw as a denial of Australian history and especially its British inheritance: 'The department of immigration and ethnic affairs could well be called the department of immigration and anti-British affairs'. This might have raised a wry smile among Canberra insiders who believed that Immigration has always had an Irish Catholic bias. Otherwise, there is not the slightest evidence for his extraordinary claim. Finally, in a thesis which was to become common to critics, he dismisses multiculturalism as 'this Canberra daydream'.[18] Reverting to Sir Henry Parkes' notion of 'the crimson thread of kinship', Blainey has gone on holding the same views and expressing them regularly through the media, to which he has excellent access.

Blainey's critique is classically conservative, resting on shared values and ethnic solidarity. He accepts that European immigrants have developed a loyalty to Australia, but cannot extend this to Asians. Why this should be so, when many Asians share languages and religions with many Europeans and have done very well economically, he does not reveal. Another popular denunciation from an academic came in 1988 with the publication of Katharine Betts' *Ideology and Immigration*, which she revised as *The Great Divide* in 1999.[19]

Blainey, as a rather old-fashioned historian, looks back to a British Australia which had shared values and origins. Betts is more impressed by American arguments and especially by the proposition that support for immigration and multiculturalism comes from a 'new class'. In her view, 'a commitment to cosmopolitanism and multiculturalism has also had status advantages for the upwardly mobile professional classes'.[20] She further argues that bipartisanship had stifled debate, a proposition which was becoming quite untrue by 1988 when attacks on multiculturalism were at their height. As she notes, however, bipartisanship remained in favour of a 'high intake', even when the consensus had been broken on multiculturalism and Asian numbers. Her conclusion was that, in the face of opinion polls showing declining support for immigration, this support was largely confined to the tertiary educated and to some minority ethnic groups. This gave credence to the journalistic argument, becoming popular by the late 1980s, that policy was being driven by the 'powerful ethnic lobby'.

Popular critiques

Much popular criticism of multiculturalism confuses public policy with the consequences of immigration. The best-known example of this was Pauline Hanson's repeated claim that multiculturalism should be 'abolished'. This would save 'billions', a claim she based on figures originally developed by Rimmer and expanded on by Paul Sheehan in *Among the Barbarians* in 1998. Sheehan, a journalist on the *Sydney Morning Herald*, summarises many of the populist attacks on multiculturalism as 'the dividing of Australia'.[21]

Sheehan had already attacked multiculturalism in his newspaper in 1996 as 'an industry of tax-fed lawyers, political operatives and racial axe-grinders that has grown like an enormous parasite out of Australia's heroic commitment to cultural diversity'.[22] This largely repeated Barnett's criticism of ten years before. He details grants to ethnic organisations under Keating. He claims that most of these go on salaries and (correctly) that they were concentrated in Labor-held electorates. Accepting that Liberal Premier Jeff Kennett followed similar policies in Victoria, he still held that 'playing the race card is primarily Labor's game'. He attacks the Bureau of Immigration Research, which 'came to be regarded as so politicised that the Howard government shut it down', and the Department of

Immigration, as having 'a vested interest in making Australia's immigration policy look like a model of virtue and efficiency'.[23]

While based in a disparate collection of essays, Sheehan's critique essentially concludes that Howard government reforms would gradually reverse 'a nation increasingly divided along racial lines, cultural enclaves, high unemployment and high crime'.[24] At the same time he praises the positive impact of Asian migration. His populist (and popular) views embrace most of the major arguments of opponents of multiculturalism in the 1990s – that immigration was producing social problems and division; that official policy was divisive and aimed at ethnic voters; and that most of this was Labor's fault, which the Howard government could reverse. Similar themes were repeated by conservative journalists such as Alan Jones, Stan Zemanek and Piers Ackerman, all of them aimed, like Sheehan's, primarily at a Sydney audience. Sheehan relied heavily on more academic arguments by Bob Birrell, Richard Basham and Tim Flannery, although without their approval. His attitude to Pauline Hanson was both critical and defensive. Of Blainey's repeated complaint about the suppression of debate on multiculturalism, 'the coalition that imposed this silence was formed by Labor, the multicultural industry and the selective news media'.[25] Sheehan's book sold very well.

Summarising the conservative critique

By 1996 a coherent conservative critique had emerged from the debates of the preceding decade. It had varying levels, from the academic approach of Blainey and Betts, through the politicians such as Howard and John Stone, and on to journalists and popularisers such as Barnett, Sheehan, Ackerman and the talk-back radio jockeys. Part of the critique was that debate had been suppressed in the interest of political correctness and that opponents of current policy had been denounced as racists or otherwise discouraged. There had certainly been very little serious analysis of the kind common among academics in Canada, the United States or Britain such as Will Kymlicka, Bikhu Parekh or Thomas Sowell. Apart from a work in untranslated Japanese, the only major analysis came from Andrew Theophanous, a former academic but also a Labor politician at the time of writing. Most defence of multiculturalism came from official research and reports. This was often inhibited by political or bureaucratic caution. The influential analysis of Stephen Castles and his Wollongong colleagues was ambivalent and did not confront the conservative critics.[26]

Debate has obviously not been suppressed, but this claim gained credence when John Howard, on becoming prime minister in 1996, expressed the hope that people would now be able to speak freely on this and associated issues. No doubt he was referring to the experience of Blainey, who had been treated rather roughly by student demonstrators and severely criticised by academic colleagues from Monash University in a collection published in 1985.[27] But he had gone on to become a Companion in the Order of Australia, chancellor of Ballarat University and chairman of the National Council for the Centenary of Federation, the latter an influential position directly approved through the prime minister's office to ensure that the celebrations did not 'deny Australia's heritage' as had allegedly happened in 1988.

Other critics did well out of the new government. David Barnett was a personal friend of Howard and wrote his official biography. Stephen Rimmer and Stephen Joske were appointed as ministerial staffers. Alan Jones enjoyed a very regular radio slot with the prime minister. Paul Sheehan and Katharine Betts enjoyed no doubt well-deserved sales and publicity. Those who were 'persecuted' after 1996 were the staffs of the Office of Multicultural Affairs and the Bureau of Immigration, Multicultural and Population Research, whose jobs were abolished.

A second accusation was that multiculturalism was divisive. This was an assertion without evidence. The concept of 'social division' is hard to substantiate in a peaceful democracy. It could refer to many cleavages which have nothing to do with ethnicity, such as rich and poor, workers and bosses, educated and ignorant, metropolitan and provincial, male and female, and so on. These have all been important at various times. There was undoubtedly some concern, as expressed in *Australians Speak* for instance, that Australia was going 'off the rails' because of diversity. By many measures Australia is the most stable, united and self-satisfied society on earth, but it is also haunted by an inexplicable sense that the ship will sink at any moment. Leadership, solidarity, homogeneity, common values, all assume prominence in public responses to this fear. They are frequently mobilised by politicians, most notably by Howard in the 2001 elections. But official multiculturalism has always been concerned with alleviating social tensions. What critics were referring to was not official programs but the observed increase in ethnic variety which, as in other societies, often exacerbates anxiety.

A third accusation, most fully canvassed by Betts, is that multiculturalism is advocated mainly by the élites or the 'new class', rather improbably allied with ethnic activists. This belief is based to a large extent on opinion polls. It builds on an argument by the American conservative, Irving Kristol, which he developed ten years before Betts wrote. As in other countries, the educated middle classes tend to express more tolerant views than do the uneducated working classes. This does not necessarily mean that their behaviour is quite different. Working-class Australians have usually worked amicably with immigrants and Aborigines. Most racial tensions have been exacerbated by relatively well-educated politicians and journalists. Betts does not seem to have consulted many ethnic activists, trade unionists or welfare workers. Her familiarity with the 'new class' – to which she belongs – leads her to believe that there is no other basis of support for immigration or multiculturalism. Yet other surveys have found that there is more tolerance of diversity among immigrants than among native-born Australians and less opposition to immigration. A similar dichotomy arises between the major cities and rural and provincial areas. Her analysis gave comfort to those who felt that One Nation represented Aussie battlers or that those concerned about the detention of asylum seekers were bleeding heart *latte* drinkers. That does not mean that her findings should be rejected out of hand. But it does mean that the political implications of what she is saying – along with many others – need to be understood. Glorifying the common sense of the common people can lead to the crudest populism.

A rather different academic critique of multiculturalism was provided by Miriam Dixson in 1999 in *The Imaginary Australian*. As with another critic, Helen Hughes of the 1988 FitzGerald committee, Dixson's ideological origins are on the socialist left. More specifically than Betts she believes that the 'Anglo-Celtic aspects of

Australian life function as a vital cohesive centre for the whole culture'. She shares with Betts the belief that intellectuals are negative towards their own culture. But she goes further in locating the dominant culture within the Anglo-Celtic majority and questioning whether recently arrived immigrants are likely to share this culture. A similar argument was developed by another academic of former left persuasion, Geoffrey Partington.[28]

Less conservative critics

Conservative criticism was most consistent and eventually most influential. It managed to shift the Liberal Party from its consensual attitudes under Malcolm Fraser towards confrontation with supporters of multiculturalism. It laid the foundations for the attacks by One Nation. It rationalised attitudes which had remained unaltered in sections of the National Party or the Returned and Services League. Criticism of multiculturalism as 'denying the British inheritance' were prominent during the bicentennial year of 1988 and became significant again during the controversy over the republic in 1999.

There were, however, significant influences within the ALP which were less favourable to multiculturalism than the party leaders. Graeme Campbell, the MP for Kalgoorlie, attracted much media attention by his consistent attacks. Eventually he was expelled from the party altogether and joined One Nation, failing to win a Western Australian Senate seat for them in 2001. Two other West Australians, Senator Peter Walsh and John Dawkins, MP for Fremantle, were equally critical but remained safely within the ALP.[29] Both held ministerial office, Walsh under Hawke and Dawkins under Hawke and Keating. As important as the criticism within the ALP was the neglect of multicultural and immigration issues under the Opposition leadership of Kim Beazley from 1996 to 2001. The party had no distinctive policy in these areas and was caught completely by surprise by the events of 2001 surrounding the detention and arrest of asylum seekers arriving by boat. This was a controversial issue in Western Australia, which normally receives most such arrivals and from which Beazley also came.

While Labor critics of multiculturalism were most prominent in Western Australia, they probably had more influence in Sydney, which is more central to the party's power structure. After the defeat of 2001 Mark Latham MP emerged as a significant advocate of returning to the 'grass roots'. Representing Campbelltown (Werriwa), a mayor of Liverpool, and locally born, Latham is very sensitive to the difficult community relationships in his western Sydney constituency. Like some others, he attributes Labor's losses to their apparent sympathy with special interests. This leads him to denounce not only multiculturalism but also feminism and other interests and ideologies of the 'élites'. The working class is assumed not only to be hostile to these trends but also to be correct. This is close to the arguments of Campbell and Hanson, although expressed entirely in terms of loyalty to the ALP.

Several other influential Labor politicians have been less than enthusiastic about multiculturalism. The very ambivalent attitudes of New South Wales Premier Bob Carr include support for cultural variety along with opposition to increased immigration and to the use of the term 'ethnic'. Carr caused some concern in 2001 by his references to 'Lebanese youth gangs' in Sydney and by his support of 'ethnic identifiers' by the police when seeking young offenders. There is considerable ambivalence among Sydney Labor politicians, compared with the long-standing acceptance of ethnic variety and immigration by their Melbourne counterparts.

The survival of multiculturalism

While multiculturalism as public policy survived all these attacks, there was no longer the enthusiastic and widespread support for it which was evident before 1988. The name was constantly criticised as conveying no meaning, or as being bureaucratic or alienating. Basing policy on ethnic diversity was attacked as divisive. Terms such as 'ethnic' or 'NESB' were questioned from the Labor side of politics, most notably by Carr's New South Wales government in the late 1990s. Zubrzycki entered the debate to argue that he had always favoured 'cultural pluralism' and that Grassby had been responsible for enforcing the use of the Canadian terminology. FitzGerald favoured 'cosmopolitanism', but this died a natural and deserved death. The word 'multiculturalism' itself became a banner behind which rallied all those who opposed the conservative attack.

Nobody could think of an acceptable alternative which retained the central idea of accepting and managing ethnic diversity. The 1999 agenda, devised by a relatively conservative council, kept the term, renaming it 'Australian multiculturalism' at the insistence of the prime minister's office.

Eventually Howard came to use the term himself, though with considerable reluctance. Queried on television about this in 2001 he simply said: 'You have to go with the flow'. In an even more extraordinary reversal a few months later, Howard regretted his 1988 remarks on Asian immigration, disagreed with Blainey's critique of multiculturalism, argued that Muslims could integrate into Australian society and supported a modest increase in the migrant intake.[30] It was unfortunate that he had not been converted to these views fifteen years before.

Essentially, multiculturalism at the national level has had very little to do with culture and a great deal to do with immigrant settlement. To many it was a gentle form of assimilation and incorporation. But it was one of the few policy areas in which Australians of non-British origins had a major input. It produced the remarkable SBS, with the best news service and the most inclusive offerings of any channel, including the much more generously funded ABC. It alerted service deliverers and public servants to the variety of their clientele. But it never endorsed cultural relativism. It could not radically change the access of immigrants to political and social power. It did not challenge the predominance of English-speaking Australian-born politicians, public servants and opinion leaders. It is, therefore, often hard to understand why there was so much vigorous opposition. This was partly a reaction of Australian conservatives to the long years of Labor government between 1983 and 1996. But it also suggests an underlying hostility to ethnic change which was one of several factors recruiting support for One Nation in the 1990s.[31]

Notes

1 OMA, *National Agenda for a Multicultural Australia*, 19.
2 *Australian* 3 December 1988.
3 *Bulletin* 18 February 1986.
4 Sestito, *The Politics of Multiculturalism*, 15.

5 Rimmer, *Fiscal Anarchy*, 5.
6 *Canberra Times* 25 January 1988.
7 Rimmer, *Fiscal Anarchy*, 45.
8 Rimmer, *The Costs of Multiculturalism*.
9 *Australian* 30 April 1988.
10 Lopez, *The Origins of Multiculturalism in Australian Politics*, 446.
11 FitzGerald, *Immigration – A Commitment to Australia*, 3.
12 Gardiner-Garden, *The Multiculturalism and Immigration Debate*.
13 *Sydney Morning Herald* 24 June 1988.
14 Radio comment, reported in *Age* and *Financial Review* 3 August 1988.
15 *Canberra Times* 4 May 1989.
16 Hewson, *Australians Speak*.
17 Blainey, *All for Australia*, 114, 153.
18 Blainey, *All for Australia*, 155, 160.
19 Betts, *Ideology and Immigration*; Betts, *The Great Divide*.
20 Betts, *Ideology and Immigration*, 84.
21 Sheehan, *Among the Barbarians*.
22 *Sydney Morning Herald* 25 May 1996.
23 Sheehan, *Among the Barbarians*, 104, 105, 120, 125.
24 Sheehan, *Among the Barbarians*, 131.
25 Sheehan, *Among the Barbarians*, 171.
26 Castles et al., *Mistaken Identity*.
27 Markus and Ricklefs, *Surrender Australia?*
28 Partington, *The Australian Nation*.
29 Walsh, *Confessions of a Failed Finance Minister*.
30 *Weekend Australian* 4 May 2002.
31 Vasta and Castles, *The Teeth Are Smiling*.

7

The impact of One Nation

All Australian political parties had removed White Australia from their platforms by 1966. By the mid-1970s all were committed to some form of multiculturalism as public policy. The National (formerly Country) Party was the least enthusiastic and the Australian Labor Party the most. The Whitlam Labor government, which officially declared Australia to be 'multicultural', was succeeded by the Fraser Coalition which laid the institutional foundations for a multicultural public policy. None of this was seriously questioned. While there was some concern at the arrival of large numbers of Vietnamese and Lebanese in the mid-1970s, there was remarkably little disorder or disharmony. Official pronouncements from the Immigration Department stressed the need for 'cohesiveness' but also repeated that there would be no return to a discriminatory policy.

The ending of White Australia seemed to have passed without any of the backlash which many had threatened if the policy were abandoned. However, opinion polling turned against majority support for immigration and was never subsequently reversed. This opinion shift might have been explained by the disappearance of full employment. Studies in Australia and elsewhere have linked increases in unemployment with increases in ethnic tension and opposition to immigration.[1] Displaced resentment is a very common phenomenon. People cannot explain the unseen economic and social forces which are changing their lives, often for the worse. They tend to blame observable agents, especially ethnic or religious minorities. Globalisation and economic rationalism disturbed many lives, but could be neither understood nor challenged. However, for most Australians, life remained comfortable and secure and social tensions were restrained.

The racist inheritance

Australia has no fascist tradition, despite the sympathy of some conservatives and reactionaries for Hitler, Mussolini or Franco in the pre-war years. The most important extremist group in the 1930s was the New Guard which encouraged resistance to the ALP government of Jack Lang in New South Wales. In the Riverina, armed groups claimed to be ready to defeat the communists should they march down from Sydney – an indication of the paranoia in some remote provincial areas. In Queensland, Social Credit had some electoral success and some of its ideas remained influential for many years, including its anti-semitism. All this was in reaction to the worldwide depression and largely disappeared with the outbreak of the Second World War.

What was more important, especially in Queensland, was a form of Australian populism which was not incompatible with support for the ALP. This was nationalistic and xenophobic, being strongly in favour of White Australia, indifferent to Aboriginal problems and unsympathetic to non-British immigrants, especially Italians. This tradition was strong in organisations such as the Australian Workers' Union. With the decline of Labor support in the 1950s much of it became enshrined within the National Party, especially under the leadership of Joh Bjelke-Petersen, Queensland premier from 1968 to 1987.

In contrast to Britain, where Enoch Powell MP had aroused strong opposition to West Indian and Asian immigration in the 1960s, there seemed to be no comparable movement in Australia. There were no major political organisations advocating racism or a White Australia after 1966. The small League of Rights, founded in Victoria in 1946, is the oldest and best-known anti-semitic and racist organisation in Australia and had its origins in Social Credit. It actively supported White Australia and had close links with the white supremacist regimes in Rhodesia and South Africa. For many years it has functioned in rural areas of Victoria, New South Wales and Queensland and has been accused of trying to penetrate the Country Party and its National Party successor.

The League consists mainly of ageing members, and several younger and more militant groups such as the National Front, the

Australian Nationalist Movement and National Action grew up. These were much smaller than their British or American counterparts. Followers of the American Lyndon LaRouche formed Citizens Electoral Councils, mainly in rural and provincial areas. Unlike the League of Rights, which was pro-British and monarchist, the LaRouche movement is rabidly anti-British. It has substantial resources, some of them originating in the United States. It is regarded as anti-semitic by Jewish organisations. Its published pamphlets have attacked Aboriginal land rights as 'Prince Philip's racist plot to splinter Australia'; the 'British Crown plot to crush Australia's unions'; the 'Rio Tinto octopus' headed by the Queen; and the Mont Pelerin Society as a 'fascist International'. This latter obsession of the aged LaRouche attacks virtually all those Australians most closely identified with support for economic rationalism and the free market and with opposition to multiculturalism. While this is all quite weird, the Citizens Electoral Councils have considerable organisational reach and financial assets. Their influence on Queensland One Nation is probably a major cause of its anti-capitalist populism. That tradition was also historically strong in the Queensland Labor and National parties, and the Citizens Electoral Councils are able to appeal to it.

Extreme racist organisations were usually at the fringe of politics and of no electoral consequence. Militant racism first appeared within the mainstream system at the time of the public meetings to explain multiculturalism, organised by Liberal Minister for Immigration Ian Macphee and his Labor shadow, Mick Young, in 1982. These meetings also included Jerzy Zubrzycki, author of the official report *Multiculturalism for All Australians*. In Perth there was persistent heckling and threats of violence.[2] Racist stickers appeared from the Australian Nationalist Movement, attacking the 'Asian invasion'. There were attacks on Asian individuals and restaurants, and one ANM member, believed to be a police infiltrator, was killed. This led to the imprisonment of its leaders and the collapse of the organisation in 1990.

This was the most extreme case of militant racism in modern Australia. However, the daubing of synagogues and mosques, and attacks on Jews, Arabs and Asians, occur frequently and the perpetrators are rarely traced. Various openly racist organisations surface from time to time, but few have any continuity or significant resources other than the League of Rights and the Citizens Electoral Councils. Internet communications with racist counterparts in the United States and Britain are common but have little measurable impact.

The weakness of overtly racist organisations created a false sense of relaxation in the first ten years after White Australia was formally abolished. Most recorded racism and most official campaigns against racism were focused on Aborigines.[3] Critics of multiculturalism and Asian immigration, such as Geoffrey Blainey in 1984 or John Howard in 1988, emphasised that they were opposed to racism. While some public figures associated with the League of Rights, there were few politicians ready to risk being labelled as racists. It was a League tactic to use provincial newspapers and radio stations, and to seek election to shire councils but not to parliaments. They were regularly monitored by the Jewish media and the B'nai B'rith Anti-Defamation Commission. These also kept an eye on various small organisations of fascist sympathisers in some of the east European communities. These had little impact on the major parties except for some Liberal Party branches in Sydney. Unlike the situation in Britain and Europe, there were no 'skinhead' or other young racists from whom physical violence might be expected. Despite considerable youth violence and semi-criminal motorbike gangs, these have remained completely apolitical. A brief attempt by One Nation to form a youth group did not prosper.

The Human Rights and Equal Opportunity Commission inquiry into racial violence in Australia in 1991 concluded that 'most of the incidents of racial violence on the basis of ethnic origin which were reported to the Inquiry occurred in a period of increasing non-European immigration, rapid economic change and recession, and highly publicised expression of opinion on the desirability of a multicultural Australia'.[4] These three factors – a changing immigrant base, economic uncertainty and a public 'debate' – continued throughout the 1990s. However, the inquiry found that violence most frequently affected Aborigines, for whom the factors they mention are not directly relevant.

The arrival of One Nation

Reactionary and anti-semitic organisations had a very low profile before the ending of White Australia, especially compared with their influence in Britain, Europe and the United States. This led many to believe that Australia was uniquely tolerant, as indeed it seemed to be until the early 1980s. Attempts to form branches of the British National Front failed, and the Australian Nationalist Movement was decimated by police action in response to its criminal activities. Racial discrimination legislation was passed in South Australia in 1966 and by the Commonwealth in 1975. This followed the British precedent of individual complaint to a tribunal. Growing concern led to the national inquiry into racial violence which reported in 1991, recommending both legislative and educational solutions. National laws to prohibit racial defamation, although urged by the Jewish community, were not passed until 1995 after considerable delay and argument and the removal of criminal sanctions.

Insistence by the Commonwealth and most States on non-discriminatory behaviour and multicultural practices inhibited overtly racist organisations, which were also prone to splits and rivalries. Problems remained in the frequent use of racist terminology and arguments by some talk-back radio hosts.[5] None of them was ever prosecuted, although one or two have lost their sponsorship due to especially outrageous remarks, most notably Ron Casey in 1988. The print journalists and politicians in general avoided such behaviour, whatever their personal views might have been. This restraint gave rise to the myth that 'political correctness' was stifling free debate, an argument derived from the United States. This was as ridiculous in Australia as it was there, where free speech was guaranteed by the Constitution. The evidence for this claim centred mainly around the criticism of Blainey following his speech at Warrnambool in 1984. He continued, however, to be recognised with appointments and honours and was especially favoured under the Howard government.

While overt racism was unacceptable in public affairs, the increasing attacks on multiculturalism and Asian immigration which began in the early 1980s encouraged a shift in public debate. The media paid great attention to Blainey's critical remarks at Warrnambool and to his attempts to justify and expand on them in his *All for Australia*, published at the end of 1984. Blainey became a hero for many with whom he undoubtedly disagreed. His accusation of a 'strong preference for Asians' in immigration policy was especially controversial. He further claimed that Australia was afraid of 'offending' Third World nations, that it was taking 'far more than its share of refugees' and that 'millions outside parliament' did not support the current policy. Whether Blainey intended it or not, these accusations set the tone for all attacks on Asian migration and multiculturalism for the rest of the century. They were particularly attractive to the Liberal Party, which had been defeated in 1983, lost Malcolm Fraser as its leader and remained out of office for another twelve years. The party began to shift away from its previous positions and to encourage criticism of the balance of the immigration program. This became more marked when John Howard became party leader in 1985. Losing that position in 1989, partly because of his views on Asian immigration, he was re-elected in 1995 and became prime minister in 1996.

In the years between 1984 and 1996, hostility to Asian immigration and multiculturalism became more acceptable among conservatives than had been the case under Fraser. Those in the Liberal Party who deplored this, most notably former immigration minister Ian Macphee, were eased out of their positions. A decisive indicator of trends within the parliamentary party was the refusal by Howard and all but five Liberal MPs to endorse the Hawke government's affirmation against racism in 1988. This gave an 'unambiguous and unqualified commitment to the principle that whatever criteria are applied … the composition of the immigration intake, race or ethnic origin shall never, explicitly or implicitly, be among them'. Howard rejected this because it limited the 'sovereign right to determine the entry of people into this country'.[6] Among those crossing the floor to support the Labor resolution were Macphee and future immigration minister Philip Ruddock. Another former minister, Michael MacKellar, abstained. Howard's rival, Andrew Peacock, excused himself with a long-standing engagement in Melbourne.[7]

Thus, when Pauline Hanson was selected as Liberal candidate for the safe Labor seat of Oxley, she began to express views which were widely held in the Liberal and National parties, especially in Queensland. The main thrust of the remarks which obliged Howard to withdraw her endorsement in 1996 was directed against special services for Aborigines. Her electorate included about 3 per cent of voters who were Aboriginal and a similar proportion of Asians, mainly Vietnamese. This was high by Queensland urban standards and largely due to concentration in public housing. The rest of the voters were mainly in the former mining districts of Ipswich and Blackstone, which were economically depressed. Many of these voters were descendants of British immigrants from the 1880s.

Hanson's position was basically that, as all Australians were equal, there should be no special services for Aborigines or immigrants; that multiculturalism was encouraging minority cultures to stay out of the mainstream; that preference for Asians was changing the traditional character of the Australian population; and that governments did not listen to such complaints and, indeed, tried to repress them. This was not a classic racist position and Hanson always denied that she was a racist. It was firmly in the Queensland populist tradition, however. It was not far from views which had wide currency in the Liberal Party, as revealed by the major party survey, *Australia Speaks*, in 1991. Forced to run as an Independent, Hanson scored a swing of 19 per cent, the highest in the country and quite enough to take over the safest Labor seat in Queensland, once held by ALP leader Bill Hayden. This naturally attracted media attention, which scarcely flagged for the next four years.

Blainey and Howard had paved the way for Hanson's success, although that had scarcely been their intention. As she had been a Liberal, her success presented a possible threat to that party. As she had won a Labor stronghold, she was of concern to the ALP. But it was the National Party, the dominant conservative force in Queensland, which first recognised her potential for appealing to provincial and rural voters and thus undermining their traditional base.

Hanson's policies

Pauline Hanson enjoyed unprecedented media coverage for several years, but this concentrated less on her policies than on her personality. Populist movements which succeed have usually depended on a charismatic leader. Although these have normally been men,

Hanson soon developed a public persona which was worthy of serious attention. Until the creation of the One Nation party in 1997, she did not develop a very coherent and rational policy, much of it originated by others.

Her original views, expressed in her 1997 publication *The Truth*, became so controversial that the book was never republished. Somewhat disingenuously she denied authorship for the larger part of it, although her picture was on the cover and she signed many copies for her supporters. Not surprisingly she had attracted a very motley following, some of whom had been waiting for a messiah for years. Queensland contained many of these, including the short-lived Confederate Action Party, most of whose former members went into One Nation. She also attracted the extreme wing of the gun lobby. In contrast to some other conservatives, she did not make a religious appeal and had views on issues like divorce and abortion which they could not share. She was a strong supporter of the grievances of male divorcees on matters such as maintenance and access to children.

Hanson's basic position on immigration was expressed in her maiden speech to parliament on 10 September 1996, and in speeches during the same period which were reprinted in *The Truth*. In parliament she maintained that 'ordinary Australians' had been kept out of the debate on immigration by the major parties. She believed that 'we are in danger of being swamped by Asians ... They have their own culture and religion, form ghettos and do not assimilate ... I should have the right to have a say in who comes into my country'. She believed her views to be 'typical of mainstream Australia'.[8] What is notable about these phrases is that many of them were still being used five years later, often by supporters of the Coalition policy towards asylum seekers.

Defending her views a month later to the short-lived Australian Reform Party, she praised those who 'manned the barricades' on immigration and multiculturalism – 'Bruce Ruxton, Peter Walsh, John Stone and of course Graeme Campbell'. She did not want 'all Asian immigration to cease' but favoured zero net migration, with immigrants not exceeding emigrants (at that time a level of about 30 000); a five-year waiting period for naturalisation; and much more stringent selection for the spouse and family reunion cate-

gories. Asian nations would be expected to 'accept their responsibilities' for Asian refugees. Again, many of these arguments were
not only being used five years later but some had been implemented, especially the stricter standards for skilled and family
reunion immigrants.

Defending herself again in parliament on 2 December 1996,
Hanson claimed that 'I am not a racist by any definition of that
word', only asking that 'any Australian, regardless of their origin,
should give Australia their full and undivided loyalty'.[9] Her supporters were less circumspect. That part of *The Truth* which was not
directly attributed to her shocked many by its emphasis on 'migrant
crime' and even 'Aboriginal cannibalism'. Hanson was racist in
lumping together all 'Asians' and blaming them collectively for not
assimilating. This was absurd. Many Asians were middle-class sub-
urbanites, English-speakers and Christians, which she never
acknowledged. It is fair to say that she became a beacon for many
who were much more racist than she was. It was another two years
before One Nation had a coherent immigration policy. Most of her
early speeches were written by John Pasquarelli, a former Liberal
candidate and assistant to Graeme Campbell, former Labor MP for
Kalgoorlie. Her immigration policy, however, was developed (after
Hanson and Pasquarelli had parted company) by Robyn Spencer
who had organised Australians Against Further Immigration from
Melbourne in 1988. AAFI had run candidates in four by-elections
in Sydney and Adelaide with some success in 1994, although never
winning a seat.

One Nation's immigration program of 1998

The immigration program presented by One Nation for the 1998
election was the fullest for any party and was quite coherent and
consistent, compared with the party's support for a single tax or
other economic nostrums.[10] Spencer was assisted by Denis
McCormack who worked for Campbell in Kalgoorlie during the
election campaign and who was the AAFI public relations officer.
The 1998 policy repeated the claim that 'to economic, political and
intellectual elites immigration has become central to a perspective
which holds that inherited Australian institutions, culture and

identity are outmoded and expendable obstacles to the establish-ment of a borderless world'. It went on to argue that 'mass immi-gration is a concept whose time has passed', favouring a zero net policy which would admit 30 000 a year, or about one-third the number, including New Zealanders, entering in 1998. This was because 'there is no justification for population growth in Aus-tralia'. Intake would be non-discriminatory 'on condition that the numbers do not significantly alter the ethnic and cultural makeup of the country'. Genuine refugees should be treated with compas-sion, but 'temporary refuge need not extend to long-term perma-nent settlement'. One Nation believed 'in providing temporary refuge until the danger in the refugee's country is resolved'.[11] This was first implemented by the Howard government in 1999 by granting 'safe haven' status to 4000 Kosovars, who were denied the right to remain or to apply for permanent residence.

The rationale for One Nation's restrictive approach included environmental pressures, economic costs and unemployment. The business migration program would continue if better managed, a position which governments of both parties had acknowledged. Family reunion should not necessarily be an Australian obligation, as most were unskilled, and would be restricted to immediate dependent family. A two-year waiting period for welfare services was supported and was already Coalition government practice. One Nation also supported the mandatory detention of illegal immi-grants, with expedited deportation and no access to legal aid or appeal. Most of this policy, apart from the 'zero net' approach, was close to Coalition policy already.

Wrongly asserting that 70 per cent of immigrants were from Asian countries, the 1998 policy prophesied that 27 per cent of the population would be Asian within twenty-five years: 'This will lead to the bizarre situation of largely Asian cities on our coast which will be culturally and racially different from the traditional Aus-tralian nature of the rest of the country'.[12]

Some aspects of this policy were already in place, such as the two-year waiting period for welfare. Others, such as temporary protection visas for refugees, were implemented in 1999 for those arriving without visas and further tightened in 2001. The humani-tarian 'special assistance' category had already been abolished, but the 'special humanitarian' category remains. There was some confusion about refugees between Hanson and Spencer at the policy launch, as the humanitarian program was to be reduced but the refugee level would remain the same. This would not have been possible if both these humanitarian programs were abolished. A shift to temporary residence for skilled workers became Coalition practice by the end of the 1990s. However, no action has been taken to limit the entry of New Zealanders or to extend the waiting period for naturalisation. New Zealanders could only qualify for permanent residence and citizenship under the same terms as other immigrants following changes in 1999. This went part of the way desired by One Nation but will not necessarily affect the numbers crossing the Tasman. The implied threat that Australia might limit New Zealand entry was a factor in discussions between the two governments in 1999.

Much of this policy remained in place for the election of 2001. However, One Nation had become much more generous towards tourists, retirees, backpackers and students, and towards family reunion (where citizens would be able to nominate parents). Some of this was more liberal than the policies pursued by the Howard government, which had capped parental reunion at 500 a year and continued to ban settlement by self-funding retirees. Policy on refugees also seemed more liberal and was condemnatory of their being 'detained in camps for years'. But the answer was still to issue temporary residence visas, to refuse refugee status to those who had passed through other countries on the way, and to heavily punish ship crews engaged in people smuggling. Most of this became government policy in 2001.

There were some important differences between One Nation immigration policy and that of the Coalition. No major party accepted the 'zero net' proposal, although this was temporarily the policy of the Australian Democrats under the leadership of Senator John Coulter. No major party wanted to interfere with the principle of free movement across the Tasman. However, the reduction of family reunion, the denial of welfare for new arrivals, the stress on business and skilled migration, and a stronger policy towards undocumented or illegal arrivals were common to the Coalition and the previous Labor government. No major party wished to extend the waiting period for naturalisation nor was it clear how a suitable level of assimilable immigration could be measured to avoid changing the ethnic and cultural character of Australia.

One Nation support

Support for One Nation was immediately tested in the Queensland State election of 13 June 1998. The result startled the major parties even more than the initial victory in Oxley. One Nation won nearly 23 per cent of the vote and returned eleven members. The Liberal and National parties foolishly gave their preferences to One Nation ahead of the ALP, ensuring its victory in several seats. Allocation of preferences remained contentious for the next few years, not only in Queensland but also in Western Australia. In the Northern Territory in 2001, the Country Liberal Party preferred One Nation to Labor and lost government for the first time. That the Coalition preferred, over the ALP, a party widely believed to be racist was unwise. Apart from north Queensland, where National MP Bob Katter eventually left the Nationals altogether, this tactic was eventually ended. It then became necessary for the two Coalition parties to win back some of the One Nation primary vote. As One Nation opposed globalisation, the free market, and the goods and services tax, this could only be done by attracting support on Aboriginal or immigrant issues, where the Coalition was more sympathetic and Labor most vulnerable.

There has been considerable discussion of the character of the One Nation constituency. It was clearly a Queensland-based party for most of the time that Pauline Hanson remained its leader, although its national office was located in Sydney and later moved to Perth. Queensland had strong traditions of populism, religious fundamentalism and right-wing minority parties. This largely explains the mass support which One Nation enjoyed outside Brisbane. Elaborate behaviourist explanations, using socio-economic data, tend to overlook these political and ideological traditions. The simplest explanation for much One Nation support was that many people were racists and resented Aboriginal and multicultural policies. There were strong correlations between educational levels, age and masculinity, but other relationships were less clear. The 'typical' supporter could be stereotyped as middle-aged, male, a manual worker, of Anglo-Australian (or sometimes British immigrant) descent, living in a small community, employed, an early school-leaver, a gun owner and a Queenslander.[13]

No socio-economic data explains why One Nation did so well in Queensland and later in parts of New South Wales, but so badly in Victoria or Tasmania. Apart from provincial areas, there was support for the party in outer suburbs of Sydney, Brisbane and Adelaide which were suffering from a run-down in factory employment and high levels of unemployment and welfare dependency. These suburbs, such as Elizabeth, Campbelltown or Logan City, were predominantly inhabited by the Australian-born and by British immigrants.

The party reached its greatest level of support at the 1998 federal election. With 1 million votes for the Senate and slightly less for the House of Representatives, its support surpassed that of all parties except the Liberals and the ALP. But it was very uneven, being much stronger in declining areas than in city centres. It thus appeared to be most threatening to the future of the National Party.

As the party went national it began to pick up a more varied following. It was well supported in economically disadvantaged suburbs of Sydney, Brisbane and Adelaide, in farming districts of Western Australia and in retirement resorts. It had very little support in inner-city suburbs, especially those with high immigrant populations. It did have support among some outer suburban electorates with high British migrant populations, including Brand, represented by ALP leader Kim Beazley. Its suburban support was more of a threat to the ALP than its provincial following. Many of its 'Aussie battler' voters outside the major cities were probably National rather than Labor supporters.

Like many populist parties elsewhere, One Nation could claim to be an 'all class' party, as it got some support and financial donations from the well-off. Its candidates were frequently from small business. Its support was a loose coalition of the disaffected – from impoverished rural areas, affluent retirement resorts, disadvantaged outer suburbs, and a variety of extremist and sometimes paranoid minor organisations. What held these together was a series of time-honoured populist beliefs, many of which had been almost consensual a century before, and the ability of Pauline Hanson to express them in simple language.

Graeme Campbell and One Nation

One Nation has normally been discussed as the party of Pauline Hanson, and it bore her name until this was removed at her request in 2001. It is hard to imagine the movement without her as its leader and inspiration. Yet she was not alone and in the end the party tried to move on without her. As is characteristic of many populist and extreme movements, it discarded its prominent members with great frequency and often with strident denunciations. Bruce Whiteside, David Ettridge, David Oldfield, Robyn Spencer, John Pasquarelli and Graeme Campbell all passed through the party at the national level, while the entire Queensland parliamentary party had defected within three years of their election. Mass adherence was followed by mass defection and disillusion.

The most significant supporter of One Nation was former Labor MP Graeme Campbell, who offered himself as a mentor for Hanson when she was elected to parliament. He then defected, and turned up again as One Nation candidate for the Senate in Western Australia in 2001. Campbell and his loyal disciple Denis McCormack had also been major sponsors of Australians Against Further Immigration which, through Spencer, had written Hanson's 1998 immigration program. Campbell, like Hanson, was elected as an Independent in 1996, in a seat which he had already held for the ALP. His persistent attacks on Labor policy and on Paul Keating had eventually earned him a well-deserved expulsion, but it did not keep him out of parliament until his defeat in 1998. His attempt to form a distinct party, Australia First, was a failure, forcing him to seek an alliance with Hanson. However, his reputed association with the League of Rights earned her disapproval, although not that of the Western Australia One Nation branch.

Campbell's position was clearly stated in his book, *Australia Betrayed*, published in 1995. This was essentially a collection of short pieces with a common theme. Most were on immigration, multiculturalism and Aborigines, although there were sideswipes at feminists and gays and the proposed Racial Vilification Bill. All were linked by their espousal by the 'cosmopolitan Ascendancy' which held the 'old Australian' majority in contempt. This theme was still being actively pursued in the debates surrounding the *Tampa* crisis five years later and obviously resonated with many resentful Australians. At the time, Campbell put the main blame on Keating, but Liberals such as Fraser, MacKellar and Macphee were also blamed. Campbell argued that an alliance of the 'cosmopolitans' with ethnic leaders dominated immigration policy under Hawke and Keating. His main concern was with multiculturalism rather than immigration intake, using terms such as 'élites', 'professional ethnics' and the 'new class' which were becoming popular with other critics and which are still in use. His 'intelligent nationalists' 'oppose high immigration on economic, environmental and social grounds'.[14]

Campbell's importance lay in his association with AAFI, his seat in the national parliament and his association with the Labor rather than the Coalition side of politics. His approach to immigration was better researched than Hanson's and drew on a range of other critics who were using the same arguments and terminology, such as Bob Birrell, Katharine Betts, Stephen Joske, J. W. Smith and Stephen Rimmer. His weakness lay in his links with the League of Rights. His membership of One Nation was always problematic. But in the end its focus moved to Western Australia where his influence was of continuing importance.

The influence of One Nation

Media comment on One Nation tended to exaggerate its support. While some opinion polls had shown as much as 20 per cent support, this had also dipped to 1 per cent and then risen again. In the 1998 election it stood at 9 per cent, but in 2001 it was only half that, and by 2002 polls were showing it back at 1 per cent. Hanson's personal vote for the Senate in Queensland still stood at 10 per cent in 2001. Much of this reflects the extent to which she was getting favourable media coverage. Because her support was so volatile, and sometimes so high, the major parties were unsure of how to deal with her. Her own position was that she was 'the mother of the nation', a self-description which did not raise as much ribaldry as it deserved. What was undeniable was her popularity in Queensland, the third largest State and one with a long record of electoral volatility. Her following in Melbourne, Adelaide and most of Victoria was negligible. Faced with court cases over the legality of public funding applications and accepting that much of her support had moved to the

Liberal Party, Hanson withdrew as One Nation president and her name was removed from its title and propaganda at the end of 2001.

One Nation has been the most successful party in Australian history to campaign on a program of limiting immigration and abolishing multiculturalism, Aboriginal reconciliation and a humane refugee policy. It was, however briefly, the most successful third party since the founding of the Australian Democrats in 1977 or the Democratic Labor Party in 1956. In 1998 its vote surpassed the highest ever recorded for either of these. While not overtly racist, much of its appeal was to racist sentiments. Thirty years after the end of White Australia, One Nation was still represented in the Senate, the Queensland and Western Australia parliaments and on several local councils. Its vote of 1 million in the 1998 federal election temporarily made it the third most popular party in the country. Even in 2001 it could still command the same support as the Australian Democrats or the Greens. It scarcely spoke for 'the Australian people' as it often claimed. But it spoke for more of them than seems desirable in a society which believed itself to be both multicultural and tolerant.[15]

One Nation impact on policy was indirect. Among implemented changes which it originally advocated were a move from permanent residence to temporary protection for some refugees, a change in the status of New Zealanders (though not a 'zero sum' limitation), and the excision of Christmas Island from the Australian 'immigration zone' in 2001. Indirectly One Nation could claim to have alerted the National Party to its declining rural popularity. Most importantly One Nation encouraged the public expression of views on immigration, Asians, multiculturalism and refugees which had been unfashionable. For this they were indirectly thanked by John Howard. Following Hanson's maiden speech he claimed that 'people do feel free to speak a little more freely and a little more openly about what they feel … I welcome the fact that people can now talk about certain things without living in fear of being branded as a bigot or as a racist'.[16]

Tragedy or farce?

In one sense, One Nation was a farce. It was inept, incompetent, unintelligent and spurious. It earned large sums of money through donations and public funding for which it was unable to account.

Had Pauline Hanson been well advised she would have contested the Senate in 1998, been elected and remained a national figure for the next six years. Had her support been loyal and disciplined it would not have thrown away the considerable gains of 1998. The whole exercise was ridiculous.

In another sense, One Nation was a tragedy. By creating a block of 1 million voters strategically placed between Labor, the Nationals and the Liberals, it tempted the parties to pander to its prejudices. The Liberals adopted much of its refugee policy. More importantly they pursued their own similar agenda against multiculturalism and Aboriginal reconciliation. The ALP under Kim Beazley had no policy on immigration worthy of the name and followed lamely behind the Coalition when the *Tampa* crisis broke out in August 2001. The Nationals were divided and had most to lose. Some Queensland leaders, notably senators Boswell and O'Chee, took a very strong stand against One Nation, which cost O'Chee his Senate seat. Others, especially in north Queensland, did not. But the party was clever enough to argue that One Nation support rested on rural disaffection and to extract some concessions for provincial areas from the Howard government.

The worst effect of One Nation was that it gave legitimacy to those who had always opposed the changes of the past thirty years. Its message was spread by the media to the entire population. It created the belief that there was a large constituency of 'Aussie battlers' whose prejudices had to be treated seriously. It encouraged anti-intellectualism, like all populist parties. This meant that much that had been creative in national development since the 1960s had to be argued for again. By failing to do so, the Howard government consolidated its own electoral position in 2001 and legitimised the whole agenda which he and his colleagues had been developing since the early 1980s.[17] This was conservative, assimilationist, reactionary and nationalistic. It was never overtly racist. But it led directly to the punitive detention of asylum seekers and the hunger strikes of Woomera.

Notes

1 Goot, 'Migrant Numbers, Asian Immigration and Multiculturalism'.
2 DIEA, *National Consultations on Multiculturalism and Citizenship Report*.

3 HREOC, *Racial Violence.*
4 HREOC, *Racial Violence*, 172.
5 Adams and Burton, *Talkback.*
6 *Canberra Times* 26 August 1988.
7 *Sydney Morning Herald* 26 August 1988.
8 Hanson, *The Truth*, 7, 10.
9 Hanson, *The Truth*, 25.
10 One Nation, *Policy Document.*
11 One Nation, *Policy Document*, 10.
12 One Nation, *Policy Document*, 11.
13 Davidoff, *Two Nations.*
14 Campbell and Uhlmann, *Australia Betrayed*, 128.
15 Leach et al., *The Rise and Fall of One Nation.*
16 Markus, *Race*, 100.
17 Markus, *Race*; Solomon, *Howard's Race.*

8

Economic rationalism

For 150 years Australian immigration policy has been dominated by economic considerations. The recruitment of labour was a prime consideration of assisted passage schemes, directed as they were towards workers who could otherwise not have afforded the fare. While often resisted by trade unions, selection for skilled occupations was also encouraged: from the building craftsmen of the gold-rush and post-war booms, through the miners of the 1880s, to the computer programmers of the 1990s. These policies have not always worked, most notably in the 1920s when mass British recruitment caused a labour surplus as the world economy collapsed in 1929. But the expectation has always been that a free market in labour could not be relied upon to fill vacancies so far from the main centres of desirable population, and that the Australian state needed to act positively to overcome this problem. In one sense, immigration policy was 'economically rational' long before that recent term was invented. But it was rarely 'free market rationality' which dominated. The state has usually responded to and assisted labour market pressures.

Economic rationalism in immigration policy

The term 'economic rationalism' was developed in Australia by a sociologist, Michael Pusey, in 1991,[1] although occasionally used by others before that. It was meant to be a critical term and was initially rejected by most professional economists.[2] It is defined in the *Australian Oxford Dictionary* as 'the theory or practice of a government using narrow definitions of efficiency and productivity (including privatisation, deregulation and low government spending) as measures of economic success, without regard to government's traditional economic responsibilities to the public sector and the welfare state'.

Over time it came to describe an approach to public policy which was free of special interests, subsidies, uncosted services or uneconomic practices. Its intellectual basis is in classical liberalism and economic theory. It implies free competition and cost–benefit measurement. The success or failure of public policy should be benchmarked against economic criteria: budgetary savings, efficient and effective administration, and outcomes which would increase the national wealth. The role of the state, apart from defence and law and order, is to remove obstacles to a free market which will make more rational decisions than can governments. Many professional economists accept a version of this approach, although usually acknowledging a greater role for the state than did classic liberals in the nineteenth century.[3] Economic rationalism has been developed in a number of think-tanks such as the Tasman Institute, the Centre for Independent Studies and the Institute of Public Affairs, all close to the conservative wing of the Liberal Party.

There is nothing new in this administrative approach except, perhaps, its sophistication. It was common to the 'political economists' who were influencing policy in the 1830s at the point where Australia started to move from the convict system to assisted migration as the basis for settlement. At the same time, in the United Kingdom, the Poor Law was being reformed on similar principles. Poor relief would be given in workhouses which were designed to discourage welfare dependency and which often contributed the child labour on which much new industry depended. The budgetary cost of poverty was thus reduced. The origins of assisted passages in the 1830s were 'rational' in removing paupers from the parish budget and sending them out to Australia to work for labour-hungry employers.

There was always a hard edge to classical liberalism. It was justified as expanding wealth by the efficient use of resources and by ending older systems of patronage and nepotism. Civil service reforms in Britain on this basis strongly influenced British colonial administration and thus the principles on which the Australian colonies were managed. As in all modern systems, the cost of public policy was strictly scrutinised. As is also often the case, apparent benefits to the undeserving or unproductive were especially likely to be criticised and cut. Despite the origins of assisted immigration in the English Poor Law, it was not long before colonial immigration policy began rejecting paupers and anyone likely to be a charge on the Australian taxpayer. The Immigration Restriction Act of 1901 prohibited entry to 'any person likely in the opinion of the Minister or of an officer to become a charge upon the public or upon any public or charitable institution' (s. 3(b)). Current official justifications of intake policy still attempt to measure the costs and benefits of particular visa classes to the budget.[4] The exclusion of those with physical disabilities has been rigidly pursued for more than a century. Public policy has always favoured the young, healthy and employable.

Apart from limiting or preventing burdens on the taxpayer, immigration policy has always aimed at specified economic objectives: the recruitment of labour; the filling of skilled vacancies, variously defined; the avoidance of those likely to become unemployed or welfare dependent; and the encouragement of workers likely to be adaptable. As long as intake was dominated by the free entry of British subjects, many immigrants were not directly selected by public authorities. Economic criteria were thus of most relevance to assisted migration and to the control of alien immigrants. Australia was not attractive to the very poor, unskilled and illiterate, as it was too expensive to reach without public support. Far more of these went to North America or for shorter journeys within Europe. Many Asians were sent as indentured labourers to plantation economies. This type of immigrant was also specifically excluded under the 1901 Act (s. 3(g)). While policy in the nineteenth century discouraged clerical workers and the lower middle classes in general, many came from Britain nevertheless at their own expense. The level of literacy among immigrants was higher than for those left behind, despite preference in assistance being given to agricultural labourers for most of the nineteenth century, a class which had low levels of literacy in England and Ireland for most of the century.

The ability to determine the economic value of immigrants increased after the Migration Act of 1958 and with the massive assisted passage schemes between 1950 and 1980. Those who received assistance, including most from Britain and northern Europe, usually had to satisfy selection criteria which were concerned with their economic viability and the likelihood that they would be productively employed. Those who did not receive assistance, mainly southern Europeans, could be denied entry permits if they were deemed not to be productive or likely to be a social burden. They were not, however, excluded for being unskilled, as factory labour was in great demand.

Displaced Persons were allocated to work for the first two years after arrival, often without regard to their previous education or experience. All this worked very well in the full employment economy of 1945 to 1970, when unemployment rarely rose as high as 2 per cent of the workforce. As factory employment expanded, many were admitted whose education did not fit them for much else. Literacy was not tested for the unassisted and there was no test for English knowledge. Free English classes were available through the adult migrant education program, which was established in 1948 and became the largest single item in the Immigration Department budget. Through this program Australia became a pioneer in teaching English as a second language (ESL).

The overall economic impact

The overall economic effects of immigration are hard to quantify and often controversial. Most Australian economists believe them to be benign or marginal.[5] A summary for the Bureau of Immigration Research by Lynne Williams in 1995 concluded that:

> at the ... economy-wide level, most of the evidence suggests that immigration confers either slightly positive or at worst neutral effects on the economy ... Of importance to policy-makers is the consensus that
> * Immigration does not lead to an increase in the unemployment rate;
> * Immigration has relatively little effect on both prices and wages;
> * Immigration has relatively little effect on the balance of payments in the long run;
> * In the longer run immigrants are net contributors to Commonwealth and local government revenues.

She concluded that 'using immigration as a tool of macroeconomic policy is ineffectual … as it does not influence the main economic variables'.[6]

This is a fair summary of the debate at that time, although it was not a view shared by Treasury nor by Hawke's finance minister from 1984 to 1990, Peter Walsh, who believed the economic impact to be negative. The modest economic effect of immigration became more contentious as other issues – such as the effect on the environment or the assimilability of immigrants – were factored into the discussion from the late 1980s. One proposition that has always been accepted is that immigrants with poor English are likely to be disadvantaged, with an implication that they are also less productive. A Bureau of Labour Market Research report of 1986 concluded that government should give high priority to English language courses.[7] Ten years later, lack of English proficiency made it increasingly difficult to gain enough points for admission in the skill streams. Policy had shifted from improving the 'human capital' of those otherwise accepted, to simply discouraging altogether potential migrants without such capital.

Historically trade unions opposed immigration as lowering the wage level and increasing the possibility of unemployment. It was a deliberate strategy of the post-war Chifley government to incorporate union leaders into the consultative processes to alleviate this hostility. While such hostility still lingers, it has been more serious in some professions, such as medicine, than for manual workers. The control of professional associations or State government over qualifications has been a major obstacle in gaining recognition for those issued outside the English-speaking world.[8] While Australia has one of the best accreditation systems in the world, problems still remain as sources of skilled migrants expand.

The popular perception persists, as elsewhere, that migrants take jobs away from Australians; that migrants threaten wages and conditions; that migrants work in occupations which are inadequately covered by arbitration or trade unions; and that migrant employers exploit their compatriot employees. Another argument that continues to be influential on trade unions, and which has been most fully developed by Bob Birrell of Monash University, is that importing skilled labour discourages governments and employers from developing training and apprenticeships for the Australian-born.[9]

The human capital approach

As economies become more sophisticated and less reliant on primary production and manufacturing, economists have argued that 'human capital' must be developed and exploited. This position, adopted by the OECD, is clearly relevant to Australia where the majority of workers are no longer in the classical 'labouring' jobs and where the level of tertiary education has risen rapidly since the 1960s. What Australia needs is to increase its human capital by expanding education. It can also do so by selecting immigrants who are better qualified in relevant areas than the national average. As the National Population Council put it in 1991, 'immigration in particular may contribute to the clever country process if it adds citizens with skills and capital and who can provide new trading links'.[10]

The adoption of a human capital approach in immigration policy has developed consistently since the introduction of a points system for selection in 1979. By 1988 the proportion of all visaed settler arrivals in skilled occupations already exceeded that in the national workforce. It rose to a peak by 1992, having risen consistently from a low level in the first year of the Hawke government. This trend has further dominated policy since 1996, when the Coalition shifted the intake emphasis from family reunion to skilled categories.

Since the early 1990s a multicultural approach to human capital has developed into the concept of 'productive diversity'. Against critics such as Helen Hughes and John Stone, who have argued that selection should favour English-speakers, the Office of Multicultural Affairs advocated the proposition that as Australia was trading largely with non-English-speaking societies its linguistic and cultural diversity was a positive asset. A multicultural workforce would be readily adaptable to global realities. Sydney's role as a 'world city' would be sustained and advanced by its many cultural links with Asia, Europe and the Pacific.[11] This approach has had some appeal, especially to global corporations and international traders. But immigration selection has increasingly emphasised English competence, despite acknowledging the utility of Asian 'languages of commerce' – which has mainly meant Chinese, as few Japanese emigrate. Most of the languages actually spoken in Australia have not been regarded as useful human capital because they have only a limited commercial utility and do not lead to many employment opportunities. Policy shifted even against Asian languages in 2002 when the Commonwealth withdrew its subsidy for teaching such languages in schools.

Human capital theory assumes that there is no prejudice in hiring among employers, who will choose rationally. This view has been mostly fully developed in Australia by Mariah Evans.[12] It is, however, challenged by studies of prejudice, which has been much less fully analysed in Australia than elsewhere.[13] One discrimination, now written into the points system, is in favour of 'previous Australian experience'. The most serious form of discrimination has been the difficulty in recognising non-British overseas qualifications, first raised in 1950 and still a matter for concern fifty years later. This rested with the Council on Overseas Professional Qualifications between 1969 and 1989 and then with the National Office of Overseas Skills Recognition, which was transferred from Immigration to the Department of Employment, Education and Training and is supported by State agencies in New South Wales and Victoria. Practices vary between States and professional accrediting bodies, which many immigrants have found confusing.

Selection criteria

Assisted immigrants were always subject to selection criteria which included the avoidance of their becoming a charge on the public purse. Under the bounty system of New South Wales in the 1830s and 1840s, no bounty was paid to shippers for anyone found to be disabled or otherwise unemployable on arrival. The few who did get that far remained in Australia, but the incentive to recruit anyone who might want to come was removed. All assistance regulations in the nineteenth century laid down the occupations, ages and conditions which were acceptable. Preference was usually for agricultural labourers and domestic servants. However, when needed, exceptions might be made for building tradesmen, railway workers or miners. These exceptions were frequently attacked by the local trade unions, even while some British unions were aiding the emigration of their unemployed members.

For 150 years the assisted passage system dictated the selection of economically viable immigrants. For most of that time it also dictated their ethnicity. Apart from Queensland the colonies did not usually fund passages for non-British subjects. Nor, right through into the 1960s, were passages ever available for non-Europeans. A series of agreements were made with specific European governments, of which the last were with Turkey in 1967 and Yugoslavia in 1970. These obliged Australia to provide employment and welfare services, while allowing it to apply selection criteria in accordance with the demands of employers.

The use of economic criteria in granting assisted passages only allowed Australian governments to select about half of those settling. The rest entered with limited controls in the nineteenth century and under the Immigration Restriction Act of 1901 and its replacement, the Migration Act of 1958. These controls rarely applied to British immigrants of European race, but the majority of these in the post-war years came as assisted immigrants in any case. Non-British immigrants could be subject to limited restrictions, such as landing fees or permits, and these were imposed in the 1920s and 1930s.[14] There were no settlement services for such immigrants, and the landing fee was a disincentive for the poor rather than a revenue-raising measure. Essentially, unassisted immigrants were assumed to cost the taxpayer nothing in the pre-war period. If not British they were ineligible for welfare payments. Into the 1960s the Immigration Department was still negotiating with State agencies to extend their housing and welfare provisions to the increasing numbers who did not come from the United Kingdom or Ireland.[15]

Selection criteria have their origins in assisted passage schemes but were progressively extended until now they cover all immigrants except those from New Zealand. Even these were divided in 2001 between those eligible for permanent settlement and those who were not, although this related more to their welfare and citizenship entitlements than to their right to remain. The 1958 Migration Act, by introducing a general system of landing permits, allowed Australia to control the intake of unassisted immigrants, including nominally the British. From 1 November 1979 a visa was required for entry to Australia from everyone except New Zealand citizens. This was enforced by fines against carriers who issued tickets to passengers without a visa.

Of growing relevance was the introduction of the numerical multifactor assessment system (NUMAS) in January 1979. This system was adopted from Canada. On its introduction, Immigration Minister Michael MacKellar outlined the nine principles on which selection was to be based:

- Australia alone would decide who was to be admitted.
- Apart from refugees, 'Australia will not admit for settlement people who would represent an economic burden ... through inordinate claims on welfare, health or other resources'.
- The size and composition should not 'jeopardise social cohesiveness'.
- Policy should be non-discriminatory.
- Applicants are considered as individuals or family units, not as community groups (with possible exceptions in refugee situations).
- The family unit should conform to Australian norms.
- There should be no restriction on departure and the guest worker system would not be adopted.
- Enclave settlement would be discouraged.
- Immigrants should integrate but would be free 'to preserve and disseminate their ethnic heritage'.[16]

The NUMAS system was based on a flexible allocation of points which were mainly designed to select economically viable immigrants. 'Pass marks' could be adjusted to meet various quotas and new points allocated to meet particular shortages or surpluses of qualifications or occupations. The system was not applied to immediate family members or to refugees. The system, as amended, became increasingly transparent, to the point that applicants could eventually assess themselves and were encouraged to do so to save time and money. The original system, requiring a pass mark of 50, combined primarily economic criteria (recognised skills, occupational demand, economic viability, transferable assets, English competence) with much more subjective measures (sponsorship within Australia, preparedness, initiative, adaptability and personal appearance). These latter measures left a great deal of discretion to departmental interviewers and were eventually discontinued.

The first major review of the system was undertaken in 1981 under the new minister, Ian Macphee, by a committee of Charles Price, Justice Gobbo, Jim Samios and David Cox. This combination of 'ethnic' and 'academic' advisers was characteristic of policy formulation during the Fraser government. They developed a migrant settlement process model which remained influential for many years and went well beyond purely economic criteria.[17] They received many submissions and also conducted research into settlement experiences. These approaches were also characteristic of the many reviews of immigration and settlement policy in the era following the Galbally report.

Successive changes increased the economic criteria and reduced subjective measures, thus also reducing the discretion of selection officers. By 1999 non-economic factors had largely been eliminated from the points system. Immediate family (spouses, parents and dependent children) and humanitarian entrants remained free of the system and constituted half of the non–New Zealand intake. But 'concessional' family had been shifted over to the skilled categories which had become dominant after 1996. Family reunion since then has essentially meant permission to bring in spouses, fiancées and dependent children, the basic minimum requirement for permanent settlement. It remains 'demand driven' but now involves higher payments and guarantees of support than ever before. Under the Keating government parental reunion was limited to those the 'balance' of whose family were not located elsewhere. Total numbers were capped at the very limited level of 500 by the Howard government exerting political pressure on the Senate to accept applicants who could afford very high visa costs and welfare bonds. Entrants under parental visas, although not eligible for social welfare for two years or the age pension for ten, were often regarded as unproductive.

In the policy debate of the early 1990s, about limiting chain migration and family reunion, it was argued by Birrell that many parents became welfare dependent.[18] The counter argument – that parents performed useful social and economic functions, even if no longer in the workforce – had much less influence on eventual policy.[19] However, not until the election of the Howard government did it become almost impossible to bring in parents, working-age children or brothers and sisters who could not satisfy skill requirements. Birrell's argument that family 'relocation' was characteristic of Third World immigrants was not specifically stated by policy makers. But the changes after 1996 certainly impacted most severely on families from Asia, the Middle East and the Balkans.

The points system effective from 1 July 1999 required applicants to be under 45, to understand vocational English and to have a skilled occupation with qualifications recognised in Australia. Extra points were given if the spouse had the same qualifications, if the qualifications had been gained in Australia, if there were six months Australian work experience, if $100 000 were invested in government bonds and if there were fluency in a trading or community language. Not all of these would be required. This system later allowed overseas students to be recruited locally with a good chance of achieving the pass mark, instead of having to return home and apply for readmission as previously. Increasingly the skilled intake was derived from those already in Australia as students or temporary skilled workers. This reduced not only the risk of misjudgements in selection but also the need to maintain fully staffed overseas posts capable of interviewing applicants.

User pays and cost-free immigration

Australian governments, both before and after Federation, have always accepted some costs in maintaining an immigration program. The most important of these was the payment of assisted passages, but there was an increasing welfare and settlement element following the Displaced Persons intake. As settlement was for permanent residence and eventual citizenship, there was no compelling reason why immigrants should not have access to all of the available social support enjoyed by the native-born.

This principle, however, took a long time to be accepted. Until well into the 1960s many provisions, such as public housing, were not available other than to Australian and British citizens. The Immigration Department took an active role in lobbying for universal eligibility both with other Commonwealth departments and with State governments.[20] Services provided by the department, such as English education, welfare advice and referral, and on-arrival accommodation, were either free or subsidised. The system created by the Galbally report extended this principle by funding migrant resource centres and ethnic grant-in-aid workers. While these welfare and educational costs were very modest compared with the national budgets for similar provisions, they were quite substantial within the budget of the Immigration Department.

As the economic rationalist ideology took hold in the public service, so did the originally American notions of 'cost-free immigration' and 'user pays'. Some settlement services had always been provided by non-government organisations, especially refugee settlement, ethnic-specific assistance and migrant-oriented provision by mainstream charitable and religious agencies. This has continued to be the case. Without volunteer work, refugee settlement would have proved even less successful than it was. But the idea that immigrants should have equal public provision, modified to cope with language and cultural 'barriers', got caught in the cross-fire of opponents of multiculturalism and supporters of economic rationalism.

The first serious attack on migrant services came with the budget cuts of 1986. Some of these were reversed after the intervention of Prime Minister Bob Hawke. But gradually and then more rapidly, the notion of cost-free immigration gained ground, as did the exclusion of recent immigrants from welfare rights enjoyed by established Australians. These changes took the form of denying welfare, other than Medicare, to all non-humanitarian arrivals. Introduced on a six-month waiting basis by the Keating government, this was immediately extended to two years on the election of the Coalition in 1996.

One rationale for this was prejudice against migrants 'arriving and living on the dole', which was mainly relevant to humanitarian arrivals, who were exempt in any case. Another was that family reunion arrivals were expected to be supported by their sponsoring relatives. As part of the changes, migrants or their sponsors were obliged to make up-front payments against welfare dependency, as a bond deposited with the Commonwealth Bank, before getting their visas. Limited numbers of those judged to be deficient in English were also obliged to make another payment for the 510 hours of English previously provided free. Cost recovery in the adult migrant English program rose from $2.8 million in the last full year of the Keating government (1995–96) to $11.7 million two years later. Once again, those making greatest use of the English program were humanitarian migrants and spouses, who were exempt from charges. Those who had arrived before 1991 were excluded from the scheme altogether, presumably in the belief that if they had not yet learnt English they never would, or they could enter courses for adult illiterates provided by agencies other than the Immigration Department.

There is no compelling reason, other than saving money, why welfare payments should be denied migrants selected for permanent residence. This weighs most heavily on poorer NESB families and discriminates against non-citizens. It was very doubtful whether the large savings predicted by the then Department of Social Security were ever realised. However, there were such savings to Immigration that, by the late 1990s, it could claim close to full cost recovery on some services, including the issuing of visas. Some at least of these savings were transferred to the increasingly expensive costs of detaining and processing asylum seekers.

The main problem with the 'user pays' principle is that those least able to pay have most need of the services which were formerly free or subsidised. The logic of current policy is that those likely to be in need of public support are not sought after anyway. This still leaves many thousands who are already in Australia and who may need support for which they cannot pay. Their numbers have been enhanced by restrictions on welfare, work or education for asylum seekers on temporary protection visas. One solution is to extend special assistance through the mainstream emergency support systems, especially the Red Cross. The ultimate in 'user pays' was the charging of detention costs to failed refugee applicants which were not recovered but which prevented them from ever returning to Australia.

Settlement outcomes

Economic rationalism and the human capital approach have measurably achieved the aim of securing employment for many immigrants in a competitive market. The Longitudinal Survey of the Immigration Department shows that those admitted under the business and skilled categories soon become employed. The process is slower for those on family reunion visas and slowest of all for humanitarian entrants.[21] Departmental research also shows that those with a good knowledge of English have much better employment prospects than do others. As Australia remains committed to a humanitarian intake, there is a good case for special employment programs for refugees. But this has always seemed too controversial to be considered. The core of immigrant disadvantage continues to be based in populations recruited under humanitarian programs.[22]

A highly selective immigration program was not needed while there was full and secure employment. It was, however, very desirable that those coming to Australia, in competition with Canada and later with the United States, should fill skilled vacancies. This was already important in the immediate post-war years when there was a severe housing shortage requiring skilled workers to enter the building industry. So acute was this that bans on the admission of Germans were lifted for building tradesmen. While many argued that immigrants took jobs from Australians, this was scarcely plausible while there were jobs for everyone. Migrants certainly faced initial difficulties when the economy slowed, leading to the riots at Bonegilla and other migrant hostels in 1952 and 1961. The failure or refusal of accrediting agencies to recognise foreign qualifications has remained a justifiable cause of resentment into the present. Many who had been professionals before emigration went into private business when thus rejected, while a few others practised illegally. This was a serious waste of talent and certainly not 'rational'. Unable to solve the problem altogether, the Immigration Department eventually gave points for 'qualifications recognisable in Australia'.

Selection became more important and more rigorous as full employment receded. By 1976 the national unemployment rate was 4.4 per cent, which was higher than for those workers born in Italy, Poland and Germany but lower than for those born in Greece or Yugoslavia. The majority of unskilled immigrants came from these European countries. But the impact of manufacturing decline had not seriously affected them, with even the more recently arrived Yugoslavs showing only 5.5 per cent unemployment. Twenty years later the impact of unemployment on migrants was much more pronounced. Despite the introduction of the NUMAS points system in 1979, some immigrant groups had exceptionally high unemployment levels. These were mostly from humanitarian entrants who were not tested under the system. Others had been recruited to industries, such as motor manufacture, which were reducing their workforces.

The relatively unskilled southern Europeans did not face high unemployment levels in the 1990s. Many had retired, which was even more true for the former Displaced Persons. But for those remaining in the workforce, most immigrants from the European Mediterranean were as likely to be employed as the national average. In 1996 the unemployment level was 9.2 per cent for all Australians. But it was only 10.6 per cent for the Macedonian-born, 10 per cent for the Greek-born, 7.7 per cent for the Italian-born, 8.8 per cent for the Maltese-born and 8.5 per cent for the Portuguese-born. These levels were remarkably low, considering that these groups had low levels of formal qualification, education and, in many cases, English proficiency. The 'new proletariat' of the 1950s and 1960s had turned into an established working class with steady incomes and a high level of home ownership. They were, however, becoming elderly and not being replaced by new arrivals. Many had been disabled in high-risk industries and were on disability pensions.[23]

The 'uneconomic' immigrant

'Economic rationalism' has always influenced policy against accepting immigrants who are likely to become a charge on public resources through unemployment, age or disability. Some critics of immigration policy, most notably Bob Birrell, have argued that the settlement of unskilled workers recruited for factory employment created the possibility of an 'ethnic underclass'.[24] This could be comparable to those found in societies with less rigorous selection processes or with long-established disadvantaged minorities such as Afro-Americans. This argument was also used by socialist critics, such as Stephen Castles and Jock Collins, influenced by Marxist analysis of the 'reserve army of labour'.[25] Available data suggests that this has not happened for the European immigrants who came to work in industry in the 1950s and 1960s. One exception is for the Turks brought in at the end of this process in the late 1960s. Their level of unemployment has been consistently above the national average, being 24 per cent in 1996.[26]

The incidence of unemployment among recent arrivals, and of ageing among the long established, has undoubtedly increased the degree of welfare dependency of many migrants. Overall this level does not exceed that for the native-born population, even though European and British immigrants are older than the average. If anything there is a slightly lower welfare-recipient rate at comparable ages, except in Victoria and South Australia, the two States most active in recruiting to manufacturing thirty years before.[27] There is, however, a considerable difference between those from birthplace groups showing a high level of English language proficiency and those from less proficient groups. These latter groups include high proportions from Italian, Greek, Yugoslav and Displaced Persons backgrounds and from refugee situations.

As suggested above, much of the 'welfare dependency' of the long-established European groups is due to ageing rather than unemployment and is often less than for the native-born. The much younger and more recently arrived immigrants show two quite distinct patterns of settlement. Many from Asia are well educated and have well-paid employment. Those coming from disturbed situations have exceptionally high unemployment levels, despite a higher level of formal qualification than the national average in most cases. In 1996, with a national unemployment level of 9.2 per cent, unemployment for the Afghanistan-born was at 42.1 per cent, for the Iraq-born 39.7 per cent, for the Salvador-born 30.6 per cent, for the Bosnia-born 30.5 per cent, for the Cambodia-born 28.8 per cent, for the Vietnam-born 25.2 per cent and for the Lebanon-born 23.6 per cent. Even very well educated groups, such as the Iran-born (22 per cent) and the Russia-born (20.5 per cent), were still disadvantaged. As some of these groups had been established for many years, this suggests that a simple 'human capital' relationship between qualifications and employment does not exist for many who come from disturbed or dictatorial systems. There is a good case for specific employment programs for these immigrants. But neither governments nor the largely privatised employment agencies have tackled this issue. The denial of welfare payments for two years places a further burden on many new arrivals who do not come on humanitarian visas but must depend on private charity and the support of their relatives.

The human capital approach assumes that governments can predict the demand for certain types of labour well into the future. Past experience suggests that this is not always the case. As settlement in Australia has been assumed to be permanent, an effective working life of forty years lies ahead of the average immigrant. This is less important when settlement is assumed to be temporary, as under various European 'guest worker' systems. While Australia had traditionally rejected such schemes, it was moving strongly towards long-term temporary entrance by 2000, when such entrants exceeded permanent settlers for the first time.

Human capital theory also assumes that the potential of the immigrant is the key issue and is already determined at the age of entry. However, in many less developed societies there is no strong relationship between education, intelligence and capacity. For many immigrants the purpose of migration is to improve the lot of their children through education. The second generation is frequently much better qualified than the first. As the tertiary education system has expanded it has picked up large numbers of students whose parents arrived before human capital criteria were made so rigorous and who would not have been admitted under current policy. Social mobility through education or small business is very characteristic of many migrants from less developed societies. The great success of second-generation Jews, Greeks and Vietnamese suggests that the initial status of the immigrant parents is a poor indication of the future potential of their children. While social mobility between generations is not particularly rapid for Australians in general, it is often so for the children of immigrants.

The limits of rationality

The 'rational' aspect of recent intake policy is that it does lead to positive employment outcomes in a difficult labour market. United States studies have shown that, in a less selective system, the overall skill of the workforce has not been improved by immigration and this has probably led to a relative decline in the wages of all less skilled workers. This finding, associated especially with the work of George Borjas, has been influential upon the Immigration Department.[28] Minister Philip Ruddock argued against a higher intake that 'the experience of the US has shown that the most immediate effect would be the dampening of wages at the low end of the labour market or a further rise in unemployment of the low skilled unless minimum wages are removed … Do we want to become a society where the rich have an army of domestic staff and the poor are struggling to feed their families?'[29] Raising the intake level for the year 2002–03, he also raised the points required, presumably to avoid such an outcome.

However, US unemployment was at a lower level than in Australia when he wrote, and very large numbers of skilled immigrants enter the American labour market and form the basis for American domination of information technology. Ruddock's response ignores the presence in the United States of several million unauthorised Mexican immigrants, who make a considerable difference to the unskilled labour market. This situation is unlikely to arise under any currently conceivable Australian policy.

An economic rationalist intake policy makes a great deal of sense in terms of immediate employment and contribution to the tax system. There is no point in encouraging people to come to Australia to be unemployed. The shift to reliance on private employment agencies, which are paid by results, makes the situation of unskilled, non-English-speaking immigrants even worse than it might otherwise be. Government has sought to alleviate any burden on taxes by requiring undertakings of support from sponsors and by refusing welfare payments for the first two years of settlement. Up-front payments for English teaching, bonds against welfare dependency, and visa charges are all 'rational' but make life more difficult for many immigrants than it was twenty years ago. Asylum seekers recently released from detention have a particularly difficult time, being denied access to services which might enable them to improve their skills and employment prospects. Many become dependent on welfare payments provided by the Commonwealth through the Red Cross.

Classical economic theory presumes a free market in labour which will 'clear' unemployment by reducing wages to the point where it is profitable to employ extra workers. This does not happen in Australia where 'inflexibilities' caused by arbitration and trade unions prevent the depression of wages for immigrants, except illegally or through female outwork in the clothing industry. Many without language skills are likely to remain unemployed, especially those admitted under humanitarian status who have not been screened through the skilled points system.

This raises the problem that both economic theory and bureaucratic practice take little account of human diversity. Even if all immigrants were rigidly processed under a rational points system, many would not be equal and would not have equal outcomes. Such rigid processing would exclude most relatives and refugees from non-English-speaking countries and severely limit the long-term objective of maintaining a replacement level of immigration to prevent population decline in the future. It would be based on the expectation that bureaucrats can predict the potential of human beings and their children for up to forty years after arrival. This would be nice if it were true. But it is not. Because the Immigration Department focus is limited to two years after arrival, instruments such as the Longitudinal Study are quite sensitive to the early employment experience of different visa categories. These validate the findings that those competent in English or entering on skilled and business visas have little employment difficulty. There is much less evidence of what subsequently happens. The experience of southern Europeans suggests that they remain in full employment for most of their working lives, buy property, start small businesses and send their children to university at higher levels than the average. Yet their 'human capital' was often very limited by the standards of today.

Policy has become much more 'economically rational' in many respects since 1980: selection on employability criteria; abolition of assisted passages; restriction of family reunion; limitation of welfare rights and services; selling of on-arrival hostels; competitive tendering and charges for English tuition; agency user pays for translating and interpreting; and, finally, in 1997, the privatisation of detention centres and deportation. But it has never included the free entry of most immigrants and has become increasingly restrictive in recent years. There is no 'free competition' or 'borderless world' for entry to Australia comparable to free trade in goods or even as for white British subjects in the past or New Zealanders more recently. By 2002 the protection of the border was eating up hundreds of millions of dollars which might otherwise have improved 'human capital' through migrant settlement, education and training.

An economically rational intake policy is obviously attractive to governments and to much of the public. It helps to justify a continuing program against the sceptics who became so influential in the 1990s. It makes sense to exploit the surplus applying for entry by selecting those most likely to benefit the economy. However, there are some necessary contradictions and problems. In 1996 nearly 69 per cent of admissions were in the family stream and only 29 per cent in the skilled. By 2001–02 this had been completely reversed, with 57 per cent in the skilled stream and only 41 per cent in the family, almost all of them spouses whose admission was demand driven. This is rational but inhumane, as it virtually excludes the possibility of uniting parents and older children with those already in Australia. It is incompatible with the family values espoused by the Coalition government. The assumption that bureaucrats can predict demand for specific occupations is also questionable, as witness oscillating policy towards the admission of medical doctors. It was not rational to reduce the research capacity to measure and predict outcomes in an 'evidence based' system or to limit effective consultation. Most dubious of all is the skewing of immigration expenditure and resources to deter asylum seekers and the consequent reduction in services for those who do arrive. This is neither rational nor humane.

Notes

1 Pusey, *Economic Rationalism in Canberra*.
2 Coleman and Hagger, *Exasperating Calculators*.
3 Nevile, 'Economic Rationalism'.
4 Access Economics, *Impact of Immigrants on the Commonwealth Budget*; Access Economics, *The Impact of Permanent Migrants on State and Territory Budgets*.
5 Brooks, *Understanding Immigrants and the Labour Market*; Foster, *Immigration and the Australian Economy*; Nevile, *The Effect of Immigration on Living Standards in Australia*.
6 Williams, *Understanding the Economics of Immigration*, 23.
7 BLMR, *Migrants in the Australian Labour Market*, 155.
8 Iredale and Nivison-Smith, *Immigrants' Experiences of Qualifications Recognition and Employment*; Iredale, *Skills Transfer*.
9 Birrell and Birrell, *An Issue of People*.
10 NPC, *Population Issues and Australia's Future*, 81.
11 Cope and Kalantzis, *Productive Diversity*.
12 Evans and Kelley, 'Immigrants' Work'.

13 Foster et al., *Discrimination against Immigrant Workers in Australia.*

14 Dutton, *One of Us?*

15 Jordens, *Alien to Citizen.*

16 DIEA, *Committee of Review on Migrant Assessment*, 3–4.

17 DIEA, *Committee of Review on Migrant Assessment.*

18 Birrell, *The Chains that Bind.*

19 Morrissey et al., *The Family in the Settlement Process.*

20 Jordens, *Alien to Citizen.*

21 VandenHeuvel and Wooden, *New Settlers Have Their Say.*

22 Johnson, *The Measurement and Extent of Poverty among Immigrants.*

23 Birrell and Jupp, *Welfare Recipient Patterns among Migrants.*

24 Birrell and Birrell, *An Issue of People.*

25 Castles et al., *Mistaken Identity*; Collins, *Migrant Hands in a Distant Land.*

26 Bertone and Casey, *Migrants in the New Economy.*

27 Birrell and Jupp, *Welfare Recipient Patterns among Migrants.*

28 Borjas, *Heaven's Door.*

29 *Australian* 11 March 2002.

9

Sustainability and population policy

For more than a century immigration policy has been concerned with two major issues: assimilability and employability. Would immigrants fit into existing society without friction and would they be gainfully employed for their own and society's benefit? These two concerns were obviously related. If suitable employment were not available, then immigrants could not fit into society. If immigrants took away jobs from the native-born or lowered wages and standards, then they would not be readily accepted. Racial features could prevent non-Europeans from being tolerated, as might their differing cultures and languages. But economic viability was also essential.

It was rarely argued that there was no further room in Australia for an increased population. The often quoted national anthem theme from the 1870s was that 'for those who come across the seas we've boundless plains to share'. The Millions movement of the 1920s enthusiastically looked to fill the empty spaces. Maps showing Australia divided into habitable regions optimistically included the Nullarbor Plain and the Simpson Desert. Agricultural improvement through organisations like the CSIRO, and irrigation through State water boards, were seen as solving the problem that much of Australia was arid and uninhabitable. This optimism collapsed along with the world economy in 1929 and the drift to the cities became an avalanche. But optimism revived during the Second World War. Its lasting monument was the Snowy Mountains scheme, built largely with immigrant labour from the late 1940s. This not only produced hydro-electricity but also allowed irrigation along the Murrumbidgee and Murray. Many who settled in these areas were immigrants from southern Europe. Australia applied more of its water supply to irrigation than any other developed country, with consequent salination problems. This helped to populate the 'boundless plains', but with only small numbers compared to those settling in the major cities.

Populate or perish

Post-war immigration policy was dominated by the slogan 'populate or perish'. This was inspired by the Japanese threat between 1941 and 1945 and the inability of Britain and other colonial powers in Asia to resist it. Australia would perish, presumably by foreign invasion, if it could not increase its population base and hence its ability to develop defence manufacturing. Reliance on the United States had been vital to wartime survival. But many pessimists did not believe that America could save Australia in the future, any more than Britain had done in 1942 when Singapore fell.

Numbers alone were not the only imperative. Australia had to be populated, as before, from the United Kingdom. Failing that, Europeans had to be attracted, instead of discouraged as they had been in the past. The threat to Australia came from Asia. With the victory of communism in China in 1950 it was seen as also coming from international communism. The Liberal Party, elected in 1949, and the Democratic Labor Party, created in 1956, used the concept of the 'Moscow–Peking Axis' to show a direct line of invasion which terminated in Sydney. Many Australian politicians and journalists later subscribed to the American 'domino theory', whereby the loss of Vietnam would lead to the complete communist control of all its neighbours.

This concept justified Australian military involvement in Vietnam until the final withdrawal in 1972 and the fall of Saigon three years later. Fear of Indonesia under Sukarno until 1965 had sustained these anxieties. Although Australian growth never exceeded that of its Asian neighbours, population nearly doubled between 1947 and 1986 with a sound manufacturing base heavily reliant on immigrants. Australia could therefore afford to maintain a major defence capacity, even with a relatively small population. While its foot soldiers were always outnumbered, its technical capacity was much greater than that of any probable invader.

Growing doubts

There have always been pessimists about the capacity of the Earth to support a rising population. The most important was Thomas Malthus (1766–1834). His predictions of imminent disaster were influential on the Poor Law Commission of 1834 which recommended assisted emigration as a way of staving off British overpopulation. But his threatened doomsday never arrived. Britain and other developed societies became more prosperous as they became more densely populated. This was partly achieved by importing food from Australia, other British empire colonies and the United States. The capacity of European agriculture also to support massive populations has remained into the present. North America opened up as the most productive agricultural area in the world. Thus, the pessimism of Malthus was replaced by optimism for over 150 years, although often reapplied to poor developing societies, especially India and China. Overpopulation was seen as a Third World phenomenon, while developed countries worried about declining fertility both in the 1930s and by 2000.

Australians who denied the ability of the soil to support growing numbers were usually scorned in the inter-war years. Professor Griffith Taylor, who correctly predicted that Australia's population would only reach 20 million by 2000, was effectively driven out of the country altogether in 1928 and retreated to the United States. The post-war imperative – to populate for defence or perish – further suppressed any scepticism. Although Australia was now a predominantly urban and even metropolitan society, rural development continued. Previously barren or grazing land was irrigated or fertilised to produce sugar, wine grapes, cotton and other water-thirsty crops. None of these employed enough workers to stop the overall drift from more remote areas which had been going on since the 1890s. Immigration had little direct rural impact and concentrated in the major cities. Those cities, however, had growing 'footprints' as they drew in water and food from further afield and also extended their suburbs into former farmland and bush.[1]

From the 1960s most international debate about population saw the problem in terms of an apparently irreversible increase pressing on limited resources – the same position as Malthus but without his cataclysmic predictions. This concern was focused by the 1970 report of the Club of Rome, *Limits to Growth*. The central objective of the United Nations and of many developing countries was to control and reduce birthrates, despite the opposition of the Catholic Church, American conservatives and many Islamic states. Demographers, including those in Australia, responded by developing relevant programs. In Europe and the developed world, this urgency was not felt. Fertility was declining below replacement level and many continued to lose population through emigration until the early 1970s. Australia, while certainly not a Third World society, had a younger population than most of Europe and a higher level of immigration. Its rate of population increase was thus higher than for most OECD states. By 1971 some were criticising the 'populate or perish' basis of immigration, notably Frank Fenner, Paul Sharp and Max Walsh at the 1971 annual conference of the Australian Institute of Political Science.[2] The greatest international impact came from the catastrophic predictions of the American natural scientist Paul Ehrlich in *The Population Bomb* (1968) and *The Population Explosion* (1990). States such as China and India adopted dramatic and often draconian programs of population limitation. Improved female education also started to have an effect on other developing societies in the Asia–Pacific region.

The belief that natural environments were threatened by population growth developed out of the initial concern with an inability to feed and employ Third World populations. Throughout the 1970s, scientists from various disciplines warned of the relevance of environmental degradation. Australia finally adopted a National Conservation Strategy in 1982. The idea of sustainable development was enshrined in the report *Our Common Future*, presented to the United Nations by Norwegian Prime Minister Gro Harlem Brundtland in October 1987. This was the product of a 21-member World Commission on Environment and Development and included representatives of the United States, the Soviet Union and Japan. It criticised nuclear power, requested that all UN agencies adopt sustainable development as their guideline, and called for all governments to make annual reports on the state of their environment. The World Bank also undertook to monitor the environmental impact of projects it funded. While these recommendations were not universally adopted, the impact of the report on environmental movements in Australia and elsewhere was substantial. It set the agenda of debate on sustainability for the next decade.[3]

While Australia remains (along with Mongolia) the least densely populated country on Earth, critical voices began to be raised against growing pressures upon the environment. Echoing international concerns, they were often inspired from North America, either through the writings of the Ehrlichs and David Suzuki or directly through American-born Norm Sanders, a founder of the Tasmanian 'green' movement. As information and organisation globalised, Australia became increasingly influenced by ideas from much more crowded societies in Europe, Asia and North America. Pressure from highly motivated and well-funded organisations, like Greenpeace and the Australian Conservation Foundation, persuaded politicians that they were dealing with a new movement with electoral force. This view was most strongly held during the 1990 federal election, when the ALP secured second-preference support from the Democrats and Greens.[4]

The 1990 election, won by the Hawke government, identified the ALP with the 'green' cause, especially through the work of Graham Richardson, minister for the environment between 1987 and 1990. Such an identification was by no means automatic. Several ALP affiliated unions and local branches saw conservation as limiting employment, a view strongly held in Tasmania. Historically Labor had been a developmental party, associated with both the Snowy Mountains scheme and the post-war migration program. But it had changed its character since then, especially under the influence of Whitlam. It became, and remained, susceptible to pressure from the 'green' lobbies, especially as these increased their electoral support. The unlikely figure of Richardson, once thought of as a typical Catholic-machine boss, had emerged as a 'born-again green', entering the Cabinet in 1988.

The relationship between conservationists and Labor remained complex, especially as Labor at the State level often remained committed to agricultural and mining development, like its Coalition alternatives. In 1990 the Conservation Foundation urged support for the Democrats. However, as two-thirds of Democrat and Green second preferences then went to Labor, this was of great benefit to the party. At this stage population was only one concern of 'greens' and not usually the most important. They were strongest in Tasmania, which had little population growth or immigration. It was, however, an increasing concern of the Democrat leaders. The Australian Electoral Survey of 1990 found that there was little difference between party supporters in the importance they attached to 'overpopulation'.[5] Many other environmental issues, such as pollution or soil degradation, were given much greater priority. The logging of old-growth forests and wood chipping became central concerns which also had no direct connection with population levels.

Zero population growth

The United States Commission on Population Growth and the American Future concluded in 1972 that zero population growth was a desirable goal and that 'in the long run no substantial benefits will result from further growth of the Nation's population'.[6] This finding had no immediate effect. The US population increased by 70 million in the next thirty years after prolonged immigration. This was not far from the commission's projected total thought likely to result from a decline in family size from three to two children, which happened regardless of public policy. This suggested that a population policy based only on limiting immigration levels was not very relevant. It also highlights the central political problem in adopting any population policy: that the time frame extends well beyond the present generation, let alone the present government.

Nevertheless, the idea of zero population growth (ZPG) was taken up with enthusiasm in Australia, notably by John Coulter, leader of the Democrats from 1991 to 1993. He had launched his campaign as early as 1971, appealing mainly to natural scientists. His original manifesto of May 1971 attracted the support of over 700 scientists, technologists and economists. ZPG was written into Democrat policy for a number of years and was later adopted by One Nation, following its espousal by Australians Against Further Immigration. Coulter was also president of Australians for an Ecologically Sustainable Population (now Sustainable Population Australia). By the mid-1990s there was a wide range of support for the idea. Its advocates lobbied actively for a population policy aimed at

ZPG, gaining support in organisations such as the CSIRO and the Australian Academy of Sciences. This policy was normally conceived of as restricting immigration, with One Nation specifically urging 'zero replacement', the number allowed in being equal to the number leaving permanently.

Support for limiting population through immigration ranged widely but was most concentrated in younger people otherwise likely to sympathise with Labor, many still at school or university. At one extreme was what might be called the 'Malthusian apocalypse predictors'. For them it was almost too late to do anything to stop the world collapsing into starvation and chaos. They could point to Africa or Bangladesh to support the coming cataclysm. Their greatest inspiration came from the Ehrlichs and their most influential local advocate was Coulter. However, the threatened catastrophe did not happen worldwide, and Australia continued to have an improving living standard and to export much of its food production.

A 'romantic' argument for population reduction held that the preservation of a pristine environment was a moral imperative. Aboriginal Australians had achieved this for thousands of years, while immigrants had destroyed flora, fauna and the soil at a catastrophic rate over 200 years. That they could also feed and house forty times the population of 1788 was usually overlooked or belittled. The most persuasive and influential advocate of this romantic position was Tim Flannery of the Australian Museum, later South Australian Museum director. His best-selling *Future Eaters* developed most fully the notion that Australia's carrying capacity was very limited and that an optimum population might be as low as 6–12 million. This could be achieved by a maximum immigration level of 30 000, balanced by a similar level of departures.[7] This was the zero net migration approach eventually adopted by One Nation. His argument rested on the nature of the Australian soil, the character of its fauna, and the claim that hunter-gatherer societies were 'ecologically sustainable'.[8]

These cataclysmic and romantic arguments had considerable influence on the social movement which grew rapidly around ecological issues in the 1980s and 1990s. They lacked similar influence on politicians, bureaucrats, business lobbies, trade unions and the general public. Australian politics has always been pragmatic and oriented towards increasing personal consumption, but often haunted by a sense of impending disaster. Many Australians are also conscious of their unique fauna and flora and uncomfortable about spreading cities, forestry and salination. What policy makers and politicians sought was solutions to these issues which did not damage employment or wealth creation. Those who thought such solutions could not be found were ineffective. Those who thought the solution lay in restricting immigration found themselves forced into proximity with One Nation and with xenophobes for whom they had no sympathy.

A more careful approach to sustainability characterised the work of Ian Lowe, Doug Cocks, Lincoln Day and Christabel Young. Cocks adopted a 'precautionary' approach that, as the ecological impact of population was uncertain, it was wiser to seek lower rather than higher totals.[9] The continuing opposition to mass immigration of Bob Birrell extends back for thirty years and still influences his quarterly journal *People and Place*. His objections are various but include the impact on the environment.[10] In 1981 he surveyed the arguments for continuing mass immigration and concluded that 'just as population advocates have exaggerated Australia's resource potential and the need for additional workers to develop this potential, so they have also understated the economic and environmental costs of population expansion'.[11] Young and Day argued in 1994, and subsequently, against the proposition that immigration was necessary to delay ageing, which was then a fashionable position within the Immigration Department.[12]

Most of these critics took part in the Australian Academy of Science symposium of 1994 and were associated with Australians for an Ecologically Sustainable Population. At the symposium, which was dominated by earth, plant and animal scientists, the chairman, Jonathan Stone, claimed that 'the first murmurs of that communal debate can already be discerned; they surely will grow until the issue of population size is part of the mainstream of national debate'.[13] This was certainly true of the middle years of the 1990s and influenced the incoming prime minister, John Howard, in 1996. However, as his government's environmental policies were limited, it is likely that his objections to immigration were influenced by its impact on ethnicity rather than sustainability.

A population policy

Australia has never had a population policy in the detailed sense of determining not only future numbers but their location and distribution. It was not clear whether the Commonwealth had any constitutional power in this respect, other than the power over immigration. Agriculture, mining and the land rested with the States, and urban development with the States and local government. Rural settlement schemes, tied to British immigration, had been attempted in the 1920s by State governments and had mostly been expensive failures. The expectation that migrants would go to the bush was completely outdated by the 1940s and contrary to all population movement throughout the twentieth century. While demographers regularly projected future population on the basis of selected assumptions, they had less to say about the desirable location of such a population or its occupational characteristics. Public and policy concerns moved through a fear of declining numbers in the 1930s, to fear of overpopulation in the 1980s, and back to fears of ageing and decline at the start of this century.[14]

The Gorton Coalition government created a National Population Inquiry in 1970, chaired by a demography professor, Mick Borrie, and reporting to the Whitlam government in 1975. This report was both exhaustive and tentative. It distinguished between a 'positive' approach (manipulating population variables through policy goals deemed desirable or achievable) and a 'passive' approach (letting nature take its course and adapting policy accordingly). It concluded that 'a policy designed to sustain a specific level of growth, be it zero or a given rate of increase or decrease, is not a practical proposition, particularly in a democratic society'.[15]

The most comprehensive response to arguments for a population policy came from the Population Issues committee of the National Population Council in 1991. Chaired by Professor Glenn Withers, its membership was predominantly academic, including Bob Birrell, Stephen Castles, Graeme Hugo and Robyn Iredale. In recognition of growing ecological concerns it included Philip Toyne, director of the Australian Conservation Foundation, and was advised by Professor Henry Nix of the Centre for Resource and Environmental Studies at the Australian National University. With such a varied composition its conclusions were tentative but included recommending a population policy which might develop 'a strategy on Ecologically Sustainable Development'. But it also believed that 'the complex nature of environmental issues makes it difficult to identify the major questions that will need to be addressed in the future'. Environmental, urban and regional issues were surveyed but without agreed recommendations. Rather than accepting that population growth would be damaging in itself, the National Population Council called for 'significant improvements in the efficiency with which resources are utilised'.[16]

Faced with growing concern about population growth and environmental degradation, the House of Representatives Standing Committee on Long-term Strategies set up an inquiry into Australia's 'carrying capacity' in February 1994, chaired by Labor MP Barry Jones, former minister for science in the Hawke government. This followed the rejection of the National Population Council recommendation of 1991 favouring a population policy but without specifying any particular numerical targets.

The Jones committee was lobbied actively by a range of organisations committed to ZPG and the restriction of immigration accordingly. Its secretariat was also sympathetic to this approach, producing a 'scenario' which concluded that the expansion of Sydney could create a mega city stretching as far as Goulburn, 200 kilometres away. Of the 271 submissions, most came from individuals. Only Immigration and Employment, Education and Training responded among Commonwealth departments. Of twenty-two witnesses called, at least five were publicly identified with opposition to mass immigration, including Rodney Spencer of Australians Against Further Immigration. Strong support came for a stable population of between 17 and 23 million; many submitted that population should remain at 17 million or even be returned to 5 million; and an 'extreme position' was argued in several submissions for a return to '1788 carrying capacity' to 'safeguard Australia's unique flora and fauna'. In the chairman's view, 'the overwhelming majority of submissions provided statements of opinion rather than analyses of the issues'.[17]

This sustained lobbying had little direct influence on the committee's ultimate recommendations. It 'rejected the view that Australia is close to its maximum population already ... There is no numerical population level beyond which the social fabric and environmental quality might be expected to go into precipitate decline'. The committee 'rejects the sense of fatalism in most submissions – that we have no choices, that we cannot manage better, and that immigration is the only factor that can change the impact of population on environment'.[18]

The Jones committee marks a high point in attempted reversal of immigration policy and adoption of a restrictive population policy in its place. It predated the rise of One Nation, which was to repeat some of the arguments of those making submissions in 1994. It recommended that immigration and population policy be conceptually and administratively separated. Population should be a responsibility of the prime minister, and the Bureau of Immigration Research should be transferred from Immigration to his department and renamed the Bureau of Population Research. In rejecting zero net migration, the committee recommended that 'proponents of radical change to existing policy and practice in immigration intake should bear the burden of proof'. Noting that immigration was the easiest variable to control, the committee felt it was 'only indirectly connected' to the rate of resource use.[19] This was not the view of the committee's executive officer, Doug Cocks of the CSIRO, who subsequently held that 'the middle way, based on an explicit goal of eventual population stabilisation, is to set annual net migration (including refugees) "permanently" somewhere below 50 000; then, depending on the figure chosen, population will plateau within a generation or so somewhere between 19 and 23 million'.[20]

The Jones committee wanted a population policy which could develop free from the regular and growing controversies about immigration. Subsequent events suggest that such controversies were often tinged with racism rather than being rationally based on demographic or ecological study. However, nothing very concrete came from the report. Both the Keating and Howard governments rejected the idea of a population policy of any kind, other than projecting likely numerical scenarios. Such a policy would need a degree of research and intergovernment co-operation well beyond that currently likely. Moreover, in the view of most professional demographers, it would put too much emphasis on factors which are often imponderable.

Opposition to determining an optimum population level was expressed to the United Nations International Conference on Population and Development in Cairo in 1994. The official Australian report, prepared by a committee appointed by the minister for immigration, clearly stated that Australia had no formal population policy and did not plan to adopt one. Nor did it specify an optimal population level, for several reasons:

- there is no clear formula for a workable population in a developed country with low fertility;
- judgements concerning the carrying capacity of Australia are widely discrepant;
- forced repatriation or massive increases of immigrants might endanger social cohesion [something of a spurious dichotomy, as few in Australia were recommending either of these];
- frequent changes to targets would be forced by economic change or public opinion.[21]

Essentially the government was saying that its immigration program was working well and that matters should be left in its hands.

Growth, limitation and devolution

Advocates of a population policy had their greatest impact in the mid-1990s. The election of the Howard government in 1996 and the rise of One Nation redirected the debate. Net intake, including refugees and New Zealanders, fell in the first year but rose steadily to the same level as in the last few years of the Labor government. The new immigration minister, Philip Ruddock, stressed the selection of skilled migrants rather than numbers.[22] Like his predecessors he denied the need for a specific population policy, while in effect endorsing an intake level which would ensure a stable population of about 25 million within twenty years. The government also responded, with limited enthusiasm, to pressures from State governments to redistribute settlement away from Sydney.

The expectation that immigrants either would or should go to the 'bush' lingered on long after Australia became one of the most urbanised societies in the world. Apart from some mining towns, such as Mount Isa, or irrigation areas such as the Murrumbidgee Irrigation Area or the Riverland, post-war European migrants did not follow their pre-war counterparts in seeking work outside the cities. British, New Zealand, Dutch and German immigrants were more likely to do so than southern Europeans and much more likely to do so than those from Asia or the Middle East. Displaced Persons had been directed mainly to work in remote locations, such as the Snowy Mountains or the Queensland cane fields, but moved into the major cities by the mid-1950s. Apart from some now-abandoned attempts to settle Indochinese in Whyalla, Wodonga or Tasmania, subsequent governments had neither the authority nor the desire to direct refugees to areas and jobs which they did not want.

The traditional notion that immigrants should people rural and remote Australia was referred to by the Borrie committee in 1975. Concluding that zero growth was probable because of declining fertility, they believed that 'there is scope for considerable growth in capitals, other than Sydney and Melbourne, without necessarily causing deterioration in the "quality of life".[23] In this view, movement to the smaller cities could be encouraged by settler nominations from the smaller capitals. Thirty years later this was attempted, with modest success, through State-specific nomination within the skill stream. But as Borrie predicted, immigrants continued to favour the two largest metropolises, as in other societies. Internal migrants also tended to settle in southeastern Queensland and northern New South Wales coastal districts, a trend only in its early stages in 1975.

The relevance of devolution to conservation is not immediately apparent. Most serious land degradation was in thinly populated agricultural districts, which would presumably not benefit from additional people working and developing already strained resources. Most degradation of amenity, outside the major cities, was along the east coast. Pressure to devolve immigrants came mainly from developmentalists rather than conservationists. It appealed to political parties such as the National Party which rested on a declining rural and provincial base. Local authorities and most State governments sought Commonwealth assistance in redirecting immigrants to their provincial centres. Some adjustments to the points system were made to meet these requests, although with numerically limited results. But the Jones committee noted that metropolitan congestion was also an environmental threat. The growth of Sydney and Melbourne was approaching 4 million each, and southeast Queensland seemed likely to house 2 million within the foreseeable future. Critics of metropolitan population growth stressed the 'footprint' notion, the loss of convenience and pollution.

Ageing and decline

Australia's fertility rate fell below replacement in 1976 and has never recovered. On the example of all other developed societies, it is never likely to. On the other hand, it is still well above the level of Japan, Italy, Spain and most east European states. Population is increasing, in contrast to Russia where it is actually falling. In the longer term, Australia can expect its population to peak within twenty years and then to decline, unless sustained by a robust immigration program. The process of ageing will also increase the proportion dependent on pensions and savings and making the heaviest demands on health services. Immigration cannot prevent this without massive additions. But it can provide increased numbers in the working ages to support the dependent elderly.

The Borrie committee, noting fertility decline, predicted that population would naturally tend towards zero growth at the declining immigration rates of the 1970s. As Australia was still a relatively 'young' country this would not result in undue dependency ratios caused by ageing. With a net immigration level of about 50 000, age dependency would not be a serious problem.[24]

Thirty years later it was increasingly perceived as one. By 1998, 12 per cent of Australians were over 65. The work of Professor Peter McDonald and Rebecca Kippen of the Australian National University was increasingly influential on the Immigration Department in the late 1990s. Noting the very recent revival of enthusiasm for immigration as retarding population ageing, they concluded that 'nothing will keep Australia's population young and nothing will stop the fall in our population growth rate, short of our fertility rate rising to peak, baby boom levels'. However, 'there is a case that the first 50 000 to 100 000 migrants have a worthwhile impact on reducing the ageing of the population'. On this analysis, net migration of 80 000 'is necessary to avoid spiralling population decline and substantial falls in the size of the labour force'.[25] In so far as the

Coalition government endorses a 'population policy', this is, indeed, the level which they have adopted at the turn of the century, despite the unpredictable and demand-driven elements of New Zealand and spouse migration and of emigration.[26]

The impact of ageing and decline is already apparent in South Australia and Tasmania and is a source of concern to their governments. While life in Adelaide may be comfortable and Tasmania is a rural paradise, both States have consistently had the highest unemployment levels in Australia for many years. Consequently they lose younger people to the metropolitan cities, exacerbating the effects of population stagnation. Attempts to reverse the situation in these two States by special visa provision have had only marginal effects. Nor have they benefited from temporary migration, which might have increased their labour force. As models of ZPG they are not very reassuring.

Future stabilisation

By 2002 most interested parties were turning their backs on zero population growth. The Population Summit, called by the Victorian government in February 2002, saw a remarkable degree of agreement that declining fertility was a problem requiring public policies to sustain population growth. Whether those policies should include a broad national population policy or not was the main area of disagreement. Minister Ruddock presented the traditional departmental line, previously accepted by Labor governments, that a population policy was undesirable. The Opposition leader, Simon Crean, departed from previous party policy in endorsing such a policy, as did the Victorian Labor premier, Steve Bracks. These concerns were repeated at another Melbourne conference, called by the *Australian* in April, and at a Sydney conference organised by the Immigration Department in May.

The difference between this recent debate and that of the 1990s was that a population policy was seen as requiring continued large-scale immigration, whereas previously reduced immigration had been seen as a weapon for ZPG. Both governmental and professional demographic projections agreed that a population of about 25 million within thirty years was the most likely and desirable outcome. Whether that level would then be maintained or would start to decline would depend on whether a continuing net immigrant intake of about 80 000 should be sustained, together with 'family friendly' policies designed to encourage a higher birthrate.

Many previous ZPG supporters, like the Green Party, the Australian Democrats, and Tim Flannery, were ready to admit that their former pessimism might have been misplaced. The cataclysmic predictions of the Ehrlichs in the 1960s had not come true, any more than did those of Malthus in the 1800s. While both may yet come true for some underdeveloped societies, they seemed irrelevant to Australia. The debate on sustainability had reached a calmer and more rational plane by 2000. It was recognised that population would rise anyway, but that its subsequent decline might also be problematic. The Green Party, as its electoral support increased, became more responsive to the dilemmas of refugee migration. They were the only party to oppose mandatory detention and the *Tampa* operation during the 2001 election. Many in the broad 'green' coalition did not relish being on the same side as One Nation, however temporarily. The problems raised by conservationists and ecologists remained. But it was being realised that drastically reducing immigration would not solve them.

The sustainability movement of the 1990s had many positive aspects, alerting governments, industry and agriculture to serious long-term problems. It enrolled into political activity many young people otherwise indifferent to the major parties. It activated a concern for the natural environment among the predominantly urban population. But the vehemence of its opposition to population increase led it into the dangerous territory of opposing immigration and providing arguments to other opponents with quite different values. All but the most extreme advocates of ZPG also favoured the humanitarian and family reunion intakes. But the zero replacement slogan, taken up by One Nation among others, would have made it impossible to defend those programs without abolishing all other immigration.

By the turn of the century both the Greens and the Democrats recognised this dilemma and modified their policies accordingly. Coulter's influence on the Democrats declined and he left the party altogether in 2001.[27] The Coalition, which had come into power sceptical of the immigration level under Labor, found itself implementing a similar level and facing pressure from its business constituency to increase numbers.

Some business leaders, such as Hugh Morgan of Western Mining, let their enthusiasm for growth run riot with targets of up to 500 000 immigrants a year. A more sober approach might have looked at increasing the skilled, family reunion and humanitarian intakes by similar proportions to a gross level of perhaps 150 000. This would liberalise the family and humanitarian streams, which had become victims of economic rationalism. The outcome within twenty-five years would still be a population of about 25 million. Anything more than this as a detailed population policy seems unlikely, except perhaps for the introduction of paid maternity leave, which was being discussed by mid-2002. Australia (with the United States) was almost alone among developed societies in not having such a 'family friendly' provision.

Notes

1 Norton et al., *An Overview of Research on the Links between Human Population and the Environment*.
2 AIPS, *How Many Australians?*, 130–204.
3 Smith, *Immigration, Population and Sustainable Environments*; Papadakis, *Politics and the Environment*.
4 Bean et al., *The Greening of Australian Politics*.
5 Bean et al., *The Greening of Australian Politics*.
6 Borrie, *Population and Australia*, para 15.82.
7 Flannery, *The Future Eaters*, 374.
8 AAS, *Population 2040*, 58.
9 Cocks, *People Policy*.
10 Birrell et al., *Populate and Perish?*
11 Birrell and Birrell, *An Issue of People*, 200.
12 AAS, *Population 2040*, 63–76.
13 AAS, *Population 2040*, 16.
14 Borrie and Mansfield, *Implications of Australian Population Trends*.
15 Borrie, *Population and Australia*, para 18.74.
16 NPC, *Population Issues and Australia's Future*, 13, 57.
17 Jones, *Australia's Population 'Carrying Capacity'*, 145, Intro.
18 Jones, *Australia's Population 'Carrying Capacity'*, 143, 144.

19 Jones, *Australia's Population 'Carrying Capacity'*, recommendations 7(b) and 12, and para 7.71.
20 Cocks, *People Policy*, 314.
21 Woolcott, *Australia: National Report on Population*, 45.
22 Ruddock, 'Immigration Reform'.
23 Borrie, *Population and Australia*, paras 18.75–76.
24 Borrie, *Population and Australia*, paras 9.69–71.
25 McDonald and Kippen, 'The Impact of Immigration on the Ageing of Australia's Population', 159, 168, 174.
26 Ruddock, 'A Sustainable Population Policy for Australia'.
27 Coulter, 'Immigration – A Battle Ground within the Australian Democrats'.

10

Refugees and asylum seekers

Between 1947 and 1972 Australia had accepted 260 000 refugees and Displaced Persons as permanent settlers. Almost all of these were escaping from communist regimes, including Russian Christians escaping from China as well as those from eastern Europe. The mass emigration of 170 000 displaced persons from central European camps was completed by 1952 and had created institutions and practices which continued to be used for non-British immigrants for the next twenty years.[1] These included the use of former military camps such as Bonegilla and Bathurst, the teaching of English through the adult migrant education program, and the co-ordination of welfare agencies through the Good Neighbour movement. Refugee settlement was seen as generous and charitable. Christian and other community organisations continued to play a major role in settlement, later organised through the Community Refugee Settlement scheme of 1979. The major groups coming between 1952 and 1972 included Hungarians in 1956, Czechoslovakians in 1968, the Russian Christians from China, and Jews from the Soviet Union.[2] In accepting refugees from communist states, Australia was pursuing the same policy as the United States and Canada. Many Germans who came as assisted migrants after 1952 had also come across from the Soviet occupation zone into Western Germany.

These refugees were acceptable because they were Europeans, within the definitions already used for the White Australia policy, and because they were escaping from communism. Most arrived under the Liberal–Country Party coalition which ruled Australia between 1949 and 1972. The Hungarian and Czechoslovak refugees were generally well educated. They were exempt from the two-year labour bond imposed on European refugees in the past and came into a system which was both better organised and more receptive. Consequently they did not suffer so much from public hostility or from being forced into jobs below their qualifications. Nor had they lived in camps for any length of time. They were escaping from the Soviet repression of their communist governments' attempts at liberalisation rather than from the aftermath of the Second World War. Although traumatic, their experiences were not quite as horrendous as for many who had been pushed around between the Soviet and Nazi war machines. Most were able to fit into the full employment economy and many found security in middle-class occupations.

The 14 000 Russian Christians were brought to Australia by the Australian Council of Churches and also enjoyed support from Christian communities. Jews from the Soviet Union, Hungary and Czechoslovakia were likewise assisted by Australian Jewish Welfare. The role of voluntary organisations in refugee settlement included religious, ethnic and social welfare agencies with strong community links. All of this helped to make refugee settlement uncontroversial, compared to what had happened in the late 1930s and the early 1950s and what was to happen again from 1975.

Thirty years later the refugee situation was quite different. Between 1972 and 2002, at least 320 000 arrived under various refugee and humanitarian programs for permanent settlement. Taking these together with their predecessors, accounting for deaths and departures and adding in their locally born children, this means that about 5 per cent of Australians have some direct experience of the refugee situation. Conversely, it means that 95 per cent do not, unless they are from the relatively small minority engaged in refugee settlement work in Australia and overseas. At the heart of opposition to refugees has been lack of experience and understanding, rather than racism or even xenophobia. Most of the Australian-born have lived very sheltered lives, including most politicians and public servants. They cannot be expected to fully understand experiences which they have never witnessed and which have never impinged on Australia. Indeed, many seem sceptical that refugee claims are authentic. Television coverage of the vast refugee camps in Africa and around Afghanistan might have increased a sense of concern about the danger of being swamped by uncontrollable numbers, which goes back for over a century as a folk myth.

Refugee settlement was often seen as a charitable act, primarily by religious agencies within the Cold War context. Yet, in contrast to the situation between 1947 and 1972, a large proportion of recent refugees are not Christians or Jews, nor are they escaping from communism. Moreover, in contrast to the post-war situation, when the European camps were eventually cleared of their inmates, the refugee situation worldwide continues to escalate as brutal dictatorships flourish, civil wars are prolonged and civil society collapses in many countries. Ironically enough, the collapse of European communism often made the situation worse, rather than better as many had hoped. People who had been forbidden to emigrate from communist states were now able to do so. Jews moved in large numbers to Israel, exacerbating population pressures and Palestinian resentment. Romanies moved across Europe, introducing practices such as begging with children which had largely died out and which west Europeans found offensive. Russian professionals sought the opportunities, which other Europeans had long enjoyed, to obtain better salaries and conditions. Most important for Australia, Yugoslavia collapsed into civil war and disintegration.

The UN Convention and Protocol

Australia has taken refugees for four reasons: because it adheres to the United Nations Convention of 1951 and the Protocol of 1967; because it needs a co-operative image in the 'world community'; because refugees are often young and active and constitute a useful addition to the workforce and population; and because some religious and ethnic groups in Australia want relief for their compatriots suffering overseas. Refugee intake is not, then, a form of charity, although it is often seen as such. Refugees have been chosen in co-operation with the International Refugee Organization, and later with the United Nations High Commissioner for Refugees (UNHCR), and are often moved with assistance from the International Organization for Migration. But Australia has the final say in accepting them, within a fixed quota known as the refugee component of the humanitarian program. Family reunion is not part of this program, although sometimes described as also being 'humanitarian'. While refugee numbers may change rapidly due to local circumstances, Australia always imposes a limitation.

Problems arise when people arrive in Australia and claim refugee status, and when political situations change dramatically in countries from which temporary immigrants are already in Australia. It is open to the Australian government to expand its program or to make special visa provisions in particular circumstances. The most important example of this was the acceptance of 20 000 Chinese students in Australia at the time of the Beijing repression of 1989.

To qualify as a refugee within the terms of the UN Convention and Protocol, applicants must have 'a well founded fear of being persecuted for reasons of race, religion, nationality, membership of a particular social group or political opinion, is outside the country of his nationality and is unable or, owing to such fear, is unwilling to avail itself of the protection of that country'. This definition is open to legal interpretation. For example, some countries have accepted that forced implementation of China's one-child policy constitutes persecution, whereas Australia has not. Canada has accepted that limitations on the rights of women in Saudi Arabia or Afghanistan constitute persecution. Although Australia ratified the UN Convention in 1954 and the Protocol in 1973, it has not, unlike Canada, incorporated them into the Migration Act.

In general, Australia has adopted a literal approach and is currently arguing that the courts have been too lenient and have created precedents by accepting appeals. For at least ten years Australia has aimed at restricting appeals through the courts but has been unable to remove final appeal to the High Court, as this has been deemed to be constitutionally protected. One problem of appeals has been considerable delay. The Immigration Department has consistently resented appeals to the courts and unauthorised arrivals, as they breach the principle of orderly processing. For those who have come without documentation as asylum seekers, this has meant continued internment under the mandatory detention policy adopted in 1991.[3]

Those refugees accepted 'offshore' by Australian migration posts overseas do not present a problem, although their arrival may be delayed if the refugee quota is overfilled. Those seeking asylum and arriving 'onshore' have been more problematic. If accepted as refugees, Australia has had little option but to include them in the overall humanitarian quota. This it has only tried to evade since the *Tampa* incident of late August 2001, by declaring some offshore parts of Australia not to be part of the 'migration zone'. Those who have entered Australia nevertheless have had their rights severely curtailed. Australia is not legally obliged to give them permanent residence, as was normal in the past.

But a problem remains for those from states recognised as severely oppressive, such as Iraq or Taliban Afghanistan. Those not accepted as refugees would normally be deported back to their place of origin. Under the UN Convention, however, this cannot be done if it means *refoulement* (return to persecution). Some states will not accept their own former subjects anyway. This presents the Australian government with the dilemma of either leaving such rejected applicants in detention (theoretically for ever) or letting them free on temporary protection visas. Deportation is also possible back to the previous country of residence, which is frequently Indonesia. But there is no obligation on any country to accept deportees who are not citizens. Australia has secured the right to return deportees to Vietnam and China by agreement with their governments. As both of these governments are among the few remaining under communist control, this is an odd reversal of earlier practice.

Refugee intakes since 1975

Refugee intakes respond to unpredictable situations. Australia does not take refugees from situations in numbers which correspond to those of concern to the UNHCR. Very few have been taken from Africa, one of the main reservoirs of refugees, nor from the neighbours of Afghanistan such as Pakistan or Iran, the other major reservoir. Refugees from eastern Europe almost disappeared until the collapse of Yugoslavia in the 1990s. Few now come from the two largest providers of refugees in the past: Vietnam and Poland. Refugees are not predominantly from Asia, as public opinion often assumes. Between 1987 and 2000, of 136 000 admitted under humanitarian programs, 34 per cent were from Europe (mainly Yugoslavia), 31 per cent from Asia (tapering off to negligible numbers after 1996), 20 per cent from the Middle East (mainly Iraq and Iran), 7 per cent from Africa (mainly the Horn of Africa), and 7 per cent from the Americas (tapering off to negligible numbers after 1991).

Totals have kept very close to the planning level of 12 000, of whom only 4000 are normally UN Convention refugees. Since the election of the Howard government in 1996, European arrivals have been 48 per cent of the total, although this probably reflects the clearing of applications from former Yugoslavia rather than a deliberate move away from Asia. These totals include those granted refugee status 'onshore' – in other words, asylum seekers.

The composition of refugees in recent years is quite different from that between 1975 and 1987. These were predominantly from Asia and the Middle East and included those fleeing from Indochina and Lebanon. Between the Census years 1976 and 1986, the Vietnam-born population rose from 2427 to 83 056; the Lebanon-born population from 33 424 to 56 343; the Cambodia-born from 496 to 13 240; the China-born from 19 971 to 37 469; and the Chile-born from 9919 to 18 737. All of these increases were largely due to refugee and humanitarian arrivals or to 'onshore' asylum seekers such as the Chinese students. What had been small or non-existent ethnic groups were transformed and continued to grow through family reunion.

Existing birthplace groups in Australia which owe their strength to the humanitarian program or which have emigrated largely to escape dictatorships or civil war include quite varied nationalities, escaping for a variety of reasons. Some groups, such as Afghans and Ethiopians, consist almost entirely of those coming with humanitarian visas. Others, such as the Vietnamese, combine refugee and family reunion components. Those from former Yugoslavia combine earlier refugees from communism, later free migrants under the 1970 agreement, and recent refugees from the breakdown of civil order since 1990. Many who have come from Sri Lanka or Fiji have been well qualified and enter under skilled or family reunion categories. But their primary motivation in emigrating has often been civil disorder or ethnic persecution. There is, then, no clear line which distinguishes 'refugee' communities from 'migrant' communities. Official classification of two streams – migrant and humanitarian – is based only on visa category and does not assist in studying the reality of specific ethnic community life.[4]

Immigrants settling for primarily 'political' reasons (as refugees or fearing future persecution) over the past fifty years might be crudely divided as follows, by birthplace figures for 1996:

- Europeans escaping communism (former Soviet bloc and Soviet Union): 200 000

- Asians escaping communism (Vietnam, Laos, Cambodia, China): 300 000
- East Africans escaping civil disorder (Ethiopia, Somalia, Sudan, Eritrea): 8000
- Latin Americans escaping dictatorship (Chile, Argentina, Uruguay, El Salvador): 50 000
- Yugoslavs escaping communism or civil disorder: 100 000
- Middle Easterners escaping religious/political fundamentalism (Iran, Iraq, Afghanistan, Syria, Lebanon): 100 000
- Others, for miscellaneous reasons (Sri Lanka, Fiji, Timor): 35 000

The humanitarian programs

The above figures can only be crude estimates and do not correspond to the number of humanitarian visas issued nor to the numbers who have arrived since 1947, as many have died or left Australia. Many may have left situations which were threatening, while others may simply have acquiesced in a family decision. The total of almost 800 000 does, however, correspond well with the official figures for those entering under humanitarian categories. These categories have developed over the past twenty years to allow flexibility in dealing with crisis situations as well as to modify the definitions of the 1951 UN Convention. Under the minister's discretionary powers there have also been several special or concessional visas. The system was at its most flexible and expansive under the Fraser and Hawke governments and especially under the ministry of Ian Macphee. It has been progressively tightened under the Howard government and become more inflexible. Towards undocumented asylum seekers it is now notoriously draconian.[5]

Prior to 1981, refugees had been admitted in response to particular crises, beginning with the Evian decision of 1938 to accept a quota of mainly Jewish refugees from the Nazis. The greatest expansion of this approach was the acceptance of post-war Displaced Persons between 1947 and 1952. Special provisions were made to deal with the Hungarian (1956) and Czech (1968) situations. Most decisions were thus ad hoc or involved individuals seeking asylum under the UN Convention. The next big surge of refugees came after 1975 from the wars in Indochina and Lebanon. These were also processed as special cases. Finally, in 1981, general visa categories were designed which did not specify particular countries.

The 'global special humanitarian' program was created in 1981 for those not strictly Convention refugees but who were suffering from deprivation of human rights and supported by Australian residents or community groups. This grew out of existing systems for Soviet Jews and Timorese. The number of Convention refugees was steadily reduced and replaced by special humanitarian entrants, until by 1987 these were in the majority in an overall total of 11 000 which has remained fairly steady ever since. Between 1987 and 2001 there were 60 000 special humanitarian entrants, as against a similar level of Convention refugees processed 'offshore'.

The special humanitarian program allows some of the responsibility for settling immigrants to be taken by their families or ethnic organisations.[6] It also introduced greater flexibility and widened the number of countries sending new settlers. It did not cope with the collapse of civil order, when many would seek to flee even if not specifically persecuted. The most acute of these situations was in former Yugoslavia. The Labor government then introduced a 'special assistance' category in 1991 which could be used by relatives already in Australia to sponsor those in civil war situations elsewhere. The major beneficiaries were from former Yugoslavia and especially from Bosnia. The Opposition consistently criticised this program and abolished it in 1999 after becoming the government. It might have served to settle the claims of many from Afghanistan or Iraq had it been retained. Total intake under this program was 34 000. The final category is for those granted refugee status 'onshore', namely asylum seekers. As discussed below, these are treated differently depending on whether they arrive with a visa (by plane) or without one (by boat). Numbers of asylum seekers remained low until 1996 when more started arriving from Afghanistan and Iraq by boat, thus precipitating the crisis to which the Howard government responded with increasing ferocity.

Boat people, asylum seekers and mandatory detention

The increasing arrival of asylum seekers from Timor and Vietnam in 1975 and 1976 reactivated historic fears of a flood moving down from Asia towards weakly defended Australia. This overlooked the reality that seventy years of controlled immigration intervened between the introduction of White Australia and the end of the war in Vietnam. In the event, only 2000 arrived by boat and they were accepted as refugees by virtue of escaping from the communist victors. Refugees from Timor, which is relatively close to Darwin, were not particularly numerous either. Many were Chinese and Catholic and their case was taken up by the Catholic Church, among others. However, their status remained ambiguous. The Department of Immigration claimed that as Portuguese citizens they should seek asylum in Portugal, a country to which most had never been and for which, as Chinese, they had no special affinity. The Commonwealth, and especially the Department of Foreign Affairs, was almost unique in the world in accepting de facto Indonesian control, which the United Nations never did. Thus, for ten years almost 2000 Timorese remained effectively in limbo as Australian residents without the right to permanence – not the responsibility of Australia or Indonesia or Portugal.

The Vietnamese flow was controlled by agreement with Vietnam in 1979 under the 'orderly departure program', which was reformed as the Comprehensive Plan of Action in 1989. This reduced the possibility of leaving by boat, aided the clearance of refugee camps in the Philippines and Indonesia, and reduced pressure on Malaysia, but never fully resolved the status of many in camps in Hong Kong. The major recipient of refugees was China, to which many of Chinese origin fled to escape ethnic rather than ideological persecution. Tension with China produced another crisis and a dramatic increase in boat departures towards other Southeast Asian countries in 1989. Over 1 million people left Vietnam by various means. Under the 1989 Plan, Australia, with Canada and the United States, agreed to assist in clearing the resulting refugee camps. By 1991 there were 122 000 Vietnam-born in Australia, a fifty-fold increase since the end of the war in 1975. To these were added another 50 000 in the next five years. Some continued to come as refugees, as the result of camp clearance programs rather than as boat arrivals. The majority came for family reunion under the Comprehensive Plan of Action. Only 2000 came directly to Australia by boat between 1975 and 1989, and for nearly ten years before 1991 there were no boat arrivals at all.[7]

The apparent solution of the problem of refugee pressure from Vietnam was one factor in persuading the FitzGerald inquiry of

1988 that the Australian commitment to refugee intake could be reduced. It also suggested that the problem of unauthorised boat people had been solved. However, neither of these optimistic conclusions was justified. A sudden increase of arrivals by sea from Cambodia persuaded the then Labor minister, Gerry Hand, that all such arrivals must be interned until cleared as refugees, rather than being housed in open reception centres as in the past. In 1991 a former mine workers' camp at Port Hedland was opened, and all those arriving without documentation or authorisation were to be interned there while being processed to assess their status. Those awaiting deportation or of uncertain status had previously been detained in Sydney (Villawood) or Melbourne (Maribyrnong). But this was the first time that all boat arrivals were detained. Port Hedland provided adequate space for most of the next seven years until greater numbers arrived after 1997.

The detention system was regularly criticised, especially for long delays. However, a bipartisan parliamentary committee endorsed it in 1994, with only one dissentient, while calling for speedier processing of asylum claims.[8] Mandatory detention did not discourage boat arrivals and there were nearly 2000 between 1990 and 1995, mainly from Cambodia. In 1997 control was transferred to a private American prison corporation, reducing public accountability and encouraging a punitive approach. Two crucial decisions in 1999 were the opening of a detention centre in the South Australian desert at Woomera, and the change from permanent to temporary visas for unauthorised arrivals deemed to be refugees.

Mandatory detention means simply that anyone arriving in Australia without a visa (other than New Zealanders, who are nominally visaed on arrival) will be detained and deported unless they claim asylum. Asylum seekers will then be detained until all assessment processes are concluded, including appeals. This does not happen to those arriving by air with a visa (usually students or tourists) and then claiming asylum. They are normally issued with bridging visas, allowing them to remain freely in the community until their case is processed. The rationale for this is that they have already passed inspection at an overseas Immigration Department post. The problem is that such posts may not be accessible to many intending refugees, or that policy decisions make it much more difficult to get a visa for some nationalities than for others. Ideally, in the view of the Immigration Department, there should be no undocumented arrivals. The integrity of the visa system requires that everyone should have one before arriving.

In the real world of refugee life, however, this ideal situation is often impossible. States like Iraq follow the previous communist practice of issuing exit visas, which those fearing persecution are unlikely to apply for or receive. Others, like Afghanistan, do not have an Australian post and may not have an effective passport or birth certificate system. For these reasons the UN Convention seeks to ensure that undocumented asylum seekers are not discriminated against. Australia does not adhere to this aspiration, by distinguishing between those without a visa, who are interned, and those arriving with a visa, who are not. Moreover, those asylum seekers interned in remote locations such as Port Hedland or Woomera have greater problems in accessing legal assistance or contacting relatives or compatriots, than did previous generations of refugees.[9]

The shift to temporary protection

The UN Convention does not oblige receiving countries to give permanent residence and citizenship to refugees. Australia did so because it was aiming to increase its population and wanted to retain the loyalty of those it had brought in, often at some expense. The Convention does require that refugees be treated like other immigrants. In Australia that meant that they should be resettled, given permanence, provided with services and be eligible for citizenship on the same basis as others. The great majority of refugees have become citizens, with a higher naturalisation rate than for most other immigrants. This was mainly to ensure security, but it also marked rejection of communist governments at home. These governments, on the other hand, usually insisted that their citizenship could only be lost by decision of the state. This was an added incentive not to return home for fear of never getting away again. Thus, return rates for refugees were usually much lower than for other immigrants. It was only with the collapse of European communism and the relaxation in China and Indochina that refugees were prepared to return, even for short visits. Until they became

Australian citizens, such a return might have damaged their permanent refugee status.

By 1990 Australia had one of the most liberal naturalisation laws in the world, with citizenship available after two years under generous conditions. However, at the same time, immigration policy was moving away from the former insistence that migrants were in Australia for life. In 2001, for the first time, those entering on temporary residence visas exceeded those admitted for permanent residence. Refugees are an unsettling element in planned immigration programs. They arrive unexpectedly and often had no intention of coming to Australia. They are not subject to the same economic rationalist criteria of selection as others and are often hard to fit into the economy. They need special services. So the notion of only protecting them until the situation at home improves has some attractions. It was first seriously introduced into public debate by Pauline Hanson, who proposed that refugees only be accepted until conditions improved at home, when they should be returned. As conditions in some countries never seem to improve, this was ridiculed at the time.

The first experiment with temporary protection visas had been in 1990 for the Chinese students allowed to remain due to Bob Hawke's emotional promise to them after the Beijing repression of 1989. It was not a success. The Immigration Department had not been consulted and bent every effort to minimising what it saw as the potentially disastrous outcome of Hawke's generosity. Its solution was to issue four-year temporary protection visas, which could be renewed but which could also be used to persuade many students to return to China. This left the students in a state of suspense as they could not secure employment, invest in a house or otherwise establish themselves. Following a parliamentary inquiry in 1992 the system was abolished and the students were given permanent residence.[10] It was feared by the Immigration Department, among others, that this would cause a massive increase in family reunion applications from China. The number of China-born did increase by 32 000 between 1991 and 1996, but this was considerably less than in the preceding five years.

Having abandoned the temporary protection visa, Australia gave permanent residence status to approved refugees until the election of the Liberal–National Coalition in 1996. Those asylum seekers awaiting clearance were not so fortunate and were, in effect, kept on temporary protection without access to many settlement and welfare services, when they were not actually interned. The new government found the temporary protection device (which is not prohibited under the UN Convention) to be even more attractive than had its predecessor. Reversing the minister's decision not to take refugees from Kosovo in 1999, the Howard government accepted 4000 on the 'safe haven' basis that they could only remain until the Kosovo situation was pacified and could not apply for permanent residence. Housed often in military camps but not interned, the Kosovars were nearly all returned in time for the winter to descend on their ruined country. This was precisely what Hanson had advocated in the platform she presented for One Nation at the 1998 election. The 'safe haven' operation was expensive and complex, calling on the organisational skills of the Immigration Department and costing $100 million. Only 82 Kosovars eventually became permanent residents as refugees. This operation was primarily a response to public opinion, favourable to the Kosovars after a period of intense television coverage of the civil war.

Temporary protection continued to be extended to asylum seekers awaiting processing but not interned. If successful they are eligible for permanent residence. Prior to September 2001 those arriving by boat were also given temporary visas when released from internment. By January 2002 there were 3200 Afghans with this status in Australia who were being offered a financial incentive to return home after the defeat of the Taliban. Those coming without a visa and being interned after the *Tampa* incident were to be issued only with three-year visas which, although renewable, could 'never' be replaced by permanent residence. As previously with temporary protection, they were ineligible for many settlement services, including free English tuition, and for family reunion. Nor was it likely that they would access secure employment. They were, however, also to be given assistance to return home.

The full Hanson agenda has not been implemented nor is it likely to be for the 4000 arriving through the 'offshore' refugee program. But the principle of temporary protection has become attractive and presents a threat to anyone escaping to Australia without the approval of the Department of Immigration. The Kosovar and Afghan precedents will allow the department to decide when temporary residents can safely be returned. The basis for this is usually optimistic reports from Australian diplomatic posts, but these do not exist in all countries likely to send refugees.

Tampa and the Pacific solution

Prior to 1991, asylum seekers were processed in Australia and lodged in the hostels originally provided for assisted immigrants in the major cities, such as Enterprise in Melbourne or Wacol in Brisbane. The majority between 1975 and 1989 were from Indochina and they tended to settle around these hostels once cleared. However, with the introduction of mandatory detention, many were located in Port Hedland, remote from the population centres. The existing hostels were closed and sold off by 1993, with the exception of two detention centres (Villawood and Maribyrnong) and smaller facilities in Perth and Darwin. Under the Comprehensive Plan of Action of 1989 many were returned to Indochina. Numbers seeking to come to Australia by boat remained quite low until 1997 and the detention system was not put under serious strain. Asylum seekers could be processed within reasonable time limits.

However, in line with worldwide developments, numbers from the Middle East and central Asia began to rise in 1997, reaching a level of 3800 by the year 2000. This was largely due to the impact of UN sanctions on Iraq and the unwillingness of Iran to continue to host millions of refugees from Afghanistan and Iraq. Most movement was towards Europe over land routes. Small numbers, some of them with relatives in Australia, chose to move towards Australia through Indonesia, a route organised by people smugglers and expedited by relaxed visa conditions for Muslims in Indonesia and Malaysia. Most were transported from Indonesia by small boats and landed on Christmas Island and Ashmore Reef, which were nearer to Indonesia than to Australia.

This increase put pressure on numbers and processing and began to alarm public opinion and the Immigration Department. Most of the asylum seekers were Muslims and this sparked off a hostile reaction based on public belief in the link between that religion and terrorism. Nancy Viviani has described mandatory detention and fear of boat people as creating a 'series of policy blunders' in the 1990s.[11] The opening of Woomera in 1999 was to be one of the worst of these. As the mandatory detention system was not subject to modification, this meant the internment of more than 1000 men, women and children at Woomera, most of them fleeing from the Taliban or Saddam Hussein. The increase in numbers and the remoteness of Woomera meant that effective processing was slowed down. In another 'blunder', the minister suspended the processing of Afghans after the overthrow of the Taliban at the end of 2001, leaving many hundreds in limbo. The result was mass hunger strikes and self-mutilation in the crises which began in January 2002.

The bottleneck created by mandatory detention was a major factor in Australia's action against the Norwegian container ship, the *Tampa*, in August 2001 and in the adoption of the 'Pacific solution'. Another was the desire of Prime Minister John Howard to alleviate public concern about increasing arrivals as a general election came closer. To win that election it was necessary to attract back to the Coalition government the 1 million votes which had gone to One Nation in 1998. The people smugglers were using larger boats than before, one of which sank with a loss of over 300 lives. Naval intervention in similar situations could well have caused similar casualties, which would not have been politically acceptable to many voters. Thus, when a large and seaworthy Norwegian ship picked up 433 asylum seekers from a sinking boat, the government was presented with a unique opportunity to intervene. Refusing to allow the *Tampa* to disembark or even to stand off from Australian territory at Christmas Island, military force was used to remove the stranded passengers and to send them out of Australian waters altogether. The government claimed that the ship should have proceeded to Indonesia and disembarked its passengers there.

The boarding of Indonesian fishing boats and other suspect vessels is quite common in the Indian Ocean, under the Border Protection Act of 1999. This occupation of a large vessel from a major shipping nation created an international furore, especially in Norway. It immediately raised the question of what to do with the asylum seekers. As they had been landed on Australian territory it might have been assumed that they had the right to claim asylum in Australia. But, by an action retrospectively validated by the Border Protection (Validation and Enforcement) legislation passed in September, they were deemed not to have landed in this country. Christmas Island had been specifically included as part of Australia by amendment to the Migration Act in 1980. It was now declared to be outside the 'migration zone', along with Ashmore Reef and Cocos Island. This was originally suggested by Pauline Hanson in a radio interview on 31 August 2001.

This novel decision was consolidated by reaching agreement with Papua New Guinea and Nauru to house the asylum seekers on their sovereign territory but at Australian expense. They were then to be processed by Immigration Department and UNHCR officers, and a promise was made that nobody would be left behind. No promise was made, however, that those judged to be refugees would be accepted by Australia. New Zealand accepted 131, all but one of whom were processed as refugees and released into New Zealand society. Apart from Ireland, which undertook to take fifty, few other states could be found to accept responsibility for what most saw as an Australian problem. In April 2002 Philip Ruddock visited several European Community states – and Norway – in a failed attempt to unload some of these refugees elsewhere.

The Pacific solution was cobbled together in a hurry to deal with the *Tampa* crisis but also to create a different regime for the future. The main responsibility rested with the prime minister, the minister for defence (Peter Reith) and the minister for immigration (Philip Ruddock). Senior public servants from Prime Minister and Cabinet and the Department of Immigration were also consulted. The new policy was defended as solving the problem of 'boat people' as none arrived later than the end of 2001. Yet the Pacific solution might be seen as yet another 'blunder'. It was grossly expensive, at almost $300 million in less than one year. It depended on promises to Papua New Guinea and Nauru which could only be met either by finding other states to 'share the burden' or by Australia taking several hundred whom it could have taken in the first place under the existing system. In January 2002 the Labor Opposition called for the Pacific solution to be terminated. By then the asylum seekers had been interned for six months awaiting processing.

The official rationalisation of the new system was that used by Howard during the November election: 'We will decide who comes to Australia and under what circumstances'. This had, of course, always been the case since the first major Act of the new Commonwealth the Immigration Restriction Act of 1901. Australia had previously sent Maltese immigrants away to New Caledonia on the *Gange* in 1916 to avoid hostile opinion during the referendum on military conscription. This case was unique, although Australia, like all sovereign states, retained the right to deport illegal immigrants or those convicted of crimes. But asylum seekers under the UN Convention are not 'illegal', as it allows them to arrive without documentation if necessary. What was unique was detention on Nauru and Manus Island – from which escape is almost impossible in any case – at Australian expense and with the use of Australian staff.

The Pacific solution was rounded out by the 'border protection' legislation which legalised the *Tampa* procedure in case it was in doubt, excised the offshore territories from the migration zone, denied permanent residence 'ever' to those asylum seekers coming without documentation, and also denied them any of the social or education services extended to other refugees. The rationale, as previously with mandatory detention on the mainland, was that others would be deterred by the example of those detained. Deterrence has, of course, been used for nearly two centuries both for criminals and for welfare recipients and its effectiveness is highly questionable.

A tough solution for a small problem

Throughout the *Tampa* crisis and its aftermath, Australian politicians continued to argue that Australia was almost uniquely generous towards refugees. This they based on the large numbers settling permanently from the late 1940s into the 1980s. Most of these remained in Australia for life in contrast to other settlers, many of whom had returned to Britain and Europe as these became more settled and prosperous. The great majority took out Australian citizenship, again in contrast to many from Britain, New Zealand and other English-speaking countries, who did not. Behind the political rhetoric was the notion that Australia was exceptionally charitable and that settled refugees were evidently grateful. Further underlying the official argument was the fear that escalating world refugee totals presented the threat of Australia being swamped by people of alien culture. This fear recurs regularly in Australian history and never seems to die. Yet even the UNHCR has never expected that the 21 million under its care would be settled in third countries like Australia. In fact, at the height of the *Tampa* crisis, Australia was taking a grand total of 4000 refugees as defined by the UN Convention and the UNHCR. Up to 8000 were being accepted because they had Australian sponsors or relatives or had been regularised as Convention refugees after arrival in Australia. Of this grand total, Afghans constituted 200 permanent settlers and 650 temporary protected settlers in the year 2000–01. It was a very small problem to inspire a very radical and controversial shift in policy.

In its long history of refugee settlement Australia had never forcibly removed asylum seekers from its territory until all avenues of appeal had been exhausted; never transferred asylum seekers outside its territory to camps managed on its behalf and at its expense; never denied the possibility of permanent residence and family reunion to those eventually accepted as refugees; never experienced mass protests and hunger strikes at detention centres; never redefined its borders to exclude offshore territories; and never alienated most of those engaged in refugee settlement work or previously cooperating with the Department of Immigration. In so far as its policy was understood overseas, Australia had been accepted as a pioneer in effective multiculturalism, as a safe haven for thousands of refugees, as a pioneer in settlement services and as a humane liberal democracy. In a few short months, this reputation was destroyed. In the global village, media reports were almost uniformly critical, not least in the Norwegian press. If Australia retained international influence it was among those pressing for a revision of the UN Convention and a clamp-down on asylum seekers. Such revision was already being considered in the Immigration Department and in Foreign Affairs and Trade by February 2002.

The rationale for this dramatic change in policy and reputation was that the integrity of the system must be maintained, that a relaxation would open the floodgates to huge numbers of new arrivals, and that people smuggling was a growing criminal threat to national borders. The third rationalisation was certainly correct but of only marginal relevance to Australia. The other two are based on bureaucratic obsessions and historic fears, respectively. All overlook that the rationale for having a humanitarian program at all is a belief in human rights. These rights were increasingly being denied under a system of detention more draconian than that in most liberal democracies. The politicians' rationale – that the majority of Australians supported the policy, as proved by the Coalition victory of November 2001 – was fully in the populist tradition that 'the people are always right'. Unfortunately history suggests that this is not invariably the case. Public opinion was at least jolted by the discovery that lies had been told about children being thrown overboard by asylum seekers, which the Senate inquired into in March, April and May 2002.

Basic fallacies in the official position include: that punishing existing asylum seekers will discourage others from following the same path (which mandatory detention since 1991 has not done); that refusing to concede that women and children should not be detained upholds the integrity of the system (which simply brings into play other Conventions to which Australia is party); that states such as Indonesia, Nauru and Papua New Guinea are anxious to assist Australia in relocating asylum seekers (which has yet to be proved and seems improbable); that public opinion will remain firm even in the face of rioting, self-mutilation and potential suicides (which is rarely the case in such confrontations); and that the Opposition would be afraid to change its stance on border protection (which was already ceasing to be true by January 2002). In contrast to previous official defences of mandatory detention, nobody now claims that these policies will save money or are the most economical alternative. This is manifestly not so.

Cost estimates of the Pacific solution were obscured by the government for as long as possible. But they were already seven times the amount promised as aid to Afghanistan by the end of 2001. That Woomera was quite unsuited to long-term detention had been obvious since 1999. This was conceded after an investigation into the riots of 2002, and preparations were made to reduce it to a holding camp for potential deportees. The public servants who recommended the site remained anonymous and may well have been promoted. The government nevertheless went ahead with constructing a detention centre on Christmas Island which will perpetuate the practice of detaining asylum seekers outside of Australia's migration zone.

How did Australia get into a situation where its international reputation and credibility have been thrown away for the sake of stemming such a small flow? How did a minister once viewed as a benign and humane liberal end up operating a system as rigid as anything attempted since the end of White Australia? The answer is relatively simple but not reassuring. It lies in the need to regain the 1 million votes which went to One Nation in 1998. It was the natural outcome of a process begun by John Howard in 1988 of playing on popular fears of immigration and multiculturalism. It marked the revival of racist and xenophobic popular attitudes, encouraged by the breakdown of bipartisan consensus and by the consistent pursuit of the American strategy of 'wedge politics' which tries to dismiss all opponents as 'politically correct élites' who despise the 'ordinary Australian'. It is not uniquely Australian. Similar developments have followed increased refugee flows into western Europe, where reactionary and even neo-fascist movements have had some electoral success. But it is a sad outcome for a country which was trying to do something unique in creating a tolerant society which, like the Australia of a century ago, might be a model for the world.

Notes

1 Kunz, *Displaced Persons.*
2 Price, *Refugees.*
3 Crock and Saul, *Future Seekers.*
4 Jupp, *Exile or Refuge?*
5 Mares, *Borderline*; McMaster, *Asylum Seekers.*
6 Parliamentary Joint Standing Committee on Migration Regulations, *Australia's Refugee and Humanitarian System.*
7 Joint Standing Committee on Migration Regulations, *Illegal Entrants in Australia.*
8 Parliamentary Joint Standing Committee on Migration, *Asylum, Border Control and Detention.*
9 Crock and Saul, *Future Seekers*; HREOC, *Those Who've Come across the Seas.*
10 Parliamentary Joint Standing Committee on Migration Regulations, *Australia's Refugee and Humanitarian System.*
11 Viviani, *The Indochinese in Australia*, 24–8.

11

A past, present and future success?

Immigration policy and associated multicultural and settlement provisions have been driven through over the past thirty years with considerable success. But they have also been driven with the brake on. In all policy areas there has been resistance – either overt and destructive, as with One Nation and many conservative publicists – or quiet and subversive, as with reluctance to develop policies or to administer in accordance with multicultural principles. This strong undercurrent of resistance reflects the upbringing and collective culture of that generation of Australians born and educated before the abandoning of White Australia. It is based, however, on attitudes which are common in most societies, including xenophobia, assimilationism and lack of tolerance. These are not necessarily dominant, but they inhibit policies which must meet the realities of a globalising world, of declining fertility with consequent ageing, and of escalating human movement for business, pleasure, work, refuge and settlement.[1]

All periodisation involves fuzzy distinctions, blurred edges and continuity and change. However, the past thirty years might be divided as follows, in terms of public policy and controversy:

- 1972–1978: a transition involving the final end of White Australia and the proclamation of Australia as 'multicultural', with the reorganisation of the Immigration Department to reflect these changes.
- 1978–1988: an emphasis on settlement, with the incorporation of ethnic communities into policy advice and the growth of welfare, education, multicultural and other provisions at Commonwealth and State levels.
- 1988–1996: a more scientific approach based on research and an emphasis on careful selection, monitoring of access and equity

and a continuing commitment to multiculturalism, despite a barrage of conservative criticism, and with a relatively high intake level despite ecological criticism and high unemployment.

- 1996–2002: a rigorous emphasis on human capital selection, user pays in services, and marginalisation of the ethnic communities, with a reduction of commitment to multiculturalism, a draconian internment policy for asylum seekers and the growth of temporary intake.

- By 2002 there were signs that official scepticism about mass immigration was declining, although refugee policy remained divisive. Business pressures for a higher intake were becoming consolidated. Howard himself publicly modified some of his previous hostility to multiculturalism. The planned program announced in May 2002 aimed at 12 000 extra places in the coming year, mainly in the skilled categories. Whether this is opening up a new period, it is too early to surmise.

State governments have proceeded at their own pace and have not had to deal with the highly controversial issues surrounding intake policy. They have taken on more responsibility for settlement and multicultural policy as the Commonwealth has reduced its interest and have involved the ethnic communities more directly in the consultative process.

The three aspects of immigration policy – intake, settlement and multiculturalism – have been subject to consistent controversy, often based on ignorance, prejudice and simple lies. However, immigration has only occasionally been judged a major concern of citizens in opinion polling, being secondary to such conventional issues as the economy, employment, health and education, if more important than Aboriginal affairs or foreign policy. While official policies have emphasised numbers and qualifications, popular reaction has usually been against ethnic change.

Immigration policy in a globalised economy

Globalisation, like economic rationalism and multiculturalism, has been given many meanings over the past three decades.[2] To some it indicates that means of communication are now so sophisticated that a global village has been created. One implication of that for

Australian immigration policy is that nothing done here at the ends of the earth can remain immune from instant international comment. The importance of this was already plain when the White Australia policy was being wound down. Neighbours and business partners in Asian independent states would not tolerate an exclusion policy based so obviously on ideas of racial inferiority and incompatibility.

While this lesson has sunk in at the official level, it was slower to gain acceptance in the public arena. Thirty years later some were still arguing that Australia should limit or exclude Muslim immigrants. As a neighbour of Indonesia, the world's largest Muslim state, a defence partner of Malaysia, a seller of cars and live sheep to Saudi Arabia, a seller of wheat to Egypt, and separated from Europe by a swathe of Muslim societies, Australia could scarcely heed calls to restrict its Muslim intake. That it already had a Muslim population of 250 000 was but a minor additional factor limiting freedom of action. Exclusions based on race or religion were simply not practicable in a globalising world.

Within the global communications village, Australia was to learn at the turn of the century that it could not implement a rigorous policy of asylum-seeker detention without this being immediately criticised around the world. It could not detain and board a Norwegian ship in 2001 without the entire European media being alerted at once, with a spirited internet correspondence in the English edition of the Norwegian *Aftenposten*. Attempts to present Australia as a tolerant and welcoming society, which had featured in official propaganda for decades, were immediately brought into question. Globalisation does not simply mean free access to information and to markets. It also means acting in the full glare of media attention, from which Australia has previously been fairly immune because of its distance from the major centres of newsworthy stories.

With the world spotlight unusually and unfavourably focused on Australia, foreign relationships became complicated. Australia's standing at the United Nations, of which it had been a founding member, began to suffer as it rebuffed criticism from the High Commissioner for Refugees and the Human Rights Commissioner. This may not have mattered much to an Australian government which had been unreceptive to UN concerns in the past. But it diminished Australian influence and was thus of concern to the Department of Foreign Affairs and Trade. It made the difficult relationship with Indonesia even more sensitive than it had been over East Timor, and thus engaged not only DFAT but also the Department of Defence.

Apart from threats to Australia's international reputation as a 'good world citizen', globalisation has a myriad of dimensions which relate directly or indirectly to its conduct of immigration policy. The international tourist and education industries are both of vital economic importance and governed by Australian immigration practices. Travel and study are globalised on a scale never previously true for Australia. Foreign tourism was a negligible factor in the economy when White Australia ended, partly because prohibitions on Asian settlement also inhibited the development of Asian shipping and airline links. Regular traffic was predominantly with Europe and especially with Britain. Asian tourists did not come to Australia and Australians did not visit Asia. Asian students started coming to Australia in significant numbers under the Colombo Plan from the mid-1950s, but they were forbidden to take up permanent residence. Most were lost to Australia, although some began the process of skilled Asians securing residence which eventually undermined the rigours of White Australia in the following decade. Quite recently such students have become a major reservoir actively drawn on for skilled migrants.

Today universities, colleges and language schools are heavily dependent on overseas, predominantly Asian, students. As governments reduce the proportion of university income derived from direct grants, Asian students become indispensable to further expansion and pay higher fees than the native-born. Yet the record of Australia has been complicated by two factors: the reluctance of the Immigration Department to lose control of the student intake, and the dishonesty and incompetence of some private language colleges. Lack of trust created the most important scandal in this area in 1990. Overseas students were obliged to lodge their entire fees and expenses with colleges, some of which promptly stole the proceeds and disappeared. Neither the Immigration Department nor the Education Department had expected this outcome of a policy designed to control overseas students. They had been mistaken in trusting the Australian college owners rather than the Asian students. The result was a massive compensation payout and a loss of Australian credibility.

Fear of loss of control led to restrictions on visas following the 1989 repression in Beijing, leaving many students in China cut off from an Australian education for which they had planned and paid, with consequent rioting against the Australian consulate in Shanghai. It took some time for the market in education to be restored. As some students, especially from China, overstay their visas or seek asylum, the caution of the Immigration Department might be justified. Over 110 000 student visas are issued annually, more than the total for permanent settlement. The creation of 'country at risk' categories inhibits both the tourist and student markets by making it difficult to secure visas for legitimate purposes. Annoyance at having to do so was only recently alleviated by the issue of electronic visas along with tickets for selected countries, responding to continuing pressure from the tourist industry in both Australia and Japan. This major innovation is claimed to be the most technically sophisticated in the world and retains the element of detailed control. Few developed countries, other than Japan, expected tourists and temporary visitors to go through the process of acquiring a visa in their home country. The large number of tourists from the European Union had grown accustomed to almost free movement between the constituent states.

Globalisation essentially means that the isolation of Australia, based on distance and immigration control, is under increasing threat. Already the rising numbers from New Zealand represent the greatest 'leakage' in the system of total visa control. Concern that many New Zealand citizens were not New Zealanders by birth were expressed in 2000 by Australian Immigration Minister Philip Ruddock. As about 20 per cent of New Zealanders are overseas-born, this was hardly surprising. It was an odd response from one multicultural society to another. The expressed fear that some were using New Zealand for 'back door entry' was yet another indicator of Australian reluctance to liberalise its system of control. It reflects a quite different and more anxious attitude than is now common either in the European Union or in the North American Free Trade zone.

Certainly globalisation also means a likely increase in criminal or terrorist networks penetrating Australia. But this does not seem to concern other states to the same degree, even after the terrorist attack on the United States of 11 September 2001. The terrorist threat, although undoubtedly a possibility, is often exaggerated. Drug smuggling and trafficking in women have been ineffectually countered, despite the rigorous visa system. They are arguably more important than terrorism or the possibility that some asylum seekers may 'disappear' into the community.

Globalisation greatly increases the number and variety of those wishing to come to Australia as tourists or students. It also increases the number seeking to settle in Australia temporarily rather than permanently. All previous policy had been designed to attract 'new Australians' who would remain, become citizens and create families. This was one rationale for exercising such detailed control over who should enter. But the picture has changed rapidly. In 1998–99, 67 000 permanent settlement visas were issued, compared with 33 580 long-stay business visas and 217 870 short-stay business visas. In the following year the number of temporary resident three- to five-year visas issued exceeded the number for permanent residence for the first time.

Short-term residence has many advantages for Australia. It is possible to control the numbers more effectively in accordance with the needs of industry. Australia is under no obligation to provide jobs or social security. Families are not formed and those coming with temporary residents have no right to remain. Temporary residents can, however, transfer their status to permanence by meeting the points requirements for skilled admission. These reward Australian work experience and Australian recognised or earned qualifications. Temporary residents, and especially students, thus provide a pool from which skilled permanent residents may be chosen without the need to recruit overseas.

These 'transilient' migrants put no strain on public welfare, do not become citizens and usually leave in due course, although often remaining or changing their status. They are welcome to employers by increasing the flexibility of the labour market. They may be especially welcome to foreign-based corporations. Globalisation essentially involves the spread of such corporations, many of which prefer to give executive positions to their compatriots. This may limit the training and promotion prospects of the Australian-born. Temporary residence may also give greater scope to globalised crime and terror, but there is little current evidence in Australia of this at present and denial of entry on such grounds is usually less than one hundred annually.

Globalisation also means that more Australians are likely to seek jobs overseas. By 2001 over 40 000 were leaving permanently each year. While travel to, and work in, Britain was always common, this was inhibited to some extent by the British immigration laws of 1962 and 1968. Australians in London still make up the largest expatriate community in the world, but numbers are also increasing in non-British societies, especially in the United States. This has presented expatriate Australians with the choice of remaining aliens or of giving up their Australian citizenship. Under the Citizenship Act of 1948 those born in Australia who acquired another nationality forfeited the citizenship with which they were born. Those not born in Australia could usually retain their birthplace citizenship after naturalisation, which many did. This was increasingly anomalous. Under pressure from information technology expatriates in California and the industry in Australia, the law was changed in 2002. Dual citizenship had always been possible for United Kingdom citizens and had more recently become available for Americans. Despite initial resistance from John Howard, his government finally accepted the reality that skilled Australians were becoming mobile and would be more likely to transfer their skills and themselves back to Australia if they could hold two citizenships. The Australian Citizenship Amendment Act, implementing these changes, was signed into law in April 2002.

Globalisation is based on economic rationalism in the sense that resources are expected to flow freely and to exploit cheap labour for manufacturing previously done within protected markets. Rather than bringing unskilled migrants to work in Australia, local manufacturers now move offshore or go out of business. This shift in demand away from unskilled labour had already been experienced between the 1890s and the 1930s. All assisted schemes between the 1830s and Federation in 1901 had sought agricultural labourers and domestic servants. This was still the case for some States into the 1920s, particularly Western Australia. But mechanisation and the two depressions of the 1890s and the 1930s greatly reduced the demand for such labour. Some industries, such as public works, cane cutting and mining, still needed semi-skilled workers into the 1960s. These were provided to a major extent from Displaced Persons and southern Europeans. The building industry also called on these and on skilled British and north European craftsmen. But the trend was towards the reduction of all forms of manual labour. The manufacturing boom of the 1960s was fuelled by the greatest assisted intake of any decade. Tariff walls were reduced from 1975 and free trade replaced protection as the consensual economic ideology. The demand for factory workers declined, especially in textiles, clothing, footwear, 'white goods' and eventually steel and car production.

Globalisation and economic rationalism began to cut into the demand for immigrant labour from as early as 1975, before these terms were invented. Full employment never returned to the exceptionally high levels of the preceding thirty years. Those unskilled immigrants who had arrived already, such as Italians and Greeks, escaped this trend at least until ageing removed them from the workforce. New arrivals, and especially refugees and others who could not speak English, experienced long periods of unemployment. This had rarely been the case for post-war immigrants, although common in the 1920s. Unlike that previous era there were fewer labouring jobs in the bush. As industrial employment declined, the openings for new arrivals closed down as well.

The impact of this on public policy was becoming clear by the 1980s and Labor governments began to respond, being criticised by the Opposition for reducing the 'quality' of migration and failing to switch intake to business and skilled categories. The Fraser government had increased the humanitarian intake in response to the Indochinese and Lebanese crises. Immigrants from these areas suffered long-term unemployment at levels as high as 30 per cent in some years. Labor continued a high humanitarian intake in response to the collapse of Yugoslavia, with similar levels of unemployment among Bosnians. Labor was, however, inhibited from drastic restructuring of the program by pressure from its migrant constituency in favour of maintaining a high level of family reunion.

With the change of government in 1996, economic rationalism finally became dominant not only in the bureaucracy – where it was already well established – but also among politicians. The skilled and business categories replaced family reunion as the main component.

The humanitarian intake was rigidly preserved at a level slightly below 12 000 a year. Business migrant intake was more than doubled between 1995 and 1997. The special assistance humanitarian category was abolished and parental reunion blocked at the low level of 500 a year. Most family reunion now involves spouses, but new spouses are only granted two-year temporary visas until the relationship is shown to be 'permanent'.

The new points system of 1999 consolidated trends towards eliminating unskilled migration. Skilled applicants were to be under 45 and to have vocational English and skilled qualifications recognised in Australia. Preferably they should have Australian qualifications, a spouse with similar skills, six months Australian work experience, and be fluent in a 'language of commerce' (as well as English) or deposit $100 000 in government bonds. Their skills should be in the limited number of occupations listed as seeking workers.

Not all of these points were essential, but a combination of most of them was. This was economically rational immigration for a globalised world. It discriminated on the basis of skill rather than race, but it left refugees and some family members still exceptionally vulnerable to unemployment. It further penalised some poorer and less skilled immigrants by withdrawing most welfare benefits from them for two years after arrival – the years in which all previous research had shown the need for support to be greatest. Increasingly Australia selected its skilled intake from overseas students already in the country. This ensured that they could speak English and had acceptable qualifications and access to local employment. It also reduced the expense of maintaining overseas selection posts and the risk that those selected overseas might not be immediately productive. Whether students selected on this basis will later press for family reunion remains to be seen.

Multicultural reality

Australia is likely to continue to take in about 100 000 permanent settlers, 200 000 short-stay business visitors, 100 000 students, 60 000 working holiday makers and 4 million tourists each year. In 2000–01 nearly 18 million arrivals and departures were processed, including Australian residents leaving and returning. These totals may be affected by unpredictable international events or by local economic circumstances. A globalised world is based on increasing movement of capital, goods, services, information and people. This is not a new process but it is accelerating. Australia was founded through one form of globalisation – the spread of European empires. The United States is the largest example of these origins and is at the core of more recent trends. In both cases, Australia has been at the periphery. This has made it vulnerable to international crises and, potentially, to shifts in international power relations. But it has also enabled a system of rigorous and effective immigration control which allowed the population to be built and created through state planning. Planning was never entirely rational because it was affected by racism, xenophobia, imperialism and domestic politics. But the aspiration was rational and utilitarian. A society would be created which would be stable, productive and better than that of its progenitors at the other end of the world.

Modern globalisation contains the contradiction that free trade in capital, goods, services and information has rarely meant free trade in people. This was also true for Australia in its imperial past. British subjects were free to enter and colonise – but only if they were white. British goods and capital were free to enter – but only if they did not undermine Australian employment and profit. Preference was given to British subjects in land ownership, political rights and welfare – but, again, only if they were white. British imperial sentiment was officially encouraged alongside Australian nationalism. Australia was undoubtedly part of a globalised world from the beginning in 1788, but it also defined itself in narrow, nationalistic and often xenophobic terms.

In a modern and more sophisticated sense, that is still true today. With an increasingly multicultural population, many Australians are still susceptible to assimilationist and exclusivist notions. With more people entering Australia for a variety of purposes than ever before, the immigration and refugee program for permanent settlement is subject to ever more rigorous limitations. A thrice-elected national government has turned its back on many of the policies adopted by its predecessors. While making policy more rational in economic terms, Australia has witnessed an increase in hostility to immigration and multiculturalism, with potent political force.

In the foreseeable future the population of Australia will continue to rise, will continue to be concentrated in a small number of large cities and will be varied in its origins and culture. Complaining about any aspect of these changes is futile but will doubtless continue. Australia will never be 'white' or 'British' again, will never live in the bush, will never be dominated by male manual workers and will never be socially or culturally uniform. Whatever happens, Australia will be influenced by its proximity to Asia and the islands of the Pacific. Its current relationship with New Zealand suggests that it will go on recruiting as many new settlers from there as there are departing Australians, unless either country modifies the provisions of the Trans-Tasman agreement on free movement.

These realities will present challenges to long-established national myths and legends, many of which have shown remarkable resilience. The assumption that all Australians, or 'ordinary' Australians, share the same values and attitudes was a mainstay of conservative rhetoric for the last decades of the twentieth century. Apart from being manifestly nonsensical, this denies the impact of postwar immigrants and the continued presence of the Indigenous people. Unless they are assumed to be fully assimilated, it is highly improbable that people who were born and brought up somewhere else, or who were racially segregated in remote communities, will share all their beliefs and values with the suburban majority of the Australian-born. Nor is it likely that this majority has a great deal in common with the diminishing minority which lives in rural and provincial districts distant from the capital and coastal cities. This minority is often seen as the guardian of true Australian values, an idealisation of rural people which is common in many societies.

Australians, then, are very varied and will probably become more so, under any conceivable program of immigration. What part of that variety is 'ethnic' is a matter for debate. There is no doubt, on past experience, that some aspects of ethnic variety will decline over the generations, especially when there is little recruitment from the original homelands. This is likely to be the case for most Europeans. There is no pressing reason for leaving Europe any more and populations there are stable or declining.

Major European birthplace groups which have gone into decline in Australia include: Italians (down 51 000 between 1971 and

1996); Greeks (down 34 000 over the same period); Dutch (down 14 000 since 1961); Estonians (down 4000 since 1954); and several other nationalities, such as Ukrainians, Latvians and Lithuanians. Now that the homelands of the former Displaced Persons are freed from communism, there is little incentive to come to Australia, although many are moving into western Europe. The decline of European influence is a slow process but likely to escalate soon with the deaths of those who came in a brief period in the early 1950s.

The second generation may retain many practices and attitudes from elsewhere. Language retention varies greatly. In the decade from 1986 to 1996, Italian spoken at home lost 40 000 speakers; Dutch 21 000; Maltese 17 000; and German 12 500. But Greek lost only 7700 and Polish 6000, while Spanish gained 17 300. These language losses are of importance if ethnic media and organisations are to be sustained. Yet these still flourish, with specialised pay television channels in Greek and Italian as well as increased numbers of community radio stations using these languages. Clubs are also sustained, some of them being large and prosperous.

Language use gradually fades over the generations which are not replaced by further immigration. This loss is faster in large cities than in some ethnic enclaves in rural areas, which are much more common in Canada than in Australia. Religion also remains as an important marker of ethnicity. The majority of European immigrants are Catholics. But various national Orthodox churches are well established. These increased their declared adherents by 83 000 between 1986 and 1996; Lutherans (the majority Australian-born) grew by 42 000, and Jews by 7000. All religions with continental European origins had their own churches and many also had retirement homes or other social centres. Some contributed to cultural maintenance by providing language and cultural classes or by conducting services in European languages.

The European aspects of multiculturalism are likely to remain important for many years, if slowly declining. Languages and religions are learnt in childhood and frequently retained throughout life. This will be equally true for the non-European component of the population, which is likely to expand. Proximity to Australia, lower living standards, authoritarian governments or the collapse of civil society will probably encourage emigration. These factors are much less relevant for Europe, Britain or North America. While European influences are likely to fade slowly, Asian influences are likely to increase. This will not necessarily mean the rapid 'Asian-isation' of Australia. Qualifications for non-refugee Asians have normally been higher than for their European predecessors. Outside China, English is widely spoken by the educated classes which Australia seeks to encourage. The traditional image of Asians as poor and inferior has little basis for those settling in Australia.

Moreover, while there is no declared bias in selection, there are remarkably high numbers of Christians among those coming from Asia and the Middle East. Birthplace groups with a Christian majority in 1996 included Filipinos, Iraqis, Indians, Sri Lankans, Koreans, Indonesians and Singaporeans. Groups with a majority speaking only English at home included Indians, Sri Lankans and Singaporeans. Many others from the former British empire were also fluent in English. Students chosen within Australia as skilled settlers must also be assumed to understand English.

A significant number of those from Asia and the Middle East are likely to become incorporated into Australian society through their knowledge of English or membership of 'mainstream' churches. Between 1986 and 1996, the years of the Hawke and Keating Labor governments, there was also an increase in those using Asian languages or subscribing to Asian religions. Numbers using Chinese languages (mainly Cantonese) at home increased by 213 000; using Vietnamese, by 80 000; using Arabic, by 58 000; using Filipino (Tagalog), by 45 000; using Korean, by 21 000; and using Turkish, by 12 000. Religious followings increased by 91 000 for Muslims, by 119 000 for Buddhists, and by 46 000 for Hindus.

These shifts downwards for European cultures, and upwards for Asian and Middle Eastern, were a major factor inspiring the growth of hostility to immigration and multiculturalism during the national Labor governments. Asian communities did not, however, diminish under the Coalition successor because they were already self-recruiting through children born in Australia as well as by additions through immigration. Increases from New Zealand and South Africa kept the 'British' component significant despite the decline of recruitment from the United Kingdom. But the business migration program was overwhelmingly Chinese. Professionals from India, Sri

Lanka and Singapore, and Fiji Indians, were able to accumulate points for English proficiency and acceptable skills.

As long as Australia continues to recruit immigrants and to be open to student, tourist and short-term arrivals in large numbers, it will continue to be multicultural and to witness large numbers of Asians in metropolitan streets. It cannot, therefore, enjoy the luxury of xenophobia. Many well-educated Asians are suspicious that the White Australia policy lingers on. To dispel this belief, governments must consciously advocate multiculturalism and keep multicultural policies in place. A harmonious Australia in the future will be one in which all Australians feel comfortable. Failure to condemn One Nation caused a strong reaction in the once politically dormant Chinese community. Governments, media and education systems must accept a strong Asian presence, dispel popular fears of an 'Asian invasion' and redefine multiculturalism in the sense of equal life chances and not just food and festivals. On present indications there is no possibility that Australia will cease to be an English-speaking, nominally Christian country. Equally, there is no likelihood of it returning to the allegedly homogeneous British society of fifty years ago.

A glance at the future

Predicting future social trends is fraught with many risks. Demographers are currently satisfied that Australia will reach a population of about 25 million within fifty years if current gross levels of about 100 000 permanent settlers each year are maintained.[3] This could mean over 5 million living in Sydney and more than 4 million in Melbourne. By world standards these would not be huge cities, but they would cover a large area and consume significant resources. Without more effective planning they might also be congested to the point where economic disincentives arise. But large areas of Australia would remain thinly populated. In some, the population would have declined to the point where many small communities were no longer viable.

Immigrants go to large cities. The traditional Australian obsession that they ought to settle in provincial areas still influences attitudes but has little to do with what actually happens. It does not make sense to settle outside the major cities unless a specific employment source,

such as a mine, needs labour. There is little or no profitable land waiting to be exploited, except in some limited irrigation areas which
already have large immigrant populations. While it may be true that
the North awaits development as always, it would require a massive
input of public resources before tropical areas became attractive to the
type of immigrant that Australia now admits.[4] By raising the skill and
educational level of immigrants Australia has made it more, rather
than less, likely that they will choose to live in the larger cities. As small
towns decline they lose their railways, their shops, their hospitals and
schools, their banks, their service industries – in short, a whole range
of occupations which might otherwise attract immigrants.

Settlement in Sydney, Toronto, London, Paris or New York
might not make much sense, as they are all more expensive than
any other city in their respective countries. But there are several
reasons for supposing that existing metropolitan settlement patterns will persist for immigrants. As the skill level of migrants rises,
so it becomes harder to get suitable employment outside the so-
called 'world cities', of which Sydney is one. These cities grow on
the basis of new technologies, with well-educated, mobile and well-
paid workers. They have the best schools and universities, the best
entertainment, the most stimulating intellectual life and the greatest degree of contact with other societies and cultures. The shift
from manual workers to highly skilled immigrants, which has typi-
fied policy since the 1980s, can only reinforce trends towards settlement in the metropolitan areas. Moreover, many such migrants
already come from major cities elsewhere and prefer an urban
lifestyle. This may be even truer for Asian immigrants than for earlier
Europeans. Many come from Hong Kong, Singapore, Manila,
Bombay, Bangkok, Baghdad, Teheran, Taipei or Seoul – all of them
as big as or bigger than the metropolitan centres of Australia.

The often expressed opposition to further immigration to
Sydney by Labor Premier Bob Carr is not shared by other State premiers. There are no restrictions on residence likely in a democratic
society. What may eventually happen, as is already the case for
London, is a decline in Sydney population growth as prices become
too high and there is a movement outwards to other coastal locations. To some extent that is already happening, as the growth rate
of Sydney is below that for Melbourne, Brisbane and Perth. There

is considerable potential for growth in medium-sized cities between 30 000 and 120 000 present population. These could have an immigrant component – which most do not at present – if there were suitable jobs available. It might also be possible to issue temporary residence visas dependent on employment in such towns, although this system could break down fairly easily unless there were also guarantees of employment. Australians rejected the idea of an identity card years ago and might well reject the idea of any checks on personal movement.

The assumption behind current policy is that skilled, young, educated and employable immigrants will seek to settle in Australia into the foreseeable future. A further assumption is that there will be little public resistance to this, even if the majority are non-European. They will not come from traditional Third World rural backgrounds and will thus acculturate rapidly to middle-class society, as is already happening for many Asians. Part of the fear of non-Europeans in the past has been that they will undercut wages and conditions and be resistant to democratic and egalitarian values. This is much less likely to be true of the kind of immigrants currently being admitted, although this will not necessarily alleviate prejudice among those unaware of the facts.

Looking ahead for fifty years must necessarily raise some doubts about projections based on current policy. Refugee situations remain unpredictable. In the past thirty years large intakes have come from Vietnam, Lebanon and former Yugoslavia. Intakes from the largest reservoirs of refugees, in Africa and the Middle East, have been very limited. Moreover, since 1996 policy has further restricted the humanitarian intake by discouraging undocumented arrivals and by granting only temporary protection to many who would have become permanent under previous policies. Refugee policy towards Iraq and Iran has favoured Christians and other non-Muslims. Overwhelmingly Muslim states such as Afghanistan have found admission very difficult. A high proportion of recent refugees have been from the middle classes, many of them familiar with English.

In the future, such selection might be more difficult. Three highly probable scenarios are:
- increased Chinese and Christian pressure from Indonesia if its political system becomes strained;

- population pressures from rapidly growing Melanesian and Polynesian populations, some on islands sinking beneath the waves; and
- continuing relatively free migration from New Zealand which, by 2050, will have a population which is only half European.

Other scenarios might include increased movement out of Taiwan and Hong Kong if China remains authoritarian; a continuous impact from the Philippines, a major source of emigrant labour, if recruitment to the Middle East becomes limited; and pressures from India, Bangladesh and Sri Lanka as population expansion threatens resources and political stability. Australia would continue to be attractive to the educated middle classes of these countries and to exclude the poor, illiterate and unemployable, as it always has in the past.

These possibilities all involve movement along tracks which have only led to Australia since the end of White Australia. 'Traditional' sources are much less likely to seek an Australian outlet. Most European societies will be facing ageing and population decline, only remediable by immigration from Africa, the Middle East and the former Soviet bloc. North American emigration has only ever been a trickle, while Latin America looks to the United States. Some recruitment from Southern African European communities is likely and already in train. But the attractions of Europe and North America are strong and many have retained United Kingdom entitlements. All of this means that Australia, like New Zealand, will witness an ethnic shift away from its European origins as powerful as the previous shift away from its British roots.

Over the next few decades Australians will need to be more receptive to ethnic change and more engaged with multicultural policies and approaches. Even if current immigration policy remains in place, the skilled and educated intake will not be coming from Europe. Nor is it likely that Australia will retain this intake if it does not once again expand its family reunion program. 'Sharing the burden' of refugees and of those escaping from overpopulation and limited island societies will also put pressure on a purely economic rationalist approach. Australia is likely to be even more ethnically diverse in 2050 than it is now, an experience which it will share with New Zealand, the United States and Canada. This will require a political leadership which encourages tolerance and harmony and which refuses to advocate narrow nationalism. The political temptation to mobilise xenophobia is incompatible with a rational immigration program. Such a program also requires a more humane approach to issues like family reunion, settlement services and refugees. A 'cost-free' program sounds very attractive, but immigrants are not simply factors of production. To use a wise German saying: 'We sought only workers but we got people'. Future governments may need to be less rigid, less obsessive, less directed by public prejudice and more humane than they had become by the 1990s.

Changing attitudes and values

Many Australian attitudes to immigration and multiculturalism are strongly engrained and are similar to those in other receiving countries. Majorities are suspicious of immigration and immigrants, according to opinion polling. They have had to be persuaded that Australia needs more people and that these will no longer come from the founding British nations. They have had to accept that racial homogeneity has gone, will not return, and is not necessary to social harmony and cohesion. They will have to accept growing numbers of tourists, entrepreneurs and students from Asia, some of whom will remain permanently. This acceptance will have to go along with a recognition of Australia's dependence for trade and security on its relationship with Asian states. This does not mean severing links with Europe or the English-speaking world. They also have growing connections with Asia and with each other, of which Australia must be a part. The sensible compromise between Keating's 'Australia is part of Asia' and Howard's greater affinity with the English-speaking world is to accept that Australia is a part of both. It is a responsibility of governments to explain these realities.

Australia's immigration program is now entirely the result of state action and social engineering. This has become more, rather than less, true as public policy in other areas has moved towards greater economic freedom and flexibility. While the state may have only a minor role in changing public attitudes, it has taken on that responsibility since 1945. Arthur Calwell, as wartime minister for information, understood very well the need to change public opinion towards mass, non-British immigration. He combined the portfolios of information and immigration throughout the Chifley government between 1945 and 1949. The information ministry then disappeared but the tradition continues to the present. The Immigration Department regularly produces information and runs campaigns, designed to gain acceptance for the intake program and for the ethnic diversity which is its result. This function was also continued by the Office of Multicultural Affairs and the Bureau of Immigration Research until they were foolishly abolished in 1996. These campaigns are, however, marginally effective and poorly funded, compared with the impact of some of the commercial mass media. Regular 'Harmony Days' do no harm. But their tolerant influence can be wiped out by one headline in a major newspaper or some well-chosen words on talk-back radio.[5]

Government advocacy is likely to be most effective when it is unequivocal and has bipartisan approval. This ceased to be the case from the mid-1980s. The public was receiving conflicting messages from the state as well as from the private mass media. The media is also manipulated by the state through 'spin doctoring', press releases, public speeches and parliamentary debates. In the resulting confusion caused by mixed messages, traditional prejudices were reasserted. The arguments and terminology so effectively used by One Nation were not novel but echoed those sanctified by a century or more of Australian usage and often repeated by influential public figures, including politicians.

For attitudes to change in the future needs a greater degree of consensus and bipartisanship than has been present since the mid-1980s. This does not mean repressing debate, which democratic governments cannot do in peacetime. It does mean reasserting that Australia cannot return to the white British imperial past nor to the outback Dreamtime of rural romantics. To maintain its population and productive workforce requires a level of immigration at least as high as at present. This will necessarily increase the non-British and non-European proportion of the population. Governments which, as in the past, bear the responsibility for immigration also bear the responsibility for explaining and justifying the social and economic changes which this brings. Since 1996 the Howard government has largely lost sight of this imperative and undone much that was being fruitfully developed by its Labor and Coalition predecessors. There were few signs by 2002 that a more constructive and bipartisan approach was being developed.

Notes

1 Castles and Miller, *The Age of Migration*.
2 Dollar and Collier, *Globalization, Growth and Poverty*; Galligan et al., *Australians and Globalisation*.
3 McDonald and Kippen, 'The Impact of Immigration on the Ageing of Australia's Population'.
4 Davidson, *The Northern Myth*.
5 Adams and Burton, *Talkback*.

Appendix I
Chronology: 1972–2002

1972   Whitlam Labor government elected and declares it will end White Australia policy. Al Grassby becomes minister for immigration.

1973   Citizenship available after three years residence without distinction between British and non-British citizens. Chilean refugees accepted. Official declaration that immigration policy will not take account of race, colour or nationality. Telephone interpreter service begins.

1974   Migration program reduced. Greek Cypriots accepted after Turkish invasion. Grassby defeated in general election. Immigration Department abolished and Clyde Cameron becomes minister for labour and immigration. Other functions delegated to other departments.

1975   James McClelland becomes minister. Whitlam government removed and Labor defeated at general election. National Inquiry into Population presents its report (Borrie report). Racial Discrimination Act passed by Commonwealth parliament. Ethnic Communities' Councils established in Sydney and Melbourne.

1976   Fraser Liberal–National Country Party Coalition appoints Michael MacKellar as minister for immigration and ethnic affairs and restores former department. Amnesty for 8000 overstayers. Indochinese and Lebanese refugees accepted. Census population: 13 548 448.

1977   Australian Population and Immigration Council presents to parliament its response to Borrie report. Refugee policy revised. *Australia as a Multicultural Society* published by Australian Ethnic Affairs Council.

1978   Galbally report on migrant programs and services advocates ethnic-specific welfare and ethnic broadcasting, defines multiculturalism and is fully endorsed by Fraser government. Family reunion criteria relaxed. New South Wales Labor government publishes *Participation* and sets up an Ethnic Affairs Commission.

1979   Numerical Multifactor Assessment System (NUMAS) adopted from Canada to measure suitability and employability through a points system. Federation of Ethnic Communities' Councils of Australia (FECCA) formed. Australian Institute of Multicultural Affairs established in Melbourne.

1980   Family reunion rules relaxed. State and Territory ministers agree with Commonwealth on intake of about 80 000. Ian Macphee becomes minister. Most Good Neighbour Councils disbanded as a result of Galbally recommendations. SBS television starts broadcasting.

1981   Passports required for New Zealanders entering Australia. Special humanitarian program developed for those from disturbed situations with relatives in Australia. Agreed to end assisted passages (after 150 years) for everyone except refugees. Census population: 14 576 330.

1982   Orderly departure program agreed between Australia and Vietnam. NUMAS replaced by new points system. John Hodges becomes minister.

1983   Hawke Labor government elected. Stewart West becomes minister. Refugees accepted from El Salvador, Sri Lanka and Lebanon. Victorian Labor government publishes *Access and Equity* and sets up an Ethnic Affairs Commission. Migration Act amended to replace 'alien' with 'non-citizen'.

1984   Geoffrey Blainey attacks multiculturalism and criticises level of Asian migration. Improvements to business migration program. Increase in overseas visitors, starting long-term trend. National Population Council set up. First national congress of FECCA held. Waiting period for citizenship reduced to two years.

1985   CEDA report (Norman and Meikle) emphasises economic benefits of immigration. Chris Hurford becomes minister. Connor report on multicultural broadcasting presented.

1986   Migration program increased to planned level of 115 000. Concessional family reunion allows immigration from qualified relatives of those already in Australia. Review of Migrant and Multicultural Programs and Services. AIMA abolished. Budget cuts in some migrant services. Census population: 15 602 279.

1987   Mick Young becomes minister. Planning level set at 120 000. Office of Multicultural Affairs created in prime minister's department. Advisory Council on Multicultural Affairs set up. National Policy on Languages developed. Merger of ABC and SBS abandoned.

1988   FitzGerald report recommends three immigration streams – family, skill and humanitarian – with emphasis on skill. Professional research to be developed, new Act proposed and multiculturalism criticised. National Office of Overseas Skills Recognition established to improve acceptance of foreign qualifications. Clyde Holding becomes minister. Liberal leader John Howard criticises multiculturalism and level of Asian migration.

1989   *National Agenda for a Multicultural Australia* published. Bureau of Immigration Research established. Tien-an-men Square repression leads to grant of temporary protection visas to Chinese in Australia, mostly students. Intake (at 145 300) the highest between 1972 and 2002. Robert Ray is minister.

1990   Extended visas for visitors from Sri Lanka, Lebanon, Iraq and Kuwait due to civil disorder and the Gulf War. Gerry Hand becomes minister.

1991   Immigration program reduced. Mandatory detention for asylum seekers arriving by boat (mainly from Cambodia). Critical report on business migration program by Parliamentary Committee of Public Accounts. Port Hedland detention centre opened as numbers detained rise. Census population: 16 850 334.

1992   Special assistance category within the humanitarian program, mainly of benefit to Yugoslavs escaping civil war. Migration Reform Act passed. Commonwealth Access and Equity strategy evaluated. National Population Council report on population issues.

1993   Permanent residence given to those on temporary protection visas, who were mainly Chinese students. Nick Bolkus becomes minister. Increase in business skills entrants.

1994   Humanitarian settlement from Yugoslavia and Middle East increases. Jones committee on population policy and 'carrying capacity' reports to parliament.

1995   New Zealand replaces United Kingdom as largest national source of migrants for first time since 1788. Global Cultural Diversity conference held in Sydney.

1996   Howard Liberal–National Coalition wins general election. Pauline Hanson wins Oxley with largest swing in the country. Philip Ruddock becomes minister for immigration and multicultural affairs. OMA and BIMPR closed down. Reduction of migration program. Humanitarian program fixed at 12 000 where it remains for next six years. Census population: 17 892 429.

1997   Temporary entry exceeds 10 million movements in and out for first time. Skill stream constitutes 52 per cent of migration program. Non-humanitarian migrants to wait two years before eligible for social security support. One Nation party founded by Pauline Hanson.

1998   Residents from Kuwait, Lebanon, China, Sri Lanka and former Yugoslavia given permanent residence as a concession. Howard Coalition wins general election in which One Nation gains 1 million votes.

1999   Increasing level of emigration. New points system favours skilled migrants with Australian experience or qualifications. Woomera detention centre opened as boat arrivals of Afghans and Iraqis increase. New multicultural agenda published.

2000   Overseas students already in Australia eligible to apply for permanent residence without first returning home. Permanent departures, at 41 080, the highest for twenty-seven years.

2001   New Zealand citizens divided between those eligible for permanent residence and citizenship and those who are not, without ending previous free movement across Tasman. Norwegian container ship *Tampa* boarded, and rescued 'boat people' taken off and transferred to Nauru and Manus Island under 'Pacific solution'. Border protection legislation removes Christmas Island and other offshore islands from Australian immigration zone. Howard Coalition wins general election largely on these issues. Census population: 19 386 700 (estimate).

2002   Continuing violence and protests at detention centres, and growing concern about 'Pacific solution' and Australia's general treatment of asylum seekers. Increasing business pressure for expanded immigration program, which is announced in May. Dual citizenship allowed for Australian-born.

Appendix II
Ministers of immigration, departmental secretaries and gross annual settler intake (including New Zealand and Humanitarian entrants), 1973–2002

Year ending 30 June	Minister (party)	Secretary	Gross intake
1973	Grassby (ALP)	Armstrong	107 401
1974	Cameron (ALP)	Armstrong	112 712
1975	McClelland (ALP)	Wilenski	89 147
1976	MacKellar (Lib.)	Bott	52 748
1977	MacKellar (Lib.)	Bott	70 916
1978	MacKellar (Lib.)	Engledow	73 171
1979	MacKellar (Lib.)	Engledow	67 192
1980	Macphee (Lib.)	Engledow	80 748
1981	Macphee (Lib.)	Menadue	110 689
1982	Hodges (Lib.)	Menadue	118 030
1983	West (ALP)	McKinnon	93 010
1984	West (ALP)	McKinnon	68 820
1985	Hurford (ALP)	McKinnon	77 510
1986	Hurford (ALP)	McKinnon	92 590
1987	Young (ALP)	McKinnon	113 540
1988	Holding (ALP)	Brown	143 480
1989	Ray (ALP)	Brown	145 320
1990	Hand (ALP)	Conybeare	121 230
1991	Hand (ALP)	Conybeare	121 690
1992	Hand (ALP)	Conybeare	107 391
1993	Bolkus (ALP)	Conybeare	76 330
1994	Bolkus (ALP)	Conybeare	69 768
1995	Bolkus (ALP)	Conybeare	87 428
1996	Ruddock (Lib.)	Williams	99 139
1997	Ruddock (Lib.)	Williams	85 752
1998	Ruddock (Lib.)	Farmer	77 300
1999	Ruddock (Lib.)	Farmer	84 140
2000	Ruddock (Lib.)	Farmer	92 270
2001	Ruddock (Lib.)	Farmer	p94 343
2002	Ruddock (Lib.)	Farmer	n.a.

Note: 2001 figure provisional; 2002 not yet available.
Source: Adapted from Table 1.2 in Jupp and Kabala 1993.

References

AAS (Australian Academy of Science) 1995, *Population 2040: Australia's Choice*, Canberra: AAS.

Access Economics 2001, *Impact of Immigrants on the Commonwealth Budget*, Canberra: Department of Immigration and Multicultural Affairs.

—— 2002, *The Impact of Permanent Migrants on State and Territory Budgets*, Canberra: Department of Immigration and Multicultural and Indigenous Affairs.

Adams, P. and Burton, L. 1997, *Talkback: Emperors of Air*, Sydney: Allen & Unwin.

AEAC (Australian Ethnic Affairs Council) 1977, *Australia as a Multicultural Society*, Canberra: AGPS.

AIPS (Australian Institute of Political Science) 1971, *How Many Australians? Immigration and Growth*, Sydney: Angus & Robertson.

Australian Institute of Multicultural Affairs 1979–84, *Annual Reports*, Melbourne: AIMA.

Baker, M., Sloan, J. and Robertson, F. 1994, *The Rationale for Australia's Skilled Immigration Program*, Canberra: AGPS.

Bean, C., McAllister, I. and Warhurst, J. (eds) 1990, *The Greening of Australian Politics: The 1990 Federal Election*, Melbourne: Longman Cheshire.

Bean, C., Simms, M., Bennett, S. and Warhurst, J. (eds) 1997, *The Politics of Retribution*, Sydney: Allen & Unwin.

Bertone, S. and Casey, H. (eds) 2000, *Migrants in the New Economy*, Melbourne: Victoria University.

Betts, K. 1988, *Ideology and Immigration*, Melbourne University Press.

—— 1999, *The Great Divide*, Sydney: Duffy & Snellgrove.

Birrell, R. 1990, *The Chains that Bind*, Canberra: AGPS.

—— 1997, *Immigration Reform in Australia*, Clayton (Vic.): Monash University Centre for Population and Urban Research.

Birrell, R. and Birrell, T. 1981, *An Issue of People,* Melbourne: Longman Cheshire.

Birrell, R. and Jupp, J. 2000, *Welfare Recipient Patterns among Migrants,* Canberra: AusInfo.

Birrell, R. and Seol, B.-S. 1998, 'Sydney's Ethnic Underclass', *People and Place 6(3),* 16–29.

Birrell, R., Hill, D. and Nevill, J. (eds) 1984, *Populate and Perish?,* Melbourne: Fontana/ACF.

Birrell, R. et al. 2001, *Skilled Labour: Gains and Losses,* Canberra: DIMA.

Blainey, G. 1975, *The Tyranny of Distance,* Melbourne: Macmillan.

—— 1984, *All for Australia,* Sydney: Methuen Haynes.

BLMR (Bureau of Labour Market Research) 1986, *Migrants in the Australian Labour Market,* Canberra: AGPS.

Borjas, G. 1999, *Heaven's Door: Immigration Policy and the American Economy,* Princeton (NJ): Princeton University Press.

Borrie, W. D. (chair) 1975, *Population and Australia: First Report of the National Population Inquiry,* Canberra: AGPS.

Borrie, W. D. and Mansfield, M. (eds) 1981, *Implications of Australian Population Trends,* Canberra: Academy of the Social Sciences in Australia.

Brooks, C. 1995, *Understanding Immigrants and the Labour Market,* Canberra: AGPS.

Bruer, J. and Power, J. 1993, 'The Changing Role of the Department of Immigration', in Jupp and Kabala, *The Politics of Australian Immigration,* 105–126.

Burnley, I. 2000, *The Impact of Immigration on Australia,* Melbourne: Oxford University Press.

Campbell, G. and Uhlmann, M. 1995, *Australia Betrayed,* Perth: Foundation Press.

Campbell, W. J. (chair) 1985, *Towards Active Voice,* Canberra: AGPS.

Canada. Royal Commission on Bilingualism and Biculturalism 1970, *The Cultural Contribution of the Other Ethnic Groups,* Ottawa: Queen's Printer.

Castles, F. 1985, *The Working Class and Welfare,* Wellington (NZ): Allen & Unwin.

Castles, S. 1994, *Multicultural Citizenship,* Canberra: Parliamentary Research Service.

Castles, S. and Miller, M. 1998, *The Age of Migration,* New York: The Guilford Press.

Castles, S., Kalantzis, M., Cope, B. and Morrissey, M. 1992, *Mistaken Identity: Multiculturalism and the Demise of Nationalism in Australia,* Sydney: Pluto Press.

Clark, G., Forbes, D. and Francis, R. (eds) 1993, *Multiculturalism, Difference and Postmodernism*, Melbourne: Longman Cheshire.

Clyne, M. 1991, *Community Languages: The Australian Experience*, Cambridge University Press.

Cocks, D. 1996, *People Policy: Australia's Population Choices*, Sydney: University of New South Wales Press.

Coleman, W. and Hagger, A. 2001, *Exasperating Calculators*, Sydney: Macleay Press.

Collins, J. 1988, *Migrant Hands in a Distant Land*, Sydney: Pluto Press.

Connor, X. (chair) 1985, *Serving Multicultural Australia: The Role of Broadcasting*, Canberra: AGPS.

Cope, B. and Kalantzis, M. 1997, *Productive Diversity*, Sydney: Pluto Press.

—— 2000, *A Place in the Sun*, Sydney: HarperCollins.

Coulter, J. 2001, 'Immigration – A Battle Ground within the Australian Democrats', *People and Place* 9(3), 10–16.

Cox, D. and Martin, J. 1975, *Welfare of Migrants*, Canberra: AGPS.

Crock, M. (ed.) 1993, *Protection or Punishment*, Sydney: Federation Press.

Crock, M. and Saul, B. 2002, *Future Seekers: Refugees and the Law in Australia*, Sydney: Federation Press.

Davidoff, N. (ed.) 1998, *Two Nations*, Melbourne: Bookman Press.

Davidson, B. R. 1965, *The Northern Myth*, Melbourne University Press.

(Dawkins, J.) 1990, *The Language of Australia*, Canberra: AGPS.

Day, L. H. and Rowland, D. T. 1988, *How Many More Australians?* Melbourne: Longman Cheshire.

DIEA (Department of Immigration and Ethnic Affairs), Annual Reports, 1976–95, Canberra: AGPS.

—— 1981, *Committee of Review on Migrant Assessment*, Canberra: AGPS.

—— 1982, *National Consultations on Multiculturalism and Citizenship Report*, Canberra: AGPS.

DIMA (Department of Immigration and Multicultural Affairs), Annual Reports, 1996–2001, Canberra: DIMA.

—— 1998, *Charter of Public Service in a Culturally Diverse Society*, Canberra: AGPS.

—— 2000, *Access and Equity Annual Report*, Canberra: AusInfo.

Dixson, M. 1999, *The Imaginary Australian*, Sydney: University of New South Wales Press.

Dollar, D. and Collier, P. 2001, *Globalization, Growth and Poverty*, New York: Oxford University Press/World Bank.

Dutton, D. 2002, *One of Us? A Century of Australian Citizenship*, Sydney: University of New South Wales Press.

Econtech 2001, *The Economic Impact of 2000/01 Migration Program Changes*, Canberra: Econtech.

Edwards, J. 1996, *Keating: The Inside Story,* Ringwood (Vic.): Viking.

Ehrlich, P. and A. 1990, *The Population Explosion,* New York: Simon & Schuster.

Evans, M. D. H. and Kelley, J. 1986, 'Immigrants' Work: Equality and Discrimination in the Australian Labor Market', *ANZ Journal of Sociology* 22(2), July, 182–207.

FECCA (Federation of Ethnic Communities' Councils of Australia), Annual Reports.

FitzGerald, S. (chair) 1988, *Immigration – A Commitment to Australia (the CAAIP Report),* Canberra: AGPS.

Flannery, T. 1994, *The Future Eaters,* Sydney: Reed Books.

Foster, L. et al. 1991, *Discrimination against Immigrant Workers in Australia,* Canberra: AGPS.

Foster, W. 1996, *Immigration and the Australian Economy,* Canberra: AGPS.

Freeman, G. and Jupp, J. (eds) 1992, *Nations of Immigrants,* Melbourne: Oxford University Press.

Galbally, F. (chair) 1978, *Migrant Services and Programs,* Canberra: AGPS.

Galligan, B., Roberts, W. and Trifiletti, G. 2001, *Australians and Globalisation,* Cambridge University Press.

Gardiner-Garden, J. 1993, *The Multiculturalism and Immigration Debate 1973–1993,* Canberra: Department of the Parliamentary Library.

Goot, M. 1999, 'Migrant Numbers, Asian Immigration and Multiculturalism'. In National Multicultural Advisory Council, *Australian Multiculturalism for a New Century – Statistical Appendix,* Canberra: AusInfo, 28–60.

Grassby, Al 1979, *The Morning After,* Canberra: Judicator.

Hage, G. and Couch, R. (eds) 1999, *The Future of Australian Multiculturalism,* Sydney: University of Sydney.

Hanson, P. 1997, *The Truth,* Adelaide: St George Publications.

Hawke, R. J. L. 1994, *The Hawke Memoirs,* Melbourne: Heinemann.

Hay, C. 1996, *Managing Cultural Diversity,* Canberra: AGPS.

(Hewson, J.) 1991, *Australians Speak,* Canberra: Office of the Leader of the Opposition.

HREOC (Human Rights and Equal Opportunity Commission) 1991, *Racial Violence,* Canberra: AGPS.

—— 1998, *Those Who've Come across the Seas – Detention of Unauthorised Arrivals,* Sydney: HREOC.

Iredale, R. 1997, *Skills Transfer,* University of Wollongong Press.

Iredale, R. and Nivison-Smith, I. 1995, *Immigrants' Experiences of Qualifications Recognition and Employment,* Canberra: AGPS.

Johnson, D. 1991, *The Measurement and Extent of Poverty among Immigrants*, Canberra: AGPS.

Joint Parliamentary Committee of Public Accounts 1991, *Business Migration Program (Report 310)*, Canberra: Parliament of Australia.

Joint Standing Committee on Migration Regulations 1990, *Illegal Entrants in Australia – Balancing Control and Compassion*, Canberra: AGPS.

Jones, B. O. (chair) 1994, *Australia's Population 'Carrying Capacity'*, Canberra: AGPS.

Jordens, A.-M. 1997, *Alien to Citizen*, Sydney: Allen & Unwin.

Jupp, J. 1966, *Arrivals and Departures*, Melbourne: Cheshire-Lansdowne.

—— (chair) 1986, *Don't Settle for Less: Report of the Review of Migrant and Multicultural Programs and Services*, Canberra: AGPS.

—— 1992, 'Immigrant Settlement Policy in Australia', in Freeman and Jupp, *Nations of Immigrants*, 130–44.

—— 1994, *Exile or Refuge?*, Canberra: AGPS.

—— 1996, *Understanding Australian Multiculturalism*, Canberra: AGPS.

—— 1998, *Immigration*, Melbourne: Oxford University Press.

—— 1999, 'Seeking Whiteness: The Recruitment of Nordic Immigrants to Oceania', in Koivukangas and Westin (eds), *Scandinavian and European Migration to Australia and New Zealand*, Turku (Finland), 28–41.

—— (ed.) 2001, *The Australian People*, Cambridge University Press.

Jupp, J. and Kabala, M. (eds) 1993, *The Politics of Australian Immigration*, Canberra: AGPS.

Jupp, J. and McRobbie, A. (eds) 1992, *Access and Equity Evaluation Research*, Canberra: AGPS.

Jupp, J., McRobbie, A. and York, B. 1990, *Metropolitan Ghettoes and Ethnic Concentrations*, Wollongong: Centre for Multicultural Studies.

Kalantzis, M., Cope, B., and Slade, D. 1986, *The Language Question*, Canberra: AGPS.

Kukathas, C. (ed.) 1993, *Multicultural Citizens: The Philosophy and Politics of Identity*, Sydney: Centre for Independent Studies.

Kunz, F. 1988, *Displaced Persons: Calwell's New Australians*, Sydney: Pergamon/ANU Press.

Kymlicka, W. 1995, *Multicultural Citizenship*, Oxford: Clarendon Press.

Lack, J. and Templeton, J. (eds) 1988, *Sources of Australian Immigration History 1901–1945*, Melbourne: History Department, University of Melbourne.

—— 1995, *Bold Experiment*, Melbourne: Oxford University Press.

Leach, M., Stokes, G. and Marsh, I. (eds) 2000, *The Rise and Fall of One Nation*, Brisbane: University of Queensland Press.

Lo Bianco, J. 1987, *National Policy on Languages*, Canberra: AGPS.

Lo Bianco, J. and Wickert, R. (eds) 2001, *Australian Policy Activism in Language and Literacy*, Melbourne: Language Australia.

London, I. H. 1970, *Non-White Immigration and the 'White Australia' Policy*, New York University Press.

Lopez, M. 2000, *The Origins of Multiculturalism in Australian Politics*, Melbourne University Press.

Lowe, I. 1996, *Understanding Australia's Population Debate*, Canberra: AGPS.

Mares, P. 2001, *Borderline*, Sydney: University of New South Wales Press.

Markus, A. 2001, *Race: John Howard and the Remaking of Australia*, Sydney: Allen & Unwin.

Markus, A. and Ricklefs, M. (eds) 1985, *Surrender Australia?*, Sydney: Allen & Unwin.

Martin, J. I. 1978, *The Migrant Presence*, Sydney: George Allen & Unwin.

McDonald, P. and Kippen, R. 2001, 'The Impact of Immigration on the Ageing of Australia's Population', in Siddique, M. A. B. (ed.), *International Migration into the 21st Century*, Cheltenham (UK): Edward Elgar, 153–77.

McMaster, D. 2001, *Asylum Seekers*, Melbourne University Press.

Morrissey, M., Mitchell, C. and Rutherford, A. 1991, *The Family in the Settlement Process*, Canberra: AGPS.

Murphy, B. 1993, *The Other Australia*, Cambridge University Press/Ethnic Affairs Commission of New South Wales (Chapter 9).

Nevile, J. 1990, *The Effect of Immigration on Living Standards in Australia*, Canberra: AGPS.

—— 1998, 'Economic Rationalism', in Smyth, P. and Cass, B. (eds), *Contesting the Australian Way*, Cambridge University Press, 169–79.

NMAC (National Multicultural Advisory Council) 1995, *Multicultural Australia: The Next Steps*, Canberra: AGPS.

—— 1999, *Australian Multiculturalism for a New Century: Towards Inclusiveness*, Canberra: AusInfo.

Norman, N. R. and Meikle, K. F. 1985, *The Economic Effects of Immigration on Australia*, Melbourne: Committee for Economic Development of Australia.

Norton, T. et al. 1994, *An Overview of Research on the Links between Human Population and the Environment*, Canberra: AGPS.

NPC (National Population Council) 1985, *Access and Equity*, Canberra: AGPS.

—— 1991, *Population Issues and Australia's Future*, Canberra: AGPS.

OECD (Organisation for Economic Co-operation and Development) 1995, *Literacy, Economy and Society*, Paris: OECD.

OMA (Office of Multicultural Affairs) 1989, *National Agenda for a Multicultural Australia*, Canberra: AGPS.

—— 1992, *Access and Equity Evaluation Report*, Canberra: AGPS.

One Nation 1998, *Policy Document: Immigration, Population and Social Cohesion*, Sydney(?): Pauline Hanson's One Nation.

Ozolins, U. 1993, *The Politics of Language in Australia*, Cambridge University Press.

Papadakis, E. 1993, *Politics and the Environment: The Australian Experience*, Sydney: Allen & Unwin.

Parekh, B. 2000, *Rethinking Multiculturalism*, Basingstoke (UK): Macmillan.

Parliamentary Joint Standing Committee on Migration 1994, *Asylum, Border Control and Detention*, Canberra: AGPS.

Parliamentary Joint Standing Committee on Migration Regulations 1992, *Australia's Refugee and Humanitarian System*, Canberra: AGPS.

Partington, G. 1994, *The Australian Nation: Its British and Irish Roots*, Melbourne: Australian Scholarly Publishing.

Paul, E. C. 2001, *Australia: Too Many People?*, Aldershot (UK): Ashgate.

Price, C. (ed.) 1980, *Refugees: The Challenge of the Future*, Canberra: Academy of the Social Sciences in Australia.

Pusey, M. 1991, *Economic Rationalism in Canberra*, Cambridge University Press.

Richardson, S., Robertson, F. and Ilsley, D. 2001, *The Labour Force Experience of New Migrants*, Canberra: DIMA.

Rimmer, S. 1988, *Fiscal Anarchy: The Public Funding of Multiculturalism*, Perth: Australian Institute for Public Policy.

—— 1991, *The Costs of Multiculturalism*, Canberra: Author.

Roe, M. 1995, *Australia, Britain and Migration 1915–1940*, Cambridge University Press.

Rubinstein, W. 1991, *The Jews in Australia*, Melbourne: Heinemann.

Ruddock, P. 1998, 'Immigration Reform: The Unfinished Agenda', Speech to the Canberra Press Club, 18 March 1998, <http://www.immi.gov.au>.

—— 2000, 'A Sustainable Population Policy for Australia', Speech to the Australian Population Association Biennial Conference, 1 December, <http://www.immi.gov.au>.

Senate Standing Committee on Foreign Affairs and Defence 1976, *Australia and the Refugee Problem*, Canberra: AGPS.

Sestito, R. 1982, *The Politics of Multiculturalism*, Sydney: Centre for Independent Studies.

Sheehan, P. 1998, *Among the Barbarians*, Sydney: Random House.

Sheppard, G. (chair) 1983, *Access and Equity: The Development of Victoria's Ethnic Affairs Policies,* Melbourne: State Government Printer.

Sherington, G. 1990, *Australia's Immigrants 1788–1988,* Sydney: Allen & Unwin.

Smith, J. W. (ed.) 1991, *Immigration, Population and Sustainable Environments,* Adelaide: Flinders Press.

Solomon, D. (ed.) 2002, *Howard's Race,* Sydney: HarperCollins.

Taylor, J. and MacDonald, H. 1992, *Children of Immigrants: Issues of Poverty and Disadvantage,* Canberra: AGPS.

Theophanous, A. 1995, *Understanding Multiculturalism and Australian Identity,* Melbourne: Elikia Books.

Totaro, P. (chair) 1978, *Participation,* Sydney: New South Wales Government Printer.

United Nations High Commissioner for Refugees 2000, *The State of the World's Refugees,* New York: Oxford University Press.

VandenHeuvel, A. and Wooden, M. 2001, *New Settlers Have Their Say,* Canberra: AusInfo.

Vasta, E. and Castles, S. 1996, *The Teeth Are Smiling: The Persistence of Racism in Multicultural Australia,* Sydney: Allen & Unwin.

Viviani, N. 1984, *The Long Journey,* Melbourne University Press.

—— 1996, *The Indochinese in Australia 1975–1995,* Melbourne: Oxford University Press.

Walsh, P. 1996, *Confessions of a Failed Finance Minister,* Sydney: Vintage.

Weller, P. 2001, *The Mandarins: Frank and Fearless?,* Sydney: Allen & Unwin.

Whitlam, E. G. 1985, *The Whitlam Government 1972–1975,* Ringwood (Vic.): Penguin Books.

Williams, L. 1995, *Understanding the Economics of Immigration,* Canberra: AGPS.

Wilton, J. and Bosworth, R. 1984, *Old Worlds and New Australia,* Melbourne: Penguin Books.

Wiseman, J. 1998, *Global Nation? Australia and the Politics of Globalisation,* Cambridge University Press.

Wooden, M. et al. 1994, *Australian Immigration: A Study of the Issues,* Canberra: AGPS.

Woolcott, R. (chair) 1994, *Australia: National Report on Population for the UN International Conference on Population and Development,* Canberra: AGPS.

Index

Abeles, Sir Peter 47
Aboriginal and Torres Strait Islander
    Commission 51, 100
Aborigines 7, 8, 9, 15, 53, 91, 99, 100,
    105, 126, 129, 131, 136, 138, 168;
    see also Indigenous Australians
Access and Equity 42, 57, 69, 73, 97–8,
    101
Ackerman, Piers 116
Adelaide 30, 31, 36, 131, 135, 176; *see
    also* South Australia
Adult Migrant Education (English)
    Program 55, 57, 73, 95, 96, 152
Afghanistan 12, 181, 183, 184, 187,
    190, 193, 198, 215
Afghans 1, 11, 156, 192, 193, 197
Africa 5, 12, 15, 181, 184, 186
Aliens 143
Aliens Act (UK, 1905) 14
All for Australia 114
Anglo-Australian 3, 24, 65
Anglo-Celtic 3, 48
Anglo-Indians 18
Anglo-Saxon 3
Arabic language 25, 212
Arena, Franca 33
Argentina 5, 16, 185
Ashmore Reef 193, 195
Asia 15, 23, 35, 50, 163, 202, 203, 210,
    217
Asians 35–6, 37, 39, 42, 52, 66, 110,
    114, 121, 125, 127, 128, 130, 131,

132, 138, 143, 150, 156, 174, 184,
    186, 212, 213
assimilation 21–3, 112, 162, 200
assisted passages 16, 17, 19, 23, 45,
    141, 142, 144, 147, 206
asylum seekers 51, 130, 153, 158, 160,
    180–99; *see also* Refugees
Auburn (NSW) 34, 39
Australia as a Multicultural Society 85
Australia Betrayed 136–7
Australia First 136
Australian 176
Australian Academy of Sciences 168,
    169
Australian Broadcasting Control
    Board 26
Australian Broadcasting Corporation
    55, 81, 106, 121
Australian Bureau of Statistics 61
Australian Chamber of Commerce
    108
Australian Citizenship Amendment
    Act (2002) 206
Australian Conservation Foundation,
    166, 170
Australian Council of Churches 181
Australian Council of Trade Unions
    (ACTU) 57, 70, 90, 109
Australian Democrats 81, 133, 138,
    166, 177
Australian Ethnic Affairs Council 70,
    71, 85, 90

Australian Greek Welfare Society 85,
88
Australian Institute for Public Policy
107
Australian Institute of Multicultural
Affairs 49, 61, 64, 72, 73, 76, 77,
89–90, 109
Australian Institute of Multicultural
Affairs Act (1979) 76, 77, 89, 92
Australian Jewish Welfare 88, 181
Australian Labor Party 8, 29, 32, 33,
34, 46, 50, 54, 57, 75, 80, 85, 87,
106, 109, 119, 123, 134, 166
Australian National University 75,
170, 175
Australian Nationalist Movement 125,
127
Australian Population and
Immigration Council 44, 70, 71
Australian Reform Party 130
Australian Refugee Advisory Council
44
Australian Security and Intelligence
Organisation (ASIO) 27
Australian Workers' Union 70, 124
Australians Against Further
Immigration 131, 136, 137, 167,
171
Australians for an Ecologically
Sustainable Population 167, 169
Australians Speak 112–13, 117, 129
Australijas Latvietis 28
Austrians 15, 24

Bankstown (NSW) 38
Barnett, David 107, 113, 115, 117
Barton, Sir Edmund 10
Basham, Richard 116
Bathurst (NSW) 180
Beazley, Kim 119, 135, 139
Belconnen (ACT) 66
Betts, Katharine 102, 114, 115, 116,
117, 118, 137
Bicentennial Multicultural
Foundation 111

Birrell, Robert 102, 116, 137, 145, 150,
155, 169, 170
Bjelke-Petersen, Sir Joh 68, 80, 124
Blainey, Professor Geoffrey 10, 47, 65,
107, 109, 113, 114, 116, 121, 126,
127, 128
B'nai B'rith Anti-Defamation
Commission 126
Bolkus, Senator Nick 51, 52, 53, 55,
74, 75, 92
Bondi (NSW) 31
Bonegilla (Vic.) 27, 154, 180
Border Protection (Validation and
Enforcement) Act (2001) 195
Border Protection Act (1999) 194
Borjas, George 157
Borrie, Professor Mick 71, 72, 170,
174, 175
Bosnians 187
Boswell, Senator Ron 139
Bottomley, Dr Gillian 101
Bracks, Steve 176
Brisbane 36, 135, 214
Britain 2, 3, 8, 11, 12, 14, 16, 24, 127,
142, 142, 144; *see also* United
Kingdom
British 1, 5, 6, 7, 11, 16, 17, 19, 21, 23,
30, 31, 34, 36, 93, 135, 141, 151,
174, 209
Broadby, Rex 70
Broadmeadows (Vic.) 32
Brown, Ron 55, 67
Bruer, Jeremy 63
Brundtland, Gro Harlem 165
Brunswick (Vic.) 31, 32
Buddhists 212
Bullivant, Brian 106
Bureau of Immigration (Multicultural
and Population) Research 52, 55,
61, 62, 73, 75, 76, 77, 115, 117, 144,
172, 218
Bureau of Labour Market Research
145
Business Migration program 51, 66,
132, 207, 208, 212

Cabramatta (NSW) 36, 39
Cadman, Alan 111
Cain, John 68, 109
Calwell, Arthur 11, 12, 52, 54, 69
Cambodia 43, 47, 189
Cameron, Clyde 41, 53
Campbell, Graeme 119, 120, 130, 131,
    136–7
Campbelltown (NSW) 120, 135
Canada, -ians 5, 14, 16, 19, 23, 24, 32,
    61, 83, 84, 91, 120, 149, 154, 183
Canadian Charter of Rights and
    Freedoms 91
Canadian Royal Commission on
    Bilingualism and Biculturalism 83
Canberra 31, 36, 65
Canterbury (NSW) 38
Cantonese 25
Carlton (Vic.) 31
Carr, Bob 68, 120, 214
Casey, Ron 127
Castles, Professor Frank 38
Castles, Professor Stephen 92, 101,
    102, 106, 117, 155, 170
Catholic Church 165, 188
Catholics 17, 21, 22, 26, 32, 33, 114
Caucasians 7
Census (of Population and Housing)
    3, 25, 35
Centre for Independent Studies 107,
    142
Ceylon Burghers 18
*Charter of Public Service in a
    Culturally Diverse Society* 98
Chatswood (NSW) 36, 39
Chifley government (1945–9) 145,
    218
Child Migrant Education Program 95
Chile 16, 185
China 7, 8, 14, 25, 163, 164, 180, 184,
    185, 188, 190, 204, 212, 216
Chinese 5, 8, 10, 14, 18, 21, 28, 33, 35,
    36, 37, 51, 146, 183, 185, 188, 191,
    212, 213
Chipman, Lauchlan 105

Chisholm, Caroline 93
Christianity 6, 7, 22, 23, 180, 181, 212,
    213, 215
Christmas Island 138, 193, 194, 195,
    198
Citizenship Act (1948) 206
Citizens Electoral Councils 125,
    126
Clarey, Percy 70
Club of Rome 165
Coburg (Vic.) 32
Cocks, Doug 169, 172
Cocos Islands 195
Colbourne, Bill 71, 90
Collingwood (Vic.) 31
Collins, Jock 155
Colombo Plan 203
Colonial Land and Emigration
    Commission 17
Commission on Population Growth
    and the American Future 167
Committee to Advise on Australia's
    Immigration Policies; *see*
    FitzGerald report.
Commonwealth Bank 152
Commonwealth Hostels Ltd. 58
Commonwealth Scientific and
    Industrial Research Organisation
    162, 168, 172
Communism 180, 182, 185, 190
Community Refugee Settlement
    Scheme 44, 180
Community Relations, Commissioner
    for 41
Comprehensive Plan of Action 188
Concessional Family Reunion 19, 45
Confederate Action Party 130
Constitution of Australia 8
    Constitution s.51(v) 67
    Constitution s.51 (xix) 68
    Constitution s.51 (xxvi) 67
    Constitution s.51 (xxvii) 15, 67
    Constitution s.116 26
Conybeare, Chris 55
Cope, Bill 96, 102

Cornish Association of South Australia 28
'cost free immigration' 152
Coulter, Senator John 133, 167, 168, 177
Council for Multicultural Australia 74
Council on Overseas Professional Qualifications 147
Country Party; *see* National Party
Court, Sir Charles 68
Cox, Professor David 72, 102, 109, 149
Crean, Simon 90, 176
Croatians 28
Cronin, Kathryn 49, 63
Culturally and Linguistically Diverse (CALD) 3
Curtin (WA) 1
Czechoslovakians 18, 180

Daily Mirror 112
Daly, Fred 54
Dandenong (Vic.) 32
Danes 18
Darwin 42, 188
Darwin, Charles 2, 7
Davis, H.O. 70
Dawkins, John 46, 96, 119
Day, Lincoln 169
Deakin, Alfred 11
Defence, Department of 203
Democratic Labor Party 86, 106, 138, 163
Deportation 67, 159, 184
Dictation test 8, 9
Die Woche 28
Displaced Persons 12, 17, 18, 28, 144, 151, 155, 174, 180, 186
Dixson, Miriam 118
Doncaster (Vic.) 36, 39
Downer, Alexander 107
Downer, Sir Alexander 53
Downs, Anthony 108
Duffy, Michael 55
Dunstan, Don 68, 86
Dutch 10, 13, 18, 25, 28, 34, 174

Dutch Australian Weekly 28

East Timor 42, 186, 187, 188, 203; *see also* Timorese
economic rationalism 6, 48, 49, 59, 81, 123, 125, 141–60, 191, 206, 207
Ecumenical Migration Centre 76
Edinenie 28
Education, Department of 41, 58, 94, 96, 203
Egypt 18, 202
Ehrlich, Paul 165, 166, 168, 177
Elizabeth (SA) 31, 135
Employment, Education and Training, Department of 147, 171
England 9, 21, 143; *see also* Britain
English as a Second Language 144
English language 3, 6, 19, 22, 23, 24, 25, 26, 38, 84, 145, 171
Enterprise hostel (Vic.) 193
Essendon (Vic.) 32
Estonians 18, 211
'ethnic' 2, 3, 23–4, 79
Ethnic Affairs Act (NSW, 1976) 68
Ethnic Affairs Branch/Division 43, 64
Ethnic Affairs Commission (NSW) 68
Ethnic Affairs Commission (Vic.) 109
Ethnic Affairs, Department of (Qld.) 69
Ethnic Communities' Councils 69, 75, 77, 80, 86, 88
ethnic groups 79–82, 88, 94
ethnic lobby 79, 80, 115
ethnic organisations 27–9, 71, 88
Ettridge, David 136
European Community (later Union) 24, 36, 195, 204
Europeans 3, 12, 16, 18, 23, 24, 27, 30, 34, 35, 39, 114, 144, 185
Evans, Mariah 147
Evian conference (1938) 186
Eyles, Peter 64

Fairfield (NSW) 31, 38
family migration 17

Family Reunion 44, 45, 47, 49, 130, 150, 178, 182, 208
Federal Multiculturalism Act (Canada 1988) 91
Federation of Ethnic Communities' Councils of Australia 52, 57, 64, 74, 75, 77, 80, 92, 95, 111
Fenner, Professor Frank 165
Ferguson, Martin 90
fertility 175
Fiji, Fijians 37, 186
Filipina/os 1, 35; *see also* Philippines
Finance, Department of 54
Finns 18, 28
First World War (1914–18) 23, 68
FitzGerald report (1988) 36, 47, 48, 58, 59, 62, 64, 73, 77, 108, 109, 118, 120, 188
Fitzroy (Vic.) 31, 32
Flannery, Tim 116, 168, 177
Footscray (Vic.) 32, 39
Foreign Affairs and Trade, Department of 188, 197, 203
Fowler electorate (NSW) 39
Fraser government (1975–83) 19, 42–6, 53, 72, 85, 106, 123, 150, 207
Fraser, Malcolm 46, 54, 55, 56, 86, 105, 109, 112, 119, 128, 137
free trade 125, 159, 207, 209
Fremantle (WA) 31
French 10, 25

Galbally Implementation Task Force 45
Galbally report (1978) 42, 43, 45, 76, 85, 86–9, 94, 97, 105, 106, 150, 151
Galbally, Frank 72, 87, 89, 107, 109
Garland, Alf 111
Gellibrand electorate (Vic.) 39
Georgiou, Petro 76, 87, 89, 109
Germans 5, 10, 13, 15, 17, 18, 25, 28, 34, 154, 174, 180
Germany 14, 180
Ghettoes 30–2, 35, 36, 130

Global Cultural Diversity Conference (1995) 50
Globalisation 123, 201–8
Gobbo, Sir James 47, 71, 90, 111, 149
Gold Coast (Qld.) 112
Good Neighbour movement 13, 22, 26, 64, 80, 86, 87, 88, 93, 180
Gorton government (1968–71) 170
Grassby, Al 41, 43, 53, 54, 66, 85, 86, 120
Greece 13
Greek Orthodox Communities 28
Greeks 18, 24, 28, 30, 31, 32, 36, 107, 157, 211
Greek language 23, 96
Green Party 138, 177
Greenpeace 166
'greens' 166, 167
Greiner, Nick 111
Guest workers 157

Hage, Ghassan 102
Hand, Gerry 46, 51, 52, 53, 55, 59, 72, 74, 189
Hanson, Pauline 2, 57, 107, 108, 112, 113, 115, 116, 120, 128–39, 191, 195; *see also* One Nation
Hardgrave, Gary 105
Hawke government (1983–91) 46–9, 53, 71, 72, 74, 146, 166
Hawke, Robert 46, 54, 55, 57, 71, 107, 110, 152, 191
Hay, Andrew 108
Hayden, Bill 129
Hellenic Herald 28
Hewson, John 107, 111, 112
High Court of Australia 183
Hindmarsh (SA) 31
Hindus 212
Hodges, John 53, 55
Holding, Clyde 47, 48, 53, 110
Holt, Harold 10, 52, 69
Home Office (UK) 61
Hong Kong 7, 10, 35, 37, 188, 216

Howard government (1966–) 3, 19, 44, 51, 52, 53, 56, 58, 59, 73, 74, 75, 81, 97, 109, 116, 150, 172, 173, 185, 187

Howard, John 55, 57, 78, 91, 98, 107, 108, 109, 110, 111, 113, 116, 117, 118, 121, 126, 127, 128, 129, 132, 138, 169, 194, 196, 199, 201, 206, 217, 218

Hughes, Professor Helen 102, 110, 118, 146

Hughes, William Morris 11

Hugo, Graeme 170

human capital 36, 59, 146–7, 156, 157

Human Rights and Equal Opportunity Commission 126

Humanitarian programs; *see* Refugees

Hungarians 18, 28, 180

Hurford, Chris 47, 48, 55, 76

Il Globo 28

illegal migration, 51, 59

Immigration (Education) Act (1971) 95

Immigration (Education) Charge Act (1992) 58

Immigration Advisory Council 69

Immigration and Ethnic Affairs, Department of 42

Immigration and Nationality Act (USA 1952 and 1965) 23

Immigration and Naturalization Service (USA) 61

Immigration Department 2, 3, 41, 57, 61–7, 76, 80, 83, 86, 88, 94, 96, 105, 114, 116, 144, 148, 154, 157, 159, 169, 171, 183, 190, 193, 195, 197, 200, 204, 218

Immigration Restriction Act (1901) 8, 15, 143, 148, 196

Immigration Review Tribunal 49

India 5, 6, 18, 164, 216

Indians 14, 35, 37, 212

Indigenous Australians 21, 22, 24, 84, 99–101; *see also* Aborigines

Indochinese 37, 44, 174, 193; *see also* Vietnamese

Indonesia, -ns 5, 6, 18, 184, 188, 193, 198, 202, 203, 215

Institute of Public Affairs 142

International Organization for Migration 182

International Refugee Organisation 182

Iran, -ians 1, 184, 186, 190

Iraq 184, 186, 187, 190

Iraqis 1, 11, 12, 212

Iredale, Robyn 170

Ireland 14, 18, 21, 143, 148, 195

Irish 1, 16, 17, 21, 22

Israel 18, 182

Italians 18, 21, 24, 27, 28, 30, 31, 32, 36, 124, 210

Italian language 25, 211

Italo-Australians 24

Italy 13, 61

Jakubowicz, Dr Andrew 101

James, Michael 108

Japan 7, 8, 14

Japanese 10, 11, 18

Jayasuriya, Professor Laksiri 101

Jegorow, Bill 71, 90

Jews 14, 22, 26, 28, 29, 34, 36, 46, 125, 157, 180, 182, 186, 211

Jones, Alan 116, 117

Jones, Barry 73, 171, 172, 174

Joske, Stephen 117, 137

Kalantzis, Professor Mary 96, 101, 102

Kaldor, Dr Susan 71

Kalgoorlie (WA) 131

Katter, Bob 134

Keating government (1991–6) 49–52, 53, 58, 74, 150, 152, 172, 217

Keating, Paul 46, 50, 51, 55, 72, 115, 137

Keilor (Vic.) 31

Kennett, Jeff 111, 115

Kensington (SA) 31

Keyes, Sir William 91
Kippen, Rebecca 175
Knöpfelmacher, Frank 105
Koreans 35, 39, 212
Kosovars 132, 192, 193
Kramer, Dame Leonie 106
Kristol, Irving 118
Kukathas, Chandran 101, 106
Kwinana (WA) 31
Kymlicka, Will 116

La Fiamma 28
Labour, Department of 41
Languages other than English
    (LOTEs) 24, 25, 84, 94–7, 211
LaRouche, Lyndon 125
Latham, Mark 120
Latin America 23, 47, 186
Latvians 18, 28
Le Courrier Australien 28
League of Rights 124, 125, 126, 136
Lebanese 28, 38, 43, 50, 120, 123, 156,
    185, 207
Lebanon 18, 186
Leichhardt (NSW) 31
Liberal Party 29, 34, 54, 56, 78, 80, 86,
    87, 90, 110, 111, 112, 113, 119, 126,
    128, 129, 134, 139, 142, 163
Liberal–National Coalition 46, 79,
    106, 111, 152, 160, 177, 180, 192,
    194, 198
Lippman, Walter 47, 86
Lithuanians 18
'Little Italys' 36
Liverpool (NSW) 120
Lo Bianco, Joseph 73, 95, 102
Logan City (Qld.) 135
London 9, 19, 30, 68, 206
Longitudinal Survey of Immigrants to
    Australia 153, 159
Lopez, Mark 84, 85, 109
Lowe, Ian 169

Macedonians 107
MacKellar, Michael 42, 43, 45, 53, 54,
    56, 71, 90, 128, 137, 149

Macphee, Ian 42, 45, 47, 53, 54, 56, 90,
    92, 111, 112, 125, 128, 137, 149,
    186
Mafia 27
Magyar Elet 28
Malaysia 43, 202
Malaysians 35, 37
Maltese 24, 25, 28, 30, 32
Maltese Herald 28
Malthus, Thomas 164, 168, 177
mandatory detention 8, 66, 177, 183,
    189, 194
Manus Island (PNG) 1, 56
Maoris 15
Maribyrnong (Vic.) 31, 189, 193
Marrickville (NSW) 31
Martin, Jean 39, 86, 101, 109
Matheson, Alan 109
McClelland, Senator Jim 41
McCormack, Denis 131, 136
McDonald, Professor Peter 175
McKinnon, Bill 47
media 27, 28, 29, 129, 137, 139
Medicare 152
Melbourne 25, 29, 30, 31, 32, 33, 34,
    46, 85, 107, 174, 213, 214
Menadue, John 43
Menzies electorate (Vic.) 33
Menzies, Sir Robert 10
Mexicans 14, 158
Middle East 38, 42, 184, 185, 193, 216
Migrant Resource Centres 43, 64, 88
Migration (Health Services) Charge
    Act (1991) 58
Migration Act (1958) 8, 9, 143, 148,
    183, 195
Migration Action 76
Migration Agents Registration (Levy)
    Act (1992) 58
Migration Amendment Act (1992) 51
Migration Legislation Amendment
    Act (1995) 59
Millions movement 162
Monk, Albert 70
Moore-Wilton, Max 56
Morgan, Hugh 178

Mount Isa (Qld.) 173
Multicultural Affairs Queensland 103
Multicultural Agendas 73, 92, 93, 98–9, 107, 121
Multiculturalism 23, 25, 29, 46, 49, 65, 70, 72, 83–121, 123, 125, 127, 136, 137, 138, 201, 208–13
Multiculturalism for all Australians 125
Multifunctional Polis 111, 112
Murphy, Senator Lionel 27
Murrumbidgee Irrigation Area 162, 173
Muslims 22, 26, 121, 193, 202, 215

National Action 125
National Advisory and Co-ordinating Committee on Multicultural Education 95
National Conservation Strategy 165
National Front 124
National Multicultural Advisory Council 71, 90, 91, 92, 98
National Office of Overseas Skills Recognition 147
National Party 34, 54, 57, 119, 123, 124, 129, 134, 135, 138, 174
National Policy on Languages 73, 95
National Population Council 70, 71, 73, 75, 97, 146, 170, 171
National Population Inquiry (1975) 72, 170
naturalisation 130, 134, 191
Nauru 1, 56, 195, 198
Nazism 9, 22, 181, 186
Neos Kosmos 28
New Guard 124
New South Wales 3, 10, 17, 80, 120, 135
New Zealand, -ers 5, 12, 14, 15, 16, 19, 21, 29, 34, 38, 45, 50, 132, 133, 148, 159, 173, 176, 195, 204, 210, 212, 216
Newcastle (NSW) 30, 57
Nieuwenhuysen, John 52

Nix, Professor Henry 170
Noakes, Brian 71
Non-English-Speaking Background(NESB) 3, 25, 79, 84, 120
Northcote (Vic.) 32
Northern Territory 134
Numerical Multifactor Assessment System (NUMAS) 44, 148, 149, 154

Oakleigh (Vic.) 32
O'Chee, Senator Bill 139
Office of Multicultural Affairs 49, 54, 55, 75, 77, 91, 97, 99, 102, 110, 117, 146, 218
Oldfield, David 136
Olson, Mancur 107
One Nation 2, 23, 33, 57, 112, 118, 119, 121, 123–39, 167, 168, 169, 172, 173, 177, 192, 194, 199, 213, 218; *see also* Hanson, Pauline
Opperman, Hubert 53
Orderly departure program 44, 188
Organisation for Economic Co-operation and Development 37, 146
Our Common Future 165
Oxley electorate (Qld.) 128

Pacific Islands, - ers 7, 14, 15, 210
'Pacific solution' 59, 63, 193–6
Papadopoulos, George 71, 76, 90, 109
Papua New Guinea 5, 195, 198
Parekh, Bikhu 116
Parkes, Sir Henry 21, 114
Partington, Geoffrey 105, 119
Pasquarelli, John 131, 136
Peacock, Andrew 107, 111, 112, 128
Perth 31, 36, 125, 214; *see also* Western Australia
Philippines 37, 43, 216
Playford, Sir Thomas 68
Points system 146, 147, 151, 158, 208; *see also* NUMAS
Poland 43, 184

Poles 18, 28, 30
Polish language 25
Poor Law (UK) 142, 143
population policy 170–3
Population Summit (2002), 176
Port Hedland (WA) 1, 47, 100, 189, 190, 193
Portuguese 18, 188
Powell, Enoch 124
Powell, Janet 92
Power, John 63
Prahran (Vic.) 31, 32
Preston (Vic.) 32
Price, Dr Charles 102, 149
Prime Minister and Cabinet, Department of 54, 56, 65, 77, 99
productive diversity 102
Protestants 17, 21, 26, 33
public choice theory 79
public opinion 4, 13, 29, 123
Pusey, Dr Michael 48, 141

Quadrant 106
qualifications 35, 145, 147, 154, 156, 208, 212
Queanbeyan (NSW) 31
Queensland 17, 25, 30, 31, 113, 124, 129, 134, 135, 137, 139, 147, 174, 175

Racial Vilification Bill 136
racism 2, 6, 66, 113, 125–7, 131, 138, 187, 199
Radio 2EA 26, 27
Radio 3ZZ 27
Randwick (NSW) 36
Ray, Senator Robert 46, 47, 48, 51, 52, 53, 55, 62, 64, 67
Red Cross 94, 153, 158
Refugee Council of Australia 75
Refugee Review Tribunal 49
Refugee Settlement Advisory Committee 75
refugees 16, 19, 43, 44, 47, 50, 51, 58, 72, 131, 132, 133, 138, 154, 156,

159, 180–99, 215, 217; *see also* asylum seekers
Regularisation of Status 59
Reid electorate (NSW) 39
Reith, Peter 195
Religion 26, 84, 182
Representatives, House of 135, 171
Returned and Services League (RSL) 91, 111, 119
Review of Migrant and Multicultural Programs and Services (1986) 57, 73, 77, 97
Richardson, Senator Graham 166
Richmond (Vic.) 31, 36
Rimmer, Stephen 107, 108, 115, 137
Rubenstein, Dr Colin 102
Ruddock, Philip 46, 53, 55, 56, 57, 67, 105, 128, 157, 173, 176, 195, 204
Russia, -ans 5, 10, 14, 175, 180, 181
Ruxton, Bruce 130
Ryan, Colonel Rupert S. 70
Ryan, Susan 95, 96

Saddam Hussein 194
Samios, Jim 149
Sanders, Norm 166
Scandinavians 12, 17
Scotland 5, 21
Second World War (1939–45) 12, 14, 68, 162, 181
See Yap Society 28
Senate 135, 137, 139, 150
Serbo-Croatian 25
Serbians 28
Sestito, Raymond 105, 107, 108
Settlement Advisory Council 72
Seventh Day Adventists 26
Sham-ho, Helen 33
Sharp, Paul 165
Sheehan, Paul 115, 116, 117
Shehadie, Sir Nicholas 90
Sheldrake, Peter 76
Shergold, Peter 77
Singapore,-ans 10, 18, 35, 37, 163

skilled migration 17, 37, 146, 154, 160, 178, 201, 207
Slade, Diane 96
Smolicz,Professor Jerzy 86, 101, 102
Snowy Mountains Scheme 13, 162
Social Credit 58, 124
Social Darwinism 9
Social Security, Department of 28, 41, 58, 94, 153
social welfare 94, 132, 152, 156
South Africa 7, 8, 9, 19, 43, 85, 212
South Australia 15, 17, 68, 156; see also Adelaide
South Sea Islanders 103
Soviet Union 46 see also Russia
Sowell, Thomas 116
Spanish 18, 24, 25
Special Assistance program 132, 187, 208
Special Broadcasting Service 26, 55, 73, 81, 89, 121
Special Humanitarian program 133, 187
Spencer, Dr Rodney 171
Spencer, Robyn 131, 133, 136
spouses 130, 150, 160
Springvale (Vic.) 32
Sri Lanka 186, 216
Sri Lankans 35, 37, 212
St Kilda (Vic.) 31
St Peters (SA) 31
St Vincent de Paul 94
State Agents General 68
State governments 10, 67–9, 94, 103, 105, 151, 174, 201
Stirling (WA) 36
Stone, John 116, 130, 146
Stone, Professor Jonathan 168
Strathfield (NSW) 36
students 151, 185, 189, 191, 203, 204, 208
Sunshine (Vic.) 31
Suzuki, David 166
Sydney Morning Herald 115

Sydney 25, 29, 30, 31, 33, 34, 39, 50, 57, 116, 119–20, 173, 174, 213, 214; *see also* New South Wales

Taiwan 216
Taiwanese 35, 37
Taliban 184, 192, 194; *see also* Afghanistan
Tampa 56, 59, 136, 139, 177, 183, 192, 193–6, 197
Tasman Institute 142
Tasmania 10, 13, 30, 68, 166, 174, 176
Taylor, Professor Griffith 164
Tchen, Senator Tsebin 33
Telephone Interpreter Service (later Translating and Interpreting Service) 64, 65
temporary protection 132, 153, 191–3
temporary residents 191, 205
Thebarton (SA) 31
Themal, Uri 71
Theophanous, Dr Andrew 33, 73, 116
Thomas, Professor Trang 102
Tien-an-men square 51
Timorese 44, 188
tourism 203
Toyne, Philip 170
trade unions 64, 145, 147
Tran, Dr My-Van 92
'transilients' 205
Trans-Tasman agreement 210
Treasury 54, 145
Turkey 23, 148
Turks 15, 18, 155
Tygodnik Polski 28

Ukrainians 18, 28, 39, 83, 211
UN High Commissioner for Refugees 182, 184, 195, 197, 202
UN International Conference on Population and Development 173
UN Refugee Convention (1951) 182, 184, 186, 190, 197

UN Refugee Convention Protocol
    (1967) 182–4
United Kingdom 5, 14, 18, 21, 34, 50,
    148, 163
United Nations 165, 188, 193
United States 1, 5, 7, 8, 11, 12, 14, 15,
    16, 19, 23, 42, 79, 84, 108, 113, 125,
    127, 154, 157, 158, 205, 209
Unity 33, 34
Unsworth, Barry 57
'user pays' 152, 153
utilitarianism 6

Veliz, Professor Claudio 71
Victoria 17, 34, 156
Vietnam 42, 188
Vietnamese 38, 39, 42, 43, 50, 123,
    129, 156, 157, 185, 188
Villawood (NSW) 189, 193
visas 148, 153, 158, 159, 189, 190
Viviani, Nancy 194

Wacol hostel (Qld.) 193
Walsh, Max 165
Walsh, Senator Peter 54, 119, 130,
    145
War Precautions Act (1920) 28
welfare dependency 156, 158
West, Stuart 46, 47, 53
Western Australia 68, 119, 134, 135
White Australia 6–10, 15, 18, 19, 22,
    37, 41, 42, 44, 50, 54, 66, 113, 123,
    124, 127, 138, 180, 188, 199, 200,
    202
Whiteside, Bruce 112, 136

Whitlam government (1972–5) 10, 24,
    41, 65, 123
Whitlam, Gough 42, 43, 53, 54, 66, 70,
    86, 110, 170
Whittlesea (Vic.) 32
Whyalla (SA) 31, 174
Wilenski, Dr Peter 65, 66, 77
Williams, Lynne 144
Withers, Professor Glenn 72, 73, 170
Wodonga (Vic.) 174
Wollongong 30, 31, 47, 57
Wong, Dr Peter 33
Woomera (SA) 1, 139, 189, 190, 194,
    198
World Bank 165
World Commission on Environment
    and Development 165
Wran, Neville 68

xenophobia 2, 6, 124, 169, 199, 200,
    213, 217

Young, Christabel 169
Young, Michael 46, 47, 90, 92, 125
Yugoslavs 18, 23, 24, 25, 27, 30, 32, 50,
    52, 148, 182, 184, 186, 207

Zammit, Josephine 71
Zammit, Paul 33
Zangalis, George 109
Zemanek, Stan 116
Zero population growth 167–9, 171,
    176, 177
Zubrzycki, Professor Jerzy 71, 77, 86,
    90, 101, 102, 107, 109, 120, 125